TOWARDS WELFARE PLURALISM

For my friend and guide

Towards Welfare Pluralism

Public Services in a Time of Change

NIRMALA RAO

*Lecturer, Department of Social Policy and Politics,
Goldsmiths' College, University of London*

Dartmouth

Aldershot • Brookfield USA • Singapore • Sydney

Published by
Dartmouth Publishing Company Limited
Gower House
Croft Road
Aldershot
Hants GU11 3HR
England

Dartmouth Publishing Company
Old Post Road
Brookfield
Vermont 05036
USA

British Library Cataloguing in Publication Data
Rao, Nirmala
  Towards welfare pluralism : public services in a time of change
  1.Welfare state 2.Public welfare - Great Britain 3.Great
  Britain - Social policy - 1979-
  I. Title
  361.6'5'0941

Library of Congress Cataloging-in-Publication Data
Rao, Nirmala, 1959-
  Towards welfare pluralism : public services in a time of change /
  Nirmala Rao.
      p.   cm.
  Includes bibliographical references and index.
  ISBN 1-85521-727-9 (hardbound), – ISBN 1-85521-732-5 (pbk.)
  1. Central-local government relations–Great Britain. 2. Local
government–Great Britain. 3. Great Britain–Politics and
government–1979- 4. Great Britain–Social policy–1979-
I. Title.
JS3137.R36   1996
361.941–dc20   95-48249
                                                      CIP

ISBN 1 85521 727 9 (Hbk)
ISBN 1 85521 732 5 (Pbk)

Printed in Great Britain at the University Press, Cambridge

Contents

List of Tables

Glossary

ADLO	Association of Direct Labour Organisations
ADSS	Association of Directors of Social Services
ALA	Association of London Authorities
AMA	Association of Metropolitan Authorities
CCT	Compulsory Competitive Tendering
CPC	Conservative Political Centre
CPS	Centre for Policy Studies
CPVE	Certificate of Pre-Vocational Education
CSD	Contract Services Department (or Division)
CTC	City Technology College
DES	Department of Education and Science
DfE	Department for Education
DHA	District Health Authority
DLO	Direct Labour Organisation
DoE	Department of the Environment
DoH	Department of Health
DSO	Direct Service Organisation
DSS	Department of Social Security
EAT	Employment Appeals Tribunal
ERA	Education Reform Act
FHSA	Family Health Services Authority
GDP	Gross Domestic Product
GLC	Greater London Council

GMS	Grant Maintained School
GNI	General Needs Index
GNP	Gross National Product
GP	General Practitioner
HAT	Housing Action Trust
HIP	Housing Investment Programme
HMI	Her Majesty's Inspectorate of Schools
HRA	Housing Revenue Account
IEA	Institute of Economic Affairs
ILEA	Inner London Education Authority
Inlogov	Institute of Local Government Studies
IPF	Institute of Public Finance
JCC	Joint Consultative Committee
JPT	Joint Planning Team
LEA	Local Education Authority
LFM	Local Financial Management
LGIU	Local Government Information Unit
LGMB	Local Government Management Board
LMS	Local Management of Schools
MBO	Management Buy-Out
MORI	Market Opinion and Research International
MSC	Manpower Services Commission
NAO	National Audit Office
NCC	National Curriculum Council
NFHA	National Federation of Housing Associations
NHS	National Health Service
NVQ	National Vocational Qualification
OECD	Organisation for Economic Co-Operation and Development
Ofsted	Office of Standards in Education
PSBR	Public Sector Borrowing Requirement
RSG	Rate Support Grant
SCAA	Schools Curriculum Assessment Authority
SEAC	Schools Examinations Assessment Council
SEC	Schools Examinations Council
SLA	Service Level Agreement
SSA	Standard Spending Assessment
SSD	Social Services Department
SSI	Social Services Inspectorate
TPAS	Tenant Participation Advisory Service
TUPE	Transfer of Undertakings (Protection of Employment)
TVEI	Technical and Vocational Education Initiative

Foreword

The term *welfare pluralism* in the title of this book implies that the provision of welfare services, instead of following a tidy organisation in state or local government monopolies, strongly under the influence of the providers, has increasingly been diversified, bringing in elements of competition and in some programmes taking the point of decision closer to the final user or 'consumer'. The changes have not all been of this kind: for instance, on budgetary grounds the elderly have been denied a previous freedom to opt for residential care (within the limits of social security allowances), and now have their fate decided by case conferences in local social services departments. But there is no doubt that in every part of the 'welfare state' there has been a period of change unprecedented both in scope and in frequency of adjustment. A long-lasting Conservative government has proved to be radical and possessed by a frenetic desire for changing things; their left wing opponents have sometimes appeared as champions of a *status quo* which is no longer tenable, and sometimes as unwillingly accepting the radical ideas of the Right.

Such periods of change produce uncertainty and conflict, and these have been particularly noticeable in the relations between central and local government, which have been affected to a point which has injured the service to the citizen. The Joseph Rowntree Foundation identified this breakdown of relations as a key issue, and has for ten years financed a substantial and co-ordinated research programme intended to identify the problems more clearly and to suggest means of reducing the uncertainty and the conflict. This programme currently runs until 1996, in which year a consolidated review of the implications of the numerous reports produced will be published, the provisional title being *Members One of Another: the Problems of Local Corporate Action.* Over the same ten years there has been a considerable development of research by other bodies, notably the Economic and Social Research Council.

Dr. Nirmala Rao was an early recruit to the Rowntree research team, and has produced many studies relevant to its mission. She has shown a remarkable ability to tease out the facts and to put them in their policy context in clear and readable reports. I was therefore particularly pleased to learn that she was proposing to write this book, in which she draws on the results of a period of profound and varied study of the changes in public services. The general election, in 1997 or earlier, will intensify the debate about welfare pluralism. I commend this book particularly to politicians and to politically conscious citizens who prefer to understand what they are talking about.

Charles Carter

Acknowledgements

I started this book in the spring of 1995 shortly after completing the last of my studies for the Joseph Rowntree Foundation's research programme on Local and Central Government Relations. It was in 1989 that Sir Charles Carter asked me to carry out the first of these studies on the effects of the Housing Act, 1988. This was followed by other studies, three more of which have formed the basis of this book. A separate stream of work on elected representatives in local government was drawn together and published as *The Making and Unmaking of Local Self-Government*.

The support of the Foundation has been invaluable. I owe a considerable debt to all its members and, in particular, to Sir Charles Carter, for his unfailing support and encouragement. I also extend my gratitude to the many others who gave me helpful advice and suggestions, and to all those local authority members and officers without whose cooperation this programme of work could not have been undertaken. I give special thanks to Bob Morris for his acute and knowledgeable comments on parts of this manuscript, and to the Local Government Management Board for making available their unpublished survey data.

In the preparation of this book I would like to single out the unparalleled care I have received from Ken Young. My one-time supervisor, and my long-standing friend, his imagination and expertise have never failed me. It is to him that I now dedicate this book, in enduring friendship.

Nirmala Rao
London, July 1995

1 Introducing the New World of Welfare

The post-war welfare state in Britain originated in a remarkable political consensus, a consensus that reflected both the public mood and the nature of British society at that time. There was agreement between the political parties on the capacity of the government to increase economic growth and improve the quality of life. It was accepted that the State had a responsibility to provide a range of social services, free at the point of use, so as to ensure a basic and rising standard of care for all its citizens. It was a new and seemingly robust settlement of the problem of welfare.

The stage was set for a 30-year period of sustained growth in expenditure, personnel and in the scope of government itself. The change was as much one of style as of substance. The growth of public administration occasioned by the war-time emergency was not curtailed but rolled forward, so creating a new class of public welfare professionals. Spanning almost the whole of the political spectrum, this new political class was united by the belief that ability and expertise were the only respectable justifications for recruitment to positions of authority and responsibility.

So powerful was this consensus that it characterised an entire political generation, with a shared agreement that

> palpable injustices and differences in the life-chances of the well-to-do and of the poor could be diminished by public expenditure and redistributive taxation: and that the agents to bring about change were the bureaucracies of central and local government, under the control of elected ministers and councillors.[1]

The consequence was a period of continuous expansion in services, expenditure and employment. A very great part of it incurred within local government, the institutional vehicle chosen to deliver the widest range of services, from public infrastructure and housing, to education and social welfare.[2] The proportion of total public expenditure incurred by the local authorities rose from 22 per cent in 1947 to 32 per cent in 1975.

Service growth did not come cheap. As a proportion of GNP, public expenditure in Britain grew from under 35 per cent in 1960 to nearly 50 per cent in 1975. Local authority expenditure itself grew from 9.7 per cent of GNP to 18.8 in 1975. Between 1964 and 1970, the effective rate of tax and insurance contributions for a married man with two children on average earnings more than doubled. The architects of the welfare state had encouraged the view that social needs were finite, that a National Health Service need not be a drain on the exchequer, and that equality of economic condition could be achieved through growth. Experience was to confound that expectation, for the development of the welfare state was dogged by persistent economic crisis.

Rising rates of inflation and unemployment, when coupled with increasing demand, led to real difficulties in meeting expectations. The prospects for sustaining services continued to be threatened by the continuing decline in Britain's relative economic performance. Britain's share of world exports, still almost a fifth in the late 1950s, had fallen to less than a tenth by 1965. The deficit on the balance of payments amounted to £265 million. Only the South East of England was in a position to compete with European countries on an equal footing; the rest of Britain had become an 'unprivileged' area.[3]

Productivity had increased more slowly than in other countries. Wages were growing at the same rate or faster, so unit labour costs and consumer prices spiralled upwards. As a result, Britain's share of world markets was diminishing. The export trade was not sufficient to keep factories open, while imports struck more deeply into the domestic market. At the point at which it was no longer possible to finance a growth in real incomes, relative decline was turning into absolute decline.[4]

By 1969, the United Kingdom ranked third in the OECD in terms of public expenditure as proportion of GDP. The crisis would not be postponed indefinitely. In 1975 the International Monetary Fund forced the Labour government to curtail the growth in public expenditure so leaving it directionless and drifting. Anthony Crosland was the messenger who translated the new reality to the local authorities; financing expanding welfare services through rising rates of taxation and low economic growth was not possible. 'The party', he proclaimed, 'was over'. But what was to follow?

The coming challenge

The seemingly remorseless growth in public expenditure, employment and taxation had not gone unresisted. The apparent consensus of the post-war settlement turned out to be more fragile than imagined; from its very inception there had been an undercurrent of resistance among dissident Conservatives. Some were moved by deep anxieties about the affordability of limitless expansion, a concern which some in the Labour party shared.[5] Others had a more fundamentalist view of rising public expenditure as a threat to a free society. For a while it seemed as if Conservative ministers could be as readily intoxicated by social expenditure as their Labour opponents. But the resignation in 1957 of Treasury ministers Peter Thorneycroft, Enoch Powell and Nigel Birch from the Macmillan government, in protest over the cabinet's refusal to make cuts in public expenditure, marked a watershed. From then on, the internal opposition had its heroes.

The intellectual drive for the opposition was provided by the Institute of Economic Affairs (IEA), a free market think-tank set up in 1960. Papers published by the Institute proposed alternative policies, including the removal of rent controls, vouchers for education, the contracting out of, and charging for, public services. Their adoption seemed unimaginable during the 1960s and early 1970s. Yet, after the fall of the Heath government in the spring of 1974, the political landscape changed dramatically. Sir Keith Joseph, formerly the most enthusiastic welfarist minister of the Macmillan era, recanted. He allied himself with the free marketeers and embarked on a series of speeches setting out a new agenda for Conservatism. His 1974 Preston speech introduced 'monetarism' into British politics, highlighting the virtues of competition and markets. He preached the teaching of the IEA on the need to create an 'enterprise culture'. The reason for Britain's economic decline, he argued, was that the country was 'over-governed, over-spent, over-taxed, over-borrowed and over-manned'.[6]

The Times, recalling the resignation of the Treasury team in 1957, credited Joseph with continuing the argument 'once associated with Enoch Powell', only 'at a deeper level of understanding'.[7] Carrying that understanding into practical policy proposals was to be the task of the Centre for Policy Studies, a think-tank which he established in 1974. Yet, while Joseph promoted the revival of free market thinking within the Conservative party, he could hardly aspire to lead it. Instead, when Heath faced the expected challenge to his leadership after the Conservatives' second 1974 election defeat, Joseph stood aside and threw his support behind his protege, victor-to-be Margaret Thatcher.

The influence of Joseph was critical in shaping Mrs Thatcher's new Conservative agenda. As she recalled:

> With Keith, I had come to see more clearly that what appeared to be technical arguments about the relationship between the stock of money and the level of prices went right to the heart of the question of what the role of government in a free society should be. It was the job of government to establish a framework of stability - whether constitutional stability, the rule of law or the economic stability provided by sound money - within which individual families and businesses were free to pursue their own dreams and ambitions. We had to get out of the business of telling people what their ambitions should be and how exactly to realise them. That was up to them.[8]

The emphasis for the Conservatives under Margaret Thatcher was to be on the individual, rather than on 'corporate bodies and institutions', thinking that subsequently came to be reflected in Conservative Political Centre pamphlets such as *The Right Approach* and *The Right Approach to the Economy*.

Mrs Thatcher and her followers repudiated the so called 'middle way' policies as the cause, not the remedy, for Britain's problems. Keen to abandon the Beveridge post-war settlement, Mrs Thatcher declared that the mixed economy had become a 'nonsense', and she blamed it for Britain's economic decline. The public services were, as she saw it, a drain on the political and economic strength of the country.

Central to the Thatcher/Joseph view of the welfare state was that it had been captured by public service bureaucrats who were stifling innovation and experiment, both nationally and locally. Their interest was in expanding services and maximising their budgets. Moreover, the Labour party increasingly revealed itself as the sponsor and protector of these same services, thus building an impulse to expansion into the political system itself. The problem of Britain was, then, to some degree a problem of government, and Mrs Thatcher set out to tackle it as such:

> I was determined at least to begin work on long-term reforms of government itself. If we were to channel more of the nation's talent into wealth-creating private business, this would inevitably mean reducing employment in the public sector. Since the 1960s, the public sector had grown steadily, accounting for an increased proportion of the total workforce.[9]

Her reforms presupposed a confrontation with the entire middle ground of British society, with what Noel Annan had dubbed 'our age'.

The new agenda

The new policy agenda was to replace the welfare monolith with a slimmed-down, competitive and pluralistic sector. Services such as health, housing and education, though continuing to remain publicly financed, were now to be introduced to markets and exposed to competition. And one important rationale for marketisation was that it would shift power away from established producers and empower those on whose behalf services were provided.

The emphasis on markets was most clearly established in the privatisation programme. This sought to reverse past nationalisation measures and place public utilities in the market place as monopoly suppliers under a strong regulatory regime. Locally-provided public services were in a different situation. They were to be either reconstructed on internal market or quasi-market lines, as in the case of the National Health Service, exposed directly to market forces, as in the case of some local authority services, or decentralised through the transfer of power and responsibility outside the local authority itself. What followed were variants on the theme of marketisation.

The National Health Service was to be the proving ground for the arguments which characterised the new Conservative philosophy. Much of the drive for change came from allegations that the service was provider-dominated, and lacking in accountability for the cost and quality of output of the service. So, when Mrs Thatcher took office in 1979, she was determined to 'simplify and decentralise' the service and 'eliminate bureaucracy'. An inquiry into the management of the NHS pointed to its 'institutionalised stagnation', and its failure to meet the needs of the patients.[10]

The government looked to the United States for ideas on how to develop what have come to be known as 'internal market' systems, to liberalise the NHS and increase its efficiency.[11] The NHS and Community Care Act, 1990 introduced the separation of the purchasing of health care from its provision, so that those providing the services would compete for business, and those whose role was to purchase it monitored performance. The practical working of the reform was based on the principle that funds should follow the patient, so that the hospital providing the service would win a corresponding fee.

The Act also contained provisions for the setting up of the National Health Service Trusts, semi-autonomous bodies ultimately responsible to the Secretary of State. These trusts were to manage their own finances, appoint their own staff and plan a package of services. These they would 'sell' either to the District Health Authorities, or to fund-holding family doctors (GPs), acting as purchasers of services on behalf of their patients.

Such measures attempted to secure some of the benefits of markets within the NHS while falling short of privatisation.[12]

Increasing pressures on social security and health expenditure led to some analogous changes in the social care area. The care needs of elderly people were a matter of national concern. Growing pressures for more publicly provided or subsidised care had to be set against the costs of meeting the expanding needs of an aging population. A report on community care by the Audit Commission in 1986 pointed to the 'perverse effects of social security policies' in this area. Following a further report in 1988, local authority social services departments were given the responsibility to plan care and ensure that individuals obtained it, either from the public, private or voluntary sectors. Subsequent legislation established the key role for local authorities as 'purchasers' of packages of care for people in need, instead of supplying it themselves. The separation of purchasing and providing roles typified this approach to marketisation.

The development of market-based approach to the management of public services had first been made apparent in the introduction of compulsory competitive tendering, initially in the NHS itself and then with extension to a range of local authority services. This movement was a gradual one, beginning in 1980 with the requirement that local authorities should submit some of their manual services to open competitive tender, a process which produced some of the benefits of a competitive regime without bringing about much change in who provided the service. During the third term, and under Mrs Thatcher's successor, competition struck deeper into local authority service provision, extending the range of affected services and tightening the competition regime. The subjection of core white collar services - finance, legal and administrative and computing services - to the competition regime encouraged the adoption of internal markets within local authorities, operating through internal trading or business units.

Replacing monolithic agency provision with markets (or quasi-markets) was also seen as the principal means of restoring a more pluralistic social order through citizen empowerment.[13] In Mrs Thatcher's version, marketisation would 'promote the vigorous virtues in individuals' by extending power to ordinary people, and accustoming them to its exercise.[14] This ambitious socio-political programme was most appropriately to be pursued in the fields of education and housing.

In education, parents were first empowered through their greater representation on governing bodies. This was one of Mrs Thatcher's earliest moves, which was further extended in 1988. A system of open enrolment was introduced in which catchment areas were abolished, funding followed the pupil, and schools were required to operate to their full capacity. In this way parents could choose to send their children to any school they liked, schools would have to compete for pupils, and bad schools would find it hard to continue. Other steps were taken to make parental choice and school based decision-making a reality by transferring operational responsibility from local education authorities to the schools themselves, under the local management of schools (LMS) initiative.

Finally, parental choice was to be more fully realised in the provisions whereby parents could vote to take their school out of LEA control and opt for a new grant maintained status, as independent bodies, financed directly by central government. Through these means an attempt was made to emulate, in the public education sector, the actual market conditions within which private schools operated, with only the direct financial transfer from parent to school lacking. That too was advocated by those who thought competition could only be fully realised in public education through a system of parental vouchers. Education vouchers were in that sense the logical further extension of quasi-market arrangements.

Housing is an area where the concept of the market is far more familiar and applicable than in education, and here the Thatcher government sought to deregulate the private rented sector and thus create more incentives to increase supply. In respect of public housing, the provision of the service by local authorities was to be subjected to privatisation, complemented by other measures designed to shift the balance of power from public landlords to their tenants. Under the *Right to Buy* provisions, sitting tenants were able to buy their homes with substantial discounts. For those who chose, or who were forced, to remain as council tenants, the *Tenants' Charter* gave them some explicit rights, whilst *tenants' choice* provisions enabled them to take over the management of their council estates should they vote to do so. A more far-reaching measure was *voluntary transfer*, under which local authorities could transfer all, or some, of their housing stock to housing associations or other approved landlords.

About this book

How successful were these various innovations in marketisation and empowerment is a matter for the chapters which follow. These deal with the impact of this search for *welfare pluralism* upon the local authorities whose powers and procedures were to be so drastically transformed. The overall significance of the Thatcher project is assessed in the final chapter.

The chapters deal in turn with the reforms in education (chapter 2), housing (chapter 3), compulsory competitive tendering (chapter 4) and community care (chapter 5). The changes to the National Health Service, while providing a paradigm for the introduction of quasi-markets in public services, lie outside the scope of this book. Its focus is upon the ways in which the kind of thinking which was manifested in the NHS was, in Mrs Thatcher's third term, transposed onto local authority services.

It may at first sight be perplexing that the radical impetus of Mrs Thatcher and her free-market supporters, trumpeted so clearly following her election as Conservative leader in 1975, did not translate into governmental action until after almost a decade in power. The first two Thatcher governments were preoccupied with economic policy, public expenditure control, and trade union reform, as well as mounting a determined attack on the powers of local authorities. Even in her second administration (1983-87), radical action was constrained by the range of opinion represented in the cabinet. And throughout this period, it seemed easier to identify the problems of public service inefficiencies than to prescribe a remedy. Not until the third term did Mrs Thatcher see a real chance to 'roll back the welfare state' by tackling the ways in which basic services were provided by the local authorities.

This stream of radical legislative change, following on the heels of the apparent abandonment of the idea of local authorities as partners in government, fuelled concern in many quarters about the impact of extreme centralisation on central and local government relations and on the 'political constitution' itself. Among those troubled by these developments was the Joseph Rowntree Foundation, which established, under the chairmanship of Sir Charles Carter, a committee to promote serious consideration of their potential impact.

The chapters that follow draw upon four of the research studies commissioned by the Foundation as part of the research programme which followed. Undertaken by the author, first at the Policy Studies Institute and later at Queen Mary and Westfield College, University of London, these studies dealt successively with the impact of the Education Reform Act, 1988; of the Housing Act, 1988; of the Local Government Act, 1988; and of the National Health Service and Community Care Act, 1990. The studies were based upon fieldwork undertaken during the period 1989 to 1994 in a large number of local areas throughout Britain. Each involved interviews with the key people engaged in the initial stages of implementation. Bringing the story up to date has entailed drawing upon the later work of other writers, the credit for which will be apparent from the source references.

Notes

1. N. Annan, *Our Age: Portrait of a Generation*, London, Weidenfeld and Nicolson, 1990, p. 12.
2. R. Lowe, *The Welfare State in Britain Since 1945*, Basingstoke, Macmillan, 1993.
3. S.R. Letwin, *The Anatomy of Thatcherism*, London, HarperCollins, 1992, pp. 92-93.
4. A. Sked and C. Cook, *Post-War Britain: A Political History*, fourth edition, Harmondsworth, Penguin, 1993, p. 327.
5. C. Barnett, *The Audit of War*, London, Macmillan, 1986.
6. Letwin, *Anatomy of Thatcherism*, p. 85.
7. ibid., p. 84.
8. M. Thatcher, *The Downing Street Years*, London, HarperCollins, 1995, p. 14.
9. ibid., p. 45.
10. Department of Health and Social Security, *NHS Management Inquiry*, London, HMSO, 1983.
11. P. Mullen, 'Planning and internal markets', in P. Spurgeon (editor), *The New Face of the NHS*, Harlow, Longman, 1993, pp. 23-45.
12. C. Ham and P. Spurgeon, in Spurgeon (editor) *The New Face of the NHS*, pp. 1-22.
13. See J. Le Grand and W. Bartlett, *Quasi-markets and Social Policy*, Basingstoke, Macmillan, 1993.
14. For a full account of Margaret Thatcher's thinking on the 'vigorous virtues', see Letwin, *Anatomy of Thatcherism*, pp. 33-36; 101-104.

2 Education: Tipping the Balance of Power

In the years following 1945, and for most of the next half-century, local authorities and schools worked within the framework defined by the 1944 Education Act. There was a general consensus about the distribution of power and responsibilities in education. Local education authorities (LEAs) had the statutory responsibility for its provision, including responsibility for the curriculum in county schools. Although schools were given the freedom to determine their own curriculum, its content and its style, in practice this was influenced by the secondary school examining bodies. It was customary to talk of a partnership between central government, LEAs and teachers, in which power over the organisation and content of education was diffused among these different elements.[1] Within this consensual structure of educational policy-making, firm leadership from the centre did not invalidate the concurrent assumption of strong local government.[2]

The financial climate in the immediate post-war period was favourable to education, and until 1972 the service benefited from substantial investment. This was required by the rise in the birth rate up to 1964, and the consequent increase in the numbers of children coming forward at successive levels. The policy imperatives of the time - to increase the number of school buildings and teachers - largely resulted from this rising demographic tide.[3]

During the late 1960s and early 1970s the consensus crumbled, and the education system came under increasing criticism. Education was seen as failing to make a sufficient contribution to national objectives, and doubts were raised about the appropriateness of the diffused responsibilities created by the 1944 Act. A general discontent, voiced by employer representatives and school governors, converged with a trenchant indictment of modern education made by conservative educationalists. During the latter half of the 1970s these criticisms crystallised in a distinctive policy position which won favour within the Conservative party.[4] They provided the impetus for a programme of legislative reform once the party came to power under Margaret Thatcher in 1979. Foremost within this programme was the Education Reform Act of 1988, which decisively rejected the post-war consensus and the structure of power relations by which it had been maintained.

The road to reform

There were three main periods in the development of the new critique of post-war education. In the first phase (1969-75), the challenge to state education was offered in the radical Right's Black Papers, which criticised progressive practices and emphasised the need for educational quality and basic learning. In the second phase (1974-84) the idea of a 'parents' charter' was developed; once implemented, this gave parents for the first time statutory places on governing bodies, and the right to information on such matters as examination results. For the first time under the Education Act, 1980, an LEA had to show why a parent's preference for a school should not be satisfied.[5] The third period (1984-88) witnessed a growth in the advocacy of enhanced parental power, culminating in the Education Reform Act, 1988.[6] This Act fundamentally altered the traditional tripartite system of education based on the relationship between central government, local government, and schools, which had been undisturbed since 1944. It enhanced the powers of central government while at the same time enabling schools to become more independent of their local education authorities.

The demand for education to become more responsive to the needs of employers had been strongly expressed for some years, yet the curriculum itself remained a 'secret garden', not to be entered by non-educationalists. The taboos were first broken by Prime Minister James Callaghan's Ruskin College speech in October 1976. His speech, and the subsequent studies leading to the 'Yellow Book', launched the so-called Great Debate, which called attention to the need for more centralised control of education through the creation of a core curriculum.[7]

At the heart of the debate was the allegation that the state system had failed. There were two distinct but related concerns voiced at this time. The first was about the standards being achieved by pupils and about the relevance of what was being taught.[8] The second was that the economic well-being of the UK was being adversely affected by the inability of the education system to respond effectively to changing demands for skilled labour.

'Standards' had become a rallying cry for critics of post-war education. Dr Rhodes Boyson, a former headteacher and Conservative MP, who had contributed to the Black Papers, was a vocal critic of what he described as 'low standards of discipline and academic work'.[9] These he attributed to modern teaching methods, and to the climate of the comprehensive school, and his proposals, notably the testing of all pupils at 7, 11 and 14, were later to become party policy. Also influential in the opposition years 1975-79 was the Conservative party's education policy adviser, Stuart Sexton, who championed 'excellence' as an educational aim.[10]

Employers' dissatisfaction with the nature and quality of the education provided to school leavers converged with politicians articulating what they believed to be parents' demands for more intervention. The result was an emphasis on public accountability. There was growing pressure for public participation in the education service and for parent representation within the system. The proposal for parents to have a powerful voice on the governing bodies of schools was endorsed in 1978 by the Taylor Committee of Inquiry into the government and management of schools and in the Conservative election manifesto in the following year.[11]

The debate did not conclude with the election of a Conservative government in 1979, but rather was extended and intensified as different elements within the government struggled with each other and with the sceptical civil servants at the DES. The common ground in the Conservative philosophy of education which characterised the 1980s was the need to bring about a more responsive and more accountable education service. The argument was that education was not developing the talents and abilities of children adequately. Such critics of established policy as the Hillgate Group, and the more influential Institute of Economic Affairs, argued that market forces were the most effective way of determining a school's curriculum and of raising standards; central government intervention was necessary only as an interim strategy to undermine the power of the vested interests that threatened educational standards and traditional values.[12]

Blame for education's failings was thus laid at the door of the existing education 'establishment': the local education authorities, the teachers' organisations, the teacher training institutions and various other groups associated with shaping the education system. The critics argued that it had begun to ignore the demands of the consumers - parents and children - and responded instead to the requirements of the producers -

local education authorities, teachers and other professionals.[13] The Adam Smith Institute's *Omega File on Education* suggested in 1984 that the problems facing education, in common with other public services, were those of 'producer capture': it was organised to suit the needs of producers rather than those of consumers.[14]

The thrust of the criticism accordingly focused on poor and inadequate standards, irrelevant curricula and the need to reconstruct the education system to conform to the principles of consumer choice and accountability. Their view was that parents should be given the 'free choice' of schools and a strong voice in their management. The control of schools should not be in the hands of local authorities, and school management should be more devolved.

> If the system itself were changed to one of self-governing, self-managing, budget centres, which were obliged, for their survival, to respond to the 'market', then there would be an in-built mechanism to raise standards and change forms and types of education in accordance with the market demand.[15]

Making the education service more accountable and responsive to the choices of individuals was thus the key to improving standards. Such were the ideas which shaped the Conservatives' legislative programme instigating what Sir Keith Joseph imagined to be a new era of 'choice and excellence'.

The 1980 Education Act marked the beginning of this new era.[16] For the first time, the Act provided for at least two from among the parents of registered pupils to be included among the governors appointed by the local authority.[17] Such provisions were further enhanced in the Education (No 2) Act, 1986, which advanced the representation and power of parent governors on governing bodies, and the Education (Schools) Act, 1992, which required the publication of information on school performance. The 1980 Act also introduced the Assisted Places Scheme, which enabled academically able children whose parents had limited financial means to secure access to independent schools. As regards the content of education, central government strengthened its own influence over the curriculum by abolishing the Schools Council in 1984 and establishing the new Secondary Examinations Council and the School Curriculum Development Committee, members of which were nominated by the DES.

As part of making the education more responsive to the needs of employers, the Thatcher government sought to provide a more vocational orientation to the curriculum for 'non-academic' pupils. It introduced schemes such as the Training and Vocational Education Initiative (TVEI) for 14 to 18 year-olds, the Certificate of Pre-Vocational Education (CPVE), and the Youth Training Scheme (YTS) within colleges and industry (under the auspices of the then Manpower Services Commission). These initiatives forced institutions such as colleges of further education, maintained by the local education authorities, to compete in the market place. They, together with the later National Vocational Qualification, (NVQ), involved a shift of power from the Department of Education and Science to the Department of Employment: the DES was seen by other departments to be too remote from the problems of the 'real world' and lacking the will to impose national policy on local authorities.

After 1981, the DES began to take a more interventionist role, led by Secretary of State Sir Keith Joseph, who saw his mission as to root out opposition to the enterprise culture where it was most deeply-embedded - in the schools and teacher training colleges. The latter he addressed in his white paper *Teaching Quality* in 1983, and in the following year introduced a system of Education Support Grants.[18] The system allowed specific grants (up to 0.5 per cent of Rate Support Grant) to be paid to local education authorities in respect of expenditure incurred on certain programmes initiated by the Secretary of State. The Department also introduced criteria for in-service training; authorities had to meet these criteria before they could receive grant. In the years that followed, the centre assumed further powers. The Education Act, 1986 gave the Secretary of State power to make regulations for the appraisal of teachers in schools and colleges, and for the approval of teacher training courses.

Sir Keith Joseph's white paper *Better Schools* set out his alternative vision for education in terms that have been described as a modern 'Black Paper'.[19] Here the strategy of reversing post-war trends was expounded, the object being to restore 'a common-sense approach to education in place of Labour's dogma'.[20] These statements of values were not however followed up by much action, and when Kenneth Baker replaced Sir Keith Joseph in 1986 he set out to build upon the relatively limited achievements of the first two Thatcher governments. He was to recall in his memoirs that

> No one had yet grasped the nettle of major legislative overhaul. While Keith Joseph had planted many of the seeds... I realised that the scale of the problem could only be tackled by a coherent national programme, and time was not on our side. I knew what I wanted in the package...[21]

Baker's contribution was an Education Reform Bill which marked the most sweeping set of changes. Thereafter education policy expressed a new and radical view of education management, the essence of which was to dismantle the old power structures and tip the balance of power firmly away from producers towards the consumers of education. While subsequent legislation was to consolidate upon this base, the Education Reform Act remained the most distinctive expression of that thinking.

The Education Reform Act

The Education Reform Act, 1988 was 'the most important and far-reaching piece of educational law making in England and Wales since the Education Act of 1944'.[22] It restored to central government powers over the curriculum which had been surrendered between the wars, and set up formal machinery for exercising power at the centre. It introduced limits on the functions of the local education authority while giving greater autonomy to schools and governing bodies.

The Act prescribed a national curriculum for schools, and gave greater managerial autonomy for schools and governing bodies. It extended parental choice and delegated decision-making in locally-maintained schools. It introduced changes in the structure and funding of further and higher education.[23] The Act paved the way for directly-funded city technology colleges.[24] It also established the mechanisms for creating a new breed of centrally-funded grant maintained schools where parents chose to opt out of local authority control. The provisions of the Act reduced the powers of the LEAs and made schools more directly responsive to consumers through the delegation of school budgets to governing bodies to provide for 'the local management of schools'.

Critics of course questioned the assumption that a market-based approach would improve choice and quality. The flaw was that education is not a commodity which can be marketed. 'If education is regarded as a learning process involving the realisation of human potential', Stewart Ranson claimed, 'it is neither a product nor a process which is appropriate to the market place'.[25] He argued that choice requires surplus places; but

> If market forces fill some schools and close others then choice evaporates leaving only a hierarchy of esteem, with little actual choice for many. The market is a crude mechanism of social selection.[26]

The feared hierarchy of schools would run from independent schools through city technology colleges and grant maintained schools down to LEA-maintained schools. The critics warned that grant maintained schools might be impelled by the dynamics of the quasi-market to move into the private sector, thus making possible a largely privatised system based on education vouchers.[27]

However real these fears, the intention to decentralise by extending choice and diversity was unmistakable. Yet it was linked in the same statute with what Mrs Thatcher called 'the most important centralising measure' of all - the creation of a national curriculum.[28]

National curriculum and testing

The Act set out a framework for the school curriculum in England and Wales. It introduced a national curriculum which included three core subjects (mathematics, English and science) and seven foundation subjects (history, geography, technology, music, art, physical education and modern language), with Welsh as a core subject in Welsh-speaking schools and otherwise a foundation subject throughout Wales.

The national curriculum was designed to raise standards by ensuring that all pupils studied a broad and balanced range of subjects throughout the compulsory schooling period. The idea was that all children were entitled to a common set of educational experiences, premised on the belief that there could be a national consensus on the general aims and objectives of compulsory education. The national curriculum was also expected to facilitate the geographical mobility of families, thus removing a source of inflexibility in the labour market as well as increase the accountability of schools.

The curriculum embodied a clear definition of the objectives and standards to be expected from state education. Its introduction starts with English for five year olds and with maths and science for five to 11 year olds. The complete curriculum will not be in operation for all children from five to 16 until 1996. The Secretary of State has responsibility for specifying attainment targets, programmes of study, and arrangements for assessments to be established for each of the four key stages at 7, 11, 14 and 16. The assessments at 7 and 11 relate to the core subjects: at 14 and 16 to the full range of the national curriculum. Pupils are assessed on their performance within these programmes of study, while attainment targets establish 'what children should normally be expected to know, understand and be able to do at around the specified ages'.

The national curriculum had all-party support and general professional acceptance. Most of its proposals were also accepted by schools, parents and local authorities. Some, however, have encountered professional resistance. Critics argued that the national curriculum could prove to be concerned more with controlling the timetable than with improving the quality of teaching and learning experiences. Reservations were also expressed about its assessment provisions and staffing implications. The new powers of the Secretary of State to define and amend programmes of study represented a sharp break with recent practice and presented another challenge to the teaching profession. Headteachers and staff lost the considerable degree of freedom they formerly had to determine the curriculum.

The national curriculum was soon to run into difficulties. The Prime Minister had wanted a basic syllabus for English, maths and science and not the complex framework which Baker had negotiated. Baker's successor, John MacGregor, sought to slim down the system he had inherited, while *his* successor, Kenneth Clarke, was to move still further away from the Baker plans. In simplifying the system, Clarke brought the national curriculum proposals into closer alignment with the former Prime Minister's views and with the instincts of the Conservative party although, ironically, the former Black Paper advocates of 'excellence' were to round on the government for their betrayal of the original aims of the project.

Another aspect of the national curriculum which has been the subject of continued controversy is national testing at 7, 11 and 14. Supporters of the reforms argued that assessment is a way of giving parents a check on the teachers. Opponents claimed that the system was likely to be dominated by nationally-prescribed tests which would undermine the assessments carried out by teachers. Others criticised what they saw as the distorting effect of paper and pencil tests on children's learning, the danger that testing will lead to 'labelling' individual children, and the possibly damaging effects on schools of the publication of results.

Testing was to prove the most controversial of all the proposals and the most difficult to implement, dependent as it was on the co-operation of the teaching profession. Kenneth Baker's preference for broad entitlement curriculum had led him to agree a complex and comprehensive testing scheme. John MacGregor attempted to simplify it; his successor Kenneth Clarke was to condemn the forms of tests adopted as 'elaborate nonsense'. It fell to John Patten to try to make assessment of the national curriculum work, but by June 1993 the hostility of the teachers to the tests themselves, and to the administrative load they imposed, threatened to derail this component of the education reform programme.

Parental choice: open enrolment and opting-out

The Education Reform Act set out important measures to extend parental choice. Open enrolment was designed to give parents a stronger say in the schools their children attend by eliminating school catchment areas. Under the Act all maintained schools are required to accept a full complement of pupils up to the limit of their physical capacity. This is defined in terms of a 'standard' number of places set for each school.[29]

The local authority associations argued that these proposals made rational planning of school provision impossible. Authorities which had taken the opportunities presented by the falling rolls after 1980 to reorganise their post-primary education claimed to have demonstrated a capacity for flexibility and continuous strategic planning which the new provision would preclude. Other critics claimed that the policy would have a limited impact, arguing that choice can be exercised only in areas where there is available surplus capacity and where schools have a gap between their admissions and standard numbers. It was also felt that open enrolment would perpetuate and even amplify the divisions between schools on the basis of race and social class.

Other measures proposed to enhance parental choice included the creation of city technology colleges and grant maintained schools. City technology colleges, set up by the Secretary of State, were to be independent of the local education authority, and substantially funded by industry. They were to provide a broad curriculum for 11 to 18 year-olds and recruit pupils representing a cross section of the population in terms of ability. Their curriculum was to have a strong emphasis on science and technology and they were to 'seek to develop the qualities of enterprise, self-reliance and responsibility and secure the highest possible standards of achievement'.[30]

'Opting out' enables governors and parents of all maintained secondary and primary schools to apply to the Secretary of State for grant maintained status (GMS), under which a school escapes from LEA control and is directly funded by the DES (later the Department for Education).[31] The Act made provision for the balloting of parents on whether to apply for grant maintained status.[32] The Act specifies in detail the rules governing the transition of a local authority maintained school to grant maintained status, but makes no provision for grant maintained schools to opt back into their local education authorities.

Some schools were quick to put forward the view that by opting out they could be more responsive to the community. They argued that they would be able to employ more appropriate staff and that in general they would be better run independently of LEA control. On the negative side their reasons for applying included the wish to avert a threat of closure or amalgamation with other schools, and fear of political interference by the local authority. By 1995, over 1,000 schools nationally had achieved grant maintained status.

The implicit aim of open enrolment and opting out is to provide a pincer movement so as to encourage competition for pupils between schools. The assumption is that schools which are responsive to choices made by parents in the market are more likely to produce high levels of achievement, to the benefit of individual pupils and society. Advocates of the market philosophy argue that the exercise of parental choice would ensure that bad schools will close and good schools flourish.

Like open enrolment, the opting out provisions caused difficulties for LEAs seeking to plan their school system. The proposals frustrated several authorities such as Derbyshire and Bedfordshire in their attempts to reorganise their schools and save money by eliminating surplus places. Many LEAs feared they would be left with responsibility for the poorer and weaker schools - those least able to cope with the pressures of competition. Others argued that the very principle of opting out fatally undermined their ability to manage the local school system.[33]

More importantly, some predicted that the government would ensure that grant maintained schools would be better-funded than their LEA-maintained counterparts. The DES Circular on GMS stated that grant maintained schools should not change the financial position either of the school or of the local ratepayers; and that a 'grant maintained school be funded on the basis of the same resource allocation formula as would apply to it had it remained within the local authority'.

Nevertheless, the Act provided for some additional funding of GMS schools.[34] For example, such schools are entitled to capital grants within the government's overall limits for capital spending, and to special purpose grants, some of which are intended to compensate for the loss of LEA training grants, while the LEA loses revenue support grant and control over the property attached to schools. Because GMS schools receive an allocation to meet the costs of the support and administrative services hitherto provided by the LEA, authorities feared that their ability to provide a comprehensive service to locally-maintained schools would be constrained by widespread opting out. A special funding regime for this new education sector was introduced in the Education Act, 1993.

Local Management of Schools

The local management of schools (LMS) was a key aspect of the Conservative government's policies for improving teaching and learning in schools through the promotion of choice and competition.[35] At the same time, it reflected a much more general move to locate decision-making at the school level, enabling schools to use resources more effectively to carry out education activities according to their characteristics and needs. School systems in countries as diverse as Australia, Hong Kong, Holland and the United States were in the same period experiencing similar moves to school-level delegation.[36]

In Britain, a number of authorities, led by Solihull and Cambridgeshire, had experimented with forms of local management although this involved only financial devolution. Solihull had introduced financial delegation in 1981, when three of the authority's schools were given control over 90 per cent of their budgets under the scheme of 'local financial autonomy'. The number of schools in the scheme gradually increased over the years to include a total of 17 by 1989. In 1982 a pilot project involving six secondary schools and one primary school was set up in Cambridgeshire. A further ten primary schools were given control of their budgets in 1986, and since April 1987 all secondary schools in the county were made responsible for their budgets, in advance of the legislation.

Influenced in large part by these experiments, the Education Reform Act compelled all LEAs to accept local management as a new form of partnership with their schools.[37] In devolving management responsibilities to the school level, LEAs had to recognise that their main role in the future lay in providing overall leadership, and in enabling schools and colleges to implement the changes.

Local management of schools was intended to enable heads and governors to manage schools efficiently by providing the information and support they need to make management decisions, while giving them the freedom to determine the use of resources to meet the needs and priorities they have identified.[38] By delegating the management of cash resources, personnel and premises to the local level LMS aimed to improve the quality of education and learning for pupils and achieve better financial management. Some critics, however, thought that the overall financial arguments of the government's plans had not been adequately demonstrated.[39]

The Act required each authority to draw up its own scheme delegating to schools a budget which schools may use at their discretion. In brief, the budget was arrived at by deciding which functions and activities should be retained by the local authority and dividing the total cost of the remaining functions and activities on a formula basis between the schools themselves. All local education authorities were required to submit schemes providing for such financial delegation to the Secretary of the State for his approval by September 1989. To help the DES and the local authorities devise such schemes, the government commissioned Coopers and Lybrand to report on the practical considerations surrounding the exercise.[40] The Act required each authority to consult with the governing bodies and heads of each of its schools in preparing the scheme. By 1 February 1990, 84 authorities had either received formal approval for their schemes or were being consulted on modifications prior to approval. Fears that the new system would produce uniformity proved unwarranted; an analysis of the first 90 submissions by LEAs showed considerable differences of approach.[41]

Once their schemes were approved, local authorities had to decide their overall spending for the coming year. They were then required to subtract the amount they intended to retain for central services. These services fell into two categories: mandatory services (which must be provided centrally) and discretionary services (those which the authority could either provide centrally or delegate to schools). Mandatory items included capital spending, allocation of grants for specific purposes, essential central administration, inspectors and advisers and home-to-school transport. Such items were to account for about 12.5 per cent of the total school budget. Discretionary items included services such as school meals, repairs and maintenance, pupil support, and supply cover for sickness and maternity leave. These could account for up to 10 per cent of the total budget but it was expected that the proportion would be reduced to seven per cent within three years to provide a continuous spur to the process of delegation.

Each LEA was also required to determine a formula of its own for allocating the remaining 75 to 80 per cent of the total budget to schools. Circular 7/88 required the formula to be 'clear, simple and predictable in its impact', and to be based on an assessment of school's objective needs, rather than on historic expenditure. The formula was to take account of the number and ages of pupils, and could include other factors such as those affecting the needs of individual schools. At least 75 per cent of the money to be distributed to schools through the formula had to be based on pupil numbers and weighted by age, with the remaining 25 per cent reflecting special factors such as split sites, floor area and special needs. LEAs were also required to show clearly the way in which 'the aggregated schools budget' (the total amount to be distributed) was to be allocated to each individual school in the form of 'school budget shares'.

Six years later, Circular 2/94 went much further to draw together the scheme of delegation and the curricular duties of the schools, governing bodies and LEAs:

> Within this statutory framework, governing bodies are free to allocate resources to their own curricular priorities from delegated budgets. Schemes should not include conditions or requirements which cut across the discretion and duties that governing bodies are given in that framework. LEAs should, however, provide in their schemes that governing bodies should spend their delegated budgets in a manner which is consistent with the implementation of the National Curriculum; with the statutory requirements relating to the curriculum as a whole, including religious education and worship; and, for county and controlled schools, and special needs, with the LEA's curriculum policy as modified by the governing body...[42]

The local determination of formulae enabled LEAs to take different approaches, to retain different proportions of total budget for central services within the broad requirement, and to adopt a variety of methods for resource allocation.[43] Despite these variations in local arrangements for distribution, the formula was to be applied to all schools, and not restricted to those that became eligible for financial delegation. It was intended to be based on 'actual needs' rather than historic spending patterns. The funding of all the schools in a local authority area on the basis of a common formula prevented a local authority from intervening in favour of one school rather than another. Inevitably, though, as a result of the introduction of this new funding scheme, some schools were to gain and others lose.[44]

The Act emphasised the need for each authority to consult with the governing bodies and heads of schools in preparing the scheme. In taking responsibility for spending the school's budget, governors are bound by their duty to ensure that the national curriculum is taught, and taught in accordance with the scheme. Delegation can be suspended by the local authority if it believes the governors have been guilty of a persistent failure to do their job. However, this power is constrained by conditions which provide a right of appeal by the governors to the Secretary of State. Evidence from the survey carried out by the LGMB in 1992 showed a marked increase in the proportion of the formula based on age-weighted pupils, from just above the required minimum of 75 per cent in 1990 to almost 82 per cent in 1992.

Table 2.1
Budgetary delegation in 1990 and 1992

	1990	1992	Number of respondents
Percentage of schools budget delegated to schools	71.7	75.3	54
Percentage of budget allocated to central administration	3.3	2.4	54
Percentage of formula based on age-weighted pupils	76.6	81.7	55

Source: LGMB, unpublished data.

Restructuring education: new roles and responsibilities

The overall effect of the Education Reform Act was to bring about a fundamental shift in the balance of power between the several participants in the educational process, tipping it dramatically in favour of parents, headteachers and governors. This section of the chapter sets out the provisions which brought about that change. A later section examines how it worked in practice in a number of LEAs and schools.

The role of central government: from 'promotion' to 'control and direction'

In his major study of central-local relations, J.A.G. Griffith argued that the essential role of the Department of Education and Science in the education system was one of 'promoting' central government values and policies.[45] Since the mid 1970s, the Department of Education and Science sought to acquire the necessary steering capacity to implement its responsibility for policy under Section 1 of the 1944 Act; the Education Reform Act now provided it with those powers.

While in the past central government gave the local education authority, governing body and headteacher collective responsibility to decide what kind of curriculum was best for their school, the Act now placed the curriculum under the control of central government. The DES - later the DfE - directs the curriculum by specifying subject areas which have to be covered and programmes of study for those subjects, and by setting up standards of assessment to match them. It lays down the duty for the governing bodies, headteachers and local education authorities to ensure that the curriculum is implemented.

Under the Act two new bodies - the National Curriculum Council (NCC) and the Secondary Examinations Assessment Council (SEAC) - were set up under the control of central government. They were responsible for keeping all aspects of the schools' curriculum and assessment under review and for advising the Secretary of State on such matters concerned with curriculum and assessment as he may refer to or as they see fit. The main thrust of the NCC was to assist the introduction of national curriculum. The SEAC took over the functions of the former Secondary Examinations Council, with responsibility for developing the assessment system. These two new bodies were however fated to be short-lived. In 1991, Secretary of State for Education Kenneth Clarke rejected their joint advice on curriculum and dismissed the chairman of both. With the teaching unions launching a successful boycott of assessment of national curriculum, a new body, the School Curriculum and Assessment Authority (SCAA) replaced them. Sir Ron Dearing, chairman-designate of the new body, was first appointed to chair both SEAC and the NCC in an attempt to find an agreeable formula for assessment.

The 1988 Act also enabled central government to intervene directly to support new institutions. These include the new grant maintained schools and the city technology colleges. The multitude of powers in the hands of central government are further evident in the rights given to the Secretary of State to approve the schemes of financial and management delegation submitted by local authorities. The Secretary of State also has the power to impose a scheme when an authority fails to submit a satisfactory one. Schools were thus given the control of their own affairs but only within the established conventions approved by the ministerial authority.

New roles for the LEA: the enabling authority

The Education Reform Act redistributed powers in a way that raised important implications for local policy making and planning. The role of the local education authority changed fundamentally. Its powers to manage the education service became restricted as central government acquired greater control, and as substantial powers were transferred to schools and governing bodies. Local authorities lost direct control of their institutions and their role as 'strategic' managers became more important. Their role change could be summarised as a series of shifts from administration to management; from providing to enabling; from maintaining to quality control; and from control to influence.

In the past, local education authorities were heavily involved with administrative matters such as the upkeep of school buildings, capital programmes and school admissions. In their new role the LEAs are responsible for the provision and allocation of budgets to schools, for determining the scope and basis of allocation of budgets, and for other matters including teacher appraisals, staff development and recruitment procedures. While still concerned with a policy framework, LEAs have been less involved in the detailed administration of schools. They have to set the framework and guidelines within which institutions will operate. In matters of the curriculum, for example, they have to produce their own curriculum policy documents and they have a duty to ensure their implementation.

Local authorities also acquired the responsibility to prepare governors and headteachers for their new role and to give support, advice and guidance where necessary. They have to facilitate and help schools to promote change and enable them to make effective use of their new powers. LEAs are expected to encourage the public to become actively involved in the education system and they have the duty to provide information to and promote discussion with the public.

Governors: from 'tea party tokens' to 'company directors'

For much of the post-war period, the role of governors was largely ceremonial.[46] Governing bodies had, for example, little influence on what was taught in schools. They could not impose their views on a school without the support of the local authority. Although the Education Act, 1980 was significant in extending the powers of governing bodies, in practice they were rarely seen to have had an important role. This was changed by the Education (No 2) Act, 1986 and the Education Reform Act, 1988, which together enhanced their powers, duties and responsibilities.

The first of these two statutes gave governors responsibility for an element of the school budget which they could spend as they thought appropriate. It further changed the balance of governing bodies by reducing the numbers of local authority governors and increasing those of parent governors.

Under the Conservative reforms the governing body gained virtual control of every aspect of the school, within the framework of the policies of the local education authority and national legislation. Crucially the Education Reform Act gave governing bodies the control of the budget, and the powers to direct the spending according to its needs and priorities. They have been elevated to the status of 'directors' of a 'company', for such has the school now become.

Most importantly, governors gained the responsibility for the oversight of the curriculum, and may examine any curriculum draft put before them. They were also given the right to obtain an explanation from the teaching staff on any matter they might wish to pursue. On staffing issues the balance of power shifts to them, as they are given powers over the appointment and dismissal of teaching and non-teaching staff. However, if they wish to dismiss or suspend any senior staff, they have to consider the advice of the chief education officer and (where relevant) the headteacher.

In parallel with their new powers, the governors have also been made more accountable to parents. They must, for example, produce and keep up to date a curriculum policy document for parents, to show how they intend to meet the requirements of the national curriculum. They have to present annual reports to parents, discuss with them the progress of the school (as laid down by the 1986 Act), and provide explanations on matters such as sex education policy and the ways in which the budget has been spent. As well as giving the details to parents, the governors are also required to report to the LEA about the way in which its curriculum policy is being interpreted and the delegated money has been used.

Headteachers: from professional leaders to institutional managers

Under the Act, headteachers have taken on new management functions within schools. They are entrusted with a range of duties and responsibilities. They have to ensure the organisation and implementation of the national curriculum, participate in the selection and appointment of teaching and non-teaching staff, review the work and organisation of the school, evaluate the standards of teaching and learning, participate in staff appraisal and development, advise the governing body and liaise with the LEA and its officers.

The 1988 Coopers and Lybrand report referred to local management of schools (LMS) rather than the then-current local financial management (LFM). This was intended to emphasise the importance of policy and planning above accounting. The task for the headteacher is to prepare a development plan for the school, demonstrating how staff, resources and policies are to support the implementation of school's educational values. Apart from these duties, headteachers must now add to their range of skills financial expertise, resource management and a sufficient knowledge of accountancy and management for the day-to-day running of their schools.

Parents: from 'keep out' to 'partners'

The 1944 Education Act required LEAs to educate children in accordance with the wishes of parents. The idea of parents as partners, however, was largely ignored for much of the post-war period. The Education Reform Act brought parents centre-stage in an attempt to 'empower' them. Parents were to be seen as consumers who will judge the performance of the school on the basis of its results, and make informed choices. Schools were required to furnish information to parents on the performance of pupils by way of assessments and by publicising results. Parents can demand explanations if the school fails to implement any policy, and can make their approval or disapproval known to governing bodies and teachers. They can thus force schools to deliver the national curriculum and, if unsatisfied, can appeal to the Secretary of State. Parents have a notional right to demand a place for their child in a different school. They can, if they meet the ballot requirements, collectively seek to remove a school from the control of its local authority by achieving grant maintained status.

These developments are in addition to some of the privileges parents already enjoyed under previous legislation. For example, the 1980 Education Act required governing bodies for the first time to include parent representatives. The government argued that parents, as clients, would be better able than others to monitor standards and quality. By the very fact of their representation on the governing body, the school would become more accountable to the community. It was claimed that by including parents on governing bodies, schools would be less subject to the inefficiencies of local education authorities, and governors would be more able than the education officers to make judgements about the real needs of schools. The Education Act, 1986 increased parental representation on governing bodies. Taking these together with the Education Reform Act, 1988, parents are now in the forefront of the school education system.

From a universal to a pluralistic system

The Education Reform Act dispensed with many of the traditional controls of the local education authority and created, in its place, the mechanisms for new controls - on the one hand those imposed by the formal, legal and administrative machinery, and on the other those exercised by parents and governors. The aim was to inject plurality and diversity into the existing system - by exposing education to the free play of market forces and consumer sovereignty.

Yet there was also the steering hand of the central government. The government assumed new regulatory powers for centralised control of the curriculum. The actions of the centre now strongly condition the ability of LEAs to plan education, diminishing their powers to control enrolment and create school provision. This is evident in the various provisions of the Act designed to give parents the right to select schools; in the encouragement given to parents (and therefore schools) to opt out of local authority control; in the increase of parental representation on the governing bodies; and in the transfer of financial and managerial responsibilities to schools and governing bodies.

There is of course a tension between more central control and more autonomy at the school level. In terms of curriculum control, the 1988 Act places additional restrictions on schools which otherwise are left to operate in a free market. Prime Minister Margaret Thatcher and her ministers argued that it was possible to take the risks inherent in setting schools free from local authorities only if there were to be a clearly defined national curriculum and an established framework within which schools could exercise their independence. Centralisation *and* decentralisation were both required.[47]

Thus a situation in which the local education authorities had a near monopoly of school and college provision was replaced by one in which grant maintained schools, local education authorities, as well as independent and public schools, compete for custom. The future survival of any LEA as a meaningful player in local education would depend upon their capacity to grasp and fulfil this new role. How did they respond to this challenge?

Local authorities' approaches to change

By 1992 local authorities had conceded a greater influence to users in the running and management of local education services. The changes enforced by the Education Reform Act were unwelcome, but were recognised as irreversible. Yet adapting to them was another matter. Apart from the rhetoric of Conservative ministers, there was no guidance on how to make sense of the new power relations in education. In 1989 the Audit Commission provided that lead in a important paper *Losing an Empire, Finding a Role: The LEA of the Future.*[48] The report warned of the need to rethink the future 'against the background of a clear understanding of the new power relationships'. It emphasised the shift from monopoly provision and manager status to a pluralistic system in which the distribution of power had moved downward to schools, outward to parent groups, and upward to the Secretary of State for Education. To be effective, the LEA would have to become a guide and leader, articulating a vision of what the education service should aspire to achieve, adopting a role as partner, and assisting schools to realise that vision.

Table 2.2
The changing role characteristics of LEAs

	Agree/strongly agree	
	1988	1992
	%	%
The LEA's role was that of:		
Traditional provider	73	16
Leader/strategic manager	79	92
Partner	52	96
Enabler	39	93
Adviser	76	96

Source: LGMB, unpublished data.

Various role conceptions were offered by the Commission: those of *leader*, articulating a vision; *partner*, supporting schools and helping them realise the vision; *planner* of facilities; *provider of information* to the market; *regulator* of quality; and *banker* or resource allocator. The 1992 LGMB survey asked chief education officers to characterise their LEA's role and report on any changes since 1988. The results showed a massive disavowal of the role of the traditional provider, and huge increases in the proportions characterising their LEA as 'partner' or 'enabler'.

As the emphasis shifted in the LEA's own role from 'control' to 'influence', new styles of management and new management structures were required. The survey found that more than half of the LEAs which responded were restructuring their education departments, while another quarter had done so in the previous twelve months. The Education Reform Act, 1988 was cited as an influence on the decision to restructure by as many as 94 per cent of the responding LEAs.

'Enabling' in education: the LEA experience

These new roles and responsibilities conferred by the Education Reform Act compelled several LEAs to develop skills in the management of change, in policy development, in customer care, in leadership, in negotiation with schools and other institutions, in marketing their services, in specifying objectives and in reviewing performance. Yet although LEAs moved towards the new role envisaged in the Act, the patterns of change were diverse. Some authorities adapted more fully than others to the enabling model; some placed more emphasis on quality control, some on the advisory role; some moved smoothly towards greater competition, while others remained uneasy.

LEAs differed in the ways in which they approached the enabling role, with much greater enthusiasm in the county councils than in the Labour-controlled northern boroughs. Asked in the 1992 LGMB survey about their approaches to delegation to schools, more than half of the metropolitan districts replied that their approach was driven by the need to comply with legal requirements, while only one in five of the counties did so; the proportions were reversed in respect of the intention to achieve 'maximum feasible delegation', an approach more favoured in the counties. The county councils visited were more sympathetic to the emphasis on competition: they believed in the autonomy of schools and the advantage of their developing their own identities. To them, the crucial determinant of their relationship with their schools was the extent to which they were able to provide cost-effective, responsive and high quality services.

What accounts for these variations in approach? An obvious factor is political control, which is reflected in the authority's values and priorities. Another, closely related, is the social composition of an area's population. There are also likely to be differences in the relative influence of officers and elected members, and these, too, might affect the authority's approach. These differences were well apparent in the LEAs visited during the crucial period of initial implementation of the Education Reform Act. In Surrey, for instance, the county council actively encouraged devolved management in order to enhance locally managed services by enabling management decisions to be taken closer to 'the customer'. It sought to improve the authority's own responsiveness in terms of adapting service delivery to meet local needs. Clearer accountability for achievement was complemented by tighter corporate controls on standards, and on the use of resources and procedures.

The high priority given in Surrey to performance management, the emphasis on contractual arrangements, and the encouragement of public participation to provide greater public/customer choice were typical of this type of authority. The stress was on 'quality control', with priority given to high profile inspection. The county council encouraged open policies to permit local schools to choose whether or not to buy its central support services, after assessing how far such services are able to meet local needs in standards or costs.

Delegating to schools

Under LMS, the main task of the LEA is to allocate resources to schools. The LEA also has to set objectives and policies on curriculum matters and on the structure of educational provision, and lay down the conditions on which schools should operate their local management responsibilities.[49] Schemes of local management have to include regulations and procedures on finance, health and safety which are binding on heads and governors, and guidelines are published for good practice, particularly on the management of resources and on personnel issues, to assist heads and governors in managing their schools.

The implementation of local management began in April 1990. LEAs submitted local management schemes by September 1989 and, most received approval in early 1990. The schemes showed that they had responded to the new requirements in different ways. Leeds, for example, gave partial delegation of the budgets to all its schools from April 1990, moving to full delegation of budgets two years later. In contrast, Surrey's scheme of local management, one of the earliest schemes in the country to be approved, introduced local management into all its primary and secondary schools in stages over a three year period.

In developing these schemes, many councils gained from their experience of partial local management through pilot schemes introduced in some of their schools in earlier years. In Surrey, a pilot scheme had been introduced in 1985, extended in 1987, and offered to all secondary schools in 1988. From April 1989 a 'dry run' scheme was operated for local management, involving five primary and five secondary schools. This enabled the council to test the validity of training programmes and materials and the effectiveness of management information systems and performance indicators, and to assess the amount of administrative time necessary for schools to undertake local management.

Some LEAs sought to delegate the maximum possible financial and management responsibility within the limits permitted by the legislation. In most, about 80 per cent of the initial budget formula determining the allocation to schools was based on age-weighted pupil numbers. This was used to allocate most staffing costs, though some special elements were distributed through other mechanisms, including for instance a lump sum to protect the curriculum at small primary schools, supply teacher cover, examination fees, premises and special needs. In Surrey, which has a wide range of schools - large and small, and in urban and rural areas - the council included in its main formula a subsidy element to help small schools with the introduction of the national curriculum, and to meet the actual costs of staff salaries. Another component of the council's formula was based on a flat rate allocation to pupil units to help schools with the basic costs inherent in staffing establishments.

Supporting local management of schools

Under LMS, the role of the LEA is essentially strategic - supporting the school in the achievement of agreed local objectives. In order to support the introduction of LMS, training facilities for governors, headteachers, senior teaching staff and administrative staff were developed. Typically, LEAs provided training in management awareness and management skills for headteachers and deputies, on information systems for administrative staff and heads, and on personnel matters, pupil needs and curriculum for governors. Some authorities appointed officers to head up LMS training; governors' training co-ordinators were appointed in some cases. Resources were committed to the appointment of administrative staff in primary and secondary schools, and for the preparation of budgets and management plans. Local management of schools units were established to manage individual schools' budgets until governors were ready to take on their delegated responsibilities.

Training for governors varied considerably between authorities. The type of training facilities provided ranged from courses which introduced governors to general areas of responsibility to courses on local management dealing with the specific responsibilities of governors for management information systems, finance, personnel, and health and safety. In some authorities the governing body of each school was expected to produce a management plan for the school in order to enable the authority to identify training needs. In others, officers were appointed to co-ordinate the training of school governors, devise appropriate training schedules for each governing body and produce manuals for governors explaining the basic requirements of local management.

The new requirements of LMS placed a premium on the effective management of information at both school and LEA level. Suitable computer hardware and software were provided to all appropriate schools in many authorities. Plans to enhance and upgrade the existing systems were accelerated by local management demands. Some LEAs computerised the administrative and accountancy systems in order to minimise the workload of schools, speed up the transfer of information between the schools and the LEA and provide for monitoring. Schools information management systems were designed to facilitate full budgetary controls including allocations and the recording of investment and expenditure items.

Relations with schools

LEAs soon became aware that the effectiveness of any service they provided under LMS, and indeed the future demand for it, would depend on the quality of their relationships with schools. LEAs indeed ignore the shift to a school-led system at their peril: 'the boot is on the other foot', as one chief education officer graphically described the reversal of LEA-school relationships.[50] Undoubtedly LMS has swept away the paternalism and the bureaucracy that formally characterised LEA-school relations in many areas.[51]

Delegating management responsibilities to schools and governing bodies under the Education Reform Act has created new sets of relationships between the departments and 'their' schools. Local education authorities could not resist this change. Most realised that the days of 'telling' schools were gone and that, instead, what is required is for them to lead, persuade and influence schools to adopt their policies and objectives. Where authorities delegated the maximum degree of responsibility, locally managed schools began to exercise a greater degree of self management and develop ambitions for independence.

In Kent, for example, where 74 per cent of the budget was delegated to schools in the first year, a number of secondary schools responded by taking steps towards becoming grant maintained. The council's proposed review of secondary education threatened the future of some schools, giving further impetus to consider opting out. It was also recognised that while the educational viability of a school was inextricably linked to its financial viability, the LEA could no longer vary the funding of individual schools in order to help them survive. In the face of these considerations, local moves to opt out could only be stemmed by persuading schools of the positive benefits of the support services available from remaining within the county system.

Similarly, where authorities retained more of the budget centrally, this caused resentment on the part of some schools, which often saw little or no advantage in their staying with the local authority. The temptation to opt out and seek grant maintained status was all the stronger. In Hounslow, where the authority sought to retain as much as 37 per cent of the budget centrally - more than most other authorities in the country - some headteachers did not rule out this possibility. Local education authorities also realised that whereas in the past they always provided a range of support services to their institutions, it would be more difficult to stipulate the levels or extent to which the schools would actually use those services in future. If schools were to buy the services which education authorities provided, these would have to become more competitive, responsive, flexible and accessible. As the new role developed under LMS, some authorities were faced with providing education services to a variety of establishments ranging from locally managed schools to grant maintained schools and city technology colleges. Thus their role became less of a provider, than that of a planner and procurer of services.

This change of emphasis in the role of the LEA had implications for the role of education officers.[52] They became less involved with managing and administering in-house staff and were forced to develop new skills in purchasing and supply, quality control and in the arts of contract specification. One chief education officer, responding to the 1992 LGMB survey, noted the need to acquire staff with new skills and experience, and commented that

> LMS has altered the balance of power between schools and the LEA, and has ensured that only those officers who understand this fundamental shift have survived.[53]

The impact of the changes has not been limited to education officers: councillors too have been faced with new responsibilities and challenges. Education committees are now called upon to set strategies and agree policies for maintained education in their localities.

The responses of schools and governing bodies

The Education Reform Act was designed to confer on headteachers and governing bodies greater control over the running of their own schools, as well as the implementation of the national curriculum and the detailed deployment of teaching and other resources.

Headteachers as managers

The Conservative government's drive to decentralise decisions from education authorities to schools radically altered the role of headteacher. The responsibility for managing the school was more clearly and firmly located in the school, and headteachers acquired new managerial and financial powers. They were given the freedom to run the schools in their own way. Their workloads changed in character, with a corresponding impact on the management style of schools and on the location of power within the school.[54] Heads gained responsibilities for training and developing their staff, appraising their performance and providing them with feedback. They also have to manage their financial resources while being accountable to the governors, parents and the community. Their need for management training and comparative information was widely recognised.[55]

This transformation of the headteacher into a manager was met with varying reactions by headteachers. Generally, it seems that heads and governors were more favourably disposed to the decentralisation of power than the average classroom teacher.[56] Yet while most headteachers welcomed the new responsibilities, they were aware of the pressures of coping with the organisational changes. The growing importance of having a strong management team and strategy was also recognised by the headteachers interviewed, and all were responding consciously to the changed situation. Most had been involved in reorganising their schools and had set up comprehensive review systems to improve performance, identify good practice, and pinpoint training needs. Most had also undertaken staff development programmes.

Despite these developments, some headteachers appeared to have a positive distaste for new ideas and practices drawn from the world of management. The idea that performance can be measured by examination results and standards of literacy and numeracy alone was resisted by some as undesirable. They put forward the view that, while the 'school manager' would be less concerned with the educational processes and more with results and products, the focus of the 'educational professional' would be on the development of the individual pupil in the classroom. In their concern with the educational role, the aim to develop the potential of the pupil was valued more highly than managerial skills. The world of business and management was perceived by these headteachers as antithetical.

For those sharing such a view, it would be inconceivable to look at education in terms of cost-effectiveness, profit and loss, as education cannot be seen as an end product which is saleable. A headteacher who was opposed to the very idea of marketing the school said:

Education, like health and welfare, does not operate within the same parameters as commercial markets. By its very nature it is quite clearly an exception in trying to operate the normal market forces and economic arguments. Pupils have to be put first and money has to follow.

Misgivings were expressed about the introduction of market strategies in the implementation of reforms, as exemplified by the publication of glossy brochures, and advertising through local press and television to attract pupils to schools. It was felt that competition between schools was likely to increase tensions and that schools might become more insular, less co-operative and more selfish. Expressing concern about the way in which the new changes were forcing schools to compete, some headteachers expressed the view that, while competition might encourage some schools to perform better, it could become counter-productive if headteachers become obsessed with fund-raising. 'There is danger', said one, 'that economic and financial considerations may be over stressed, at least in the early years of local management'.

This sort of resistance among headteachers was not uncommon. Another commented, 'My role as a professional headteacher is not to go out and raise money, and secure funds...but it has become a regrettable necessity of our education system'. A third, who fully supported the principle of local management, remarked that:

it is important not to lose sight of educational objectives: LMS should be looked at to improve the quality of education and not as a cost cutting exercise. There is a danger that many may spend a lot of time worrying about savings, when in fact they should be concerned about the children and the curriculum.

And in practice, the headteachers of primary schools were able to see little flexibility in budget decisions, given that more than 85 per cent of the budget was made up of teachers' salaries.

Despite the reservations that some headteachers clearly had about commercialisation, most recognised the need to reorient their professional role to a degree. Although aware that the desire to attract more pupils and budget maximisation had changed the educational ethos, they were more conscious than in the past of needing to market themselves.

We are having to view ourselves as a business enterprise. The kind of brochures we print, the form of publicity in the local press and the way we advertise on the local radio are becoming very important to us. Under LMS we are beginning to see ourselves very differently,

said a secondary headteacher in Hounslow. Indeed, even in 1990, many schools had started advertising on television and radio, setting up marketing committees, consulting with public relations advisers, looking for industrial sponsorship and producing promotional videos.

Only a minority of the headteachers interviewed saw little difference between their previous role and the new one; these few did not agree that they were now doing a different job, needing different abilities. They felt that the abilities a head needed were the same as in the past. 'What is changing is the emphasis and the methods of working'. For some, the change had come gradually and was no longer a novelty. In Solihull, where headteachers seemed more enthusiastic than their counterparts in other authorities, they had the experience of the scheme of 'financial autonomy' introduced by the authority in 1981. The headteachers interviewed there felt their past experience made it relatively easy for them to cope with the new changes that the local management of schools entailed. Heads in this authority felt positively about the increasing autonomy being given to schools. Describing some of the merits of the scheme, one commented, 'Freedom given to the heads under the present system will enable headteachers to perform better and to develop a degree of professional commitment and skill which is essential for the healthy development of the education system'. Some heads enjoyed the challenge, admitting that the new responsibilities were forcing them to improve their performance and to become more cost-conscious.

Headteachers have been faced with a number of issues over their roles, responsibilities and power. It became clear that they would have to be more accountable and perform better if they were to stay in post. A number of authorities have now introduced fixed term contracts. One headteacher of a primary school interviewed in Solihull, who was already in such a post, felt optimistic that such contracts would enhance standards in the schools. In return for a higher salary than his counterparts in similar sized schools, he was required to perform to agreed targets in respect of the school's performance, educational standards and the number of pupils registered.

Parental participation

The Education Reform Act placed the headteacher at the centre of an entirely new network of relationships in which schools have greater autonomy, and parents and governors enjoy extended powers. Parents in the past had tended to look to them as professionals to prepare their children for the future. They were now given a right to have a say in that process, while the subsequent Education (Schools) Act of 1992 fuelled their ability to contribute with its requirement that schools publish an increased range of information about their performance.

Table 2.3
Source of initiatives to promote
parental choice, involvement and accountability

	LEA initiative %	school -led %	statutory obligation %
Parent choice:			
admissions	39	4	41
appeals	21	3	54
voting	16	6	32
Parent involvement:			
in governing bodies	51	25	14
in annual parent meetings	20	35	21
in parent/teacher associations	11	68	3
within school activities	11	70	3
in commenting on pupil progress	14	52	11
Parent accountability:			
through complaints	45	6	31
through appeals	32	7	28
through school evaluation	23	24	7

Source: LGMB, unpublished data.

Headteachers now came to experience a greater involvement with parents. In the early stages of implementation many complained of a lack of parental interest and a lack of awareness among parents about the reforms. As one Manchester headteacher expressed it:

There appears to be a misunderstanding by the government about what parents want for their children. Parents visit schools only to know their children's progress and to find out whether they are being cared for. In my view they do not want to spend their time questioning me nor do they want to get involved in curriculum aspects.

Other education officers tend to express similar views, doubting that parents actually wanted more than a 'long-stop' right to complain when dissatisfied with their children's education.

Parental participation, however, is not driven solely by parent interest. LEAs themselves have in some areas discerned a considerable opportunity to open-up schools to parents, largely in the hope of strengthening their commitment to LEA-maintained status and forestalling any groundswell of opinion in favour of opting-out. Ministers, for their part, had expressed the hope that the ERA would 'galvanise' parental involvement, a hope that would have been reflected in local Conservative party circles. There is, moreover, a distinction to be drawn between *parental choice*, which has been driven by the statutory rights, conferred by the Education Reform Act, *parental involvement* in school-based activities which the schools have promoted, and *accountability to parents*, for which LEAs have themselves often taken the responsibility. Table 2.3 presents some evidence gathered by the LGMB from 71 LEAs in 1992.

The governing bodies: the process of involvement

Under the Education Reform Act, the delegation of decision-making powers to governing bodies has implications for governor involvement in areas which have traditionally been within the domain of the school's professional staff. Although there was some uncertainty about the new role in matters such as staffing, premises and finance, most governors recognised the need to become more active and sensitive, and to develop good relations with heads, staff and local education authorities. Despite the occasional well-publicised struggle, the majority of the governors interviewed expressed the need to reassure and support the headteacher and staff in order to sustain morale, avoid conflicts and promote educational development. There was consensus on the need for better training so that governors could become more familiar with all aspects of their schools.[57]

In general, governors have welcomed their stronger role. Those interviewed expressed qualified support for the local management of schools, although admitting that some of the work involved would be beyond their capabilities. For example:

> The system is flexible and enables us to get on with our jobs quickly because we do not have to depend on the local authority. It will lead to a more economical use of resources and will provide the incentive to save with much greater determination.

A majority recognised that their jobs as governors would become much more difficult and time-consuming in the future. Many were finding the extra work in preparing for local management too much of an incursion on their time. The number of meetings had already increased, and most governors felt burdened by the paper work. The nature of the work generated was posing difficulties for some governors. A governor in Rotherham described it as 'Too much responsibility, too quickly'. A chairman of governors said:

> I am extremely worried that the responsibilities placed upon governors demand a considerable amount of time, knowledge and commitment. One governor has resigned and another is considering resignation. There are professional people on my governing body in full time employment who are finding it impossible to take time off work because their employers cannot afford to, or will not, release them. I am certain that soon we will lose good people with valuable skills who will choose to discontinue their role.

Some governors felt they were being asked to do the work unpaid and reported that not even travelling expenses were paid to attend training sessions. They suggested that more incentives were required to encourage governor interest.

The heavier workload did not, however, deter all governors, even in the initial stages. 'We are delighted with these new opportunities. As governors we should take proper advantage of them, be readily inclined to support and promote the school's policies and help in a constructive way' said one Kent governor. In Surrey governors appeared similarly keen to take on the new responsibilities. A chairman of a governing body in the county who was also a parent governor in another school said 'Governors would like to be more involved in schools now than they have in the past and are challenging the new procedures'. Some governing bodies had organised themselves into sub-committees and working groups to simplify their tasks, delegating areas such as staffing, curriculum, premises and finance to these groups. On the whole, however, governors seemed generally happy to leave curriculum matters to headteachers, primarily because they felt that the professionals knew better what to do and how to do it. 'I am trying to read the national curriculum documents. They are huge volumes and very complicated. We just have to trust the professionals' lamented one. Some governors nevertheless liked to be informed about curriculum matters, as they felt they could usefully comment.

The role of school governors has been central to the changes introduced by the Education Reform Act. Yet governors have been slow in getting to grips with the new educational and management issues. The chairman of a governing body in Surrey said 'A large number of governors do not realise what they are going to take on; if they did they would not be applying'.

The Education Reform Act: problems with implementation

Due to the controversial nature of the changes made by the Education Reform Act, and the hostility with which they were received by some participants in the education system, implementation was always likely to be problematic. Indeed, as noted earlier, the government's analysis of the 'education problem' attributed many of the failures of the system to the education establishment. It accordingly aimed to counterbalance their power by increasing the number of players at the table - introducing parents and governors at the expense of the teachers and local education authorities who had hitherto occupied the strongest positions.

Opposition from some LEAs, headteachers and individual teachers was expected to put significant obstacles in the way of local implementation even before the teacher unions chose to veto assessment. There was additionally concern over professionals' capacity to implement the changes, with some fear that they might sabotage or hijack the reforms. In the event many education officers, inspectors and headteachers responded positively to the Act, and anxieties revolved around issues of the time-tabling of implementation, the adequacy of teaching resources and the consequent administrative workload. For headteachers in particular, the stress of coping with the organisational changes associated with the introduction of LMS and the national curriculum was often substantial in the initial stages. Serious concerns were expressed about the speed at which the changes were being introduced and many headteachers did not feel adequately prepared.[58]

One of the most emotive issues for governors and heads, as they faced their new responsibilities for day-to-day management of their schools, has been the retention of a full and experienced teaching staff. Under LMS, each school receives its budget on a funding formula that takes account of average, but not actual, salary costs. Thus, heads of schools with too many experienced teachers at the top of the pay scale find themselves unable to afford them. The full force of this factor was felt only in 1995, when the government decided not to fund the teachers' pay settlement, placing schools at risk of losing their more expensive and thereby more experienced staff. Schools with falling pupil numbers were to face similar problems. For headteachers of these schools, local management was not going to mean making decisions about how best to spend the money, but more difficult ones about how to make cuts.

The implementation of the national curriculum posed the biggest problems. Headteachers have been generally prepared to accept the case for a national curriculum, at least because it would remedy deficiencies arising from the wide variations in practice in different schools. Its implementation was however bedevilled by a lack of properly trained teachers and adequate resources. Some schools were already under-resourced to the point that they were unable to teach the curriculum effectively. A headteacher complained:

> Adequate time has not been allowed for preparation to implement the curriculum and there may be serious consequences of introducing too many things at once. The national curriculum is putting my school under particular stress because of the need for extra equipment and training. It is unrealistic to talk of the national curriculum when adequate resources are not provided to enable the legislated curriculum to be developed. The resource implications of the reforms have not been given sufficient consideration.

A report in 1990 by Her Majesty's Inspectorate (HMI) on the implementation of the national curriculum in primary schools, also found that in most schools resources were inadequate, that teachers were having problems with assessing and keeping achievement records, that there were insufficient teachers with the right kind of expertise and experience, and that schools were facing problems of recruiting experienced staff. Having to rely on temporary teachers was 'having damaging effects on the early stages of implementation'.[59] The prescriptive nature of the curriculum itself also provoked criticism. Many teachers were concerned about the level of detail that was emerging. A headteacher in Manchester expressed a commonly-held view:

> It is too centralist, too rigid and practically unworkable. There is no room for developing good practice in the school. Staff are extremely stressed and they are beginning to see pupils in a different way. The commitment being asked from teachers is beyond human capabilities. Keeping up the morale of the school is becoming very difficult.

It was also argued that the assessment and testing arrangements were too complex. Primary and secondary schools were initially worried about how much time and resources the new assessment would take, but subsequent proposals by the government to simplify assessment arrangements eased some of the burden. Inevitably, for a long time this created a great deal of insecurity in the minds of the teachers. Fears were expressed that schools might spend more time testing, completing complicated record-keeping schedules and planning for the future than teaching. It was just such a concern that led to the confrontation between the teacher unions and the government in 1993, with a boycott being first imposed, then lifted, then (in 1995) re-imposed.

Less obviously, the recruitment of school governors has itself proved to pose an implementation problem.[60] A Solihull headteacher pointed out that the effective implementation of the Education Reform Act presupposed a vigorous governing body; however

> My governing body is nowhere near equipped to come to terms with the new changes. They are not qualified to appoint, dismiss and suspend staff. They will rely heavily on me and my deputies. Most of them are finding it hard to give the time and the right kind of expertise. In Solihull we are concerned about losing governors. It will have a significant impact on the role of the head in the next decade.

Another headteacher from the same authority argued that the difficulty of recruiting governors with the knowledge and the skills needed to take on the new responsibilities would be exacerbated in deprived areas, where the majority of parents were unlikely to be highly educated:

> Solihull is a very divided authority. The south is very affluent, and most of the parents are educated professionals who are keen to get on to the governing body. But in the north and in an area such as ours with large council estates, how can we get the right parents to be on the governing body, who can be in a position to make important decisions and have the ability to identify the needs of schools?

While these comments were made in the early stages, they point up a more general issue of the extent to which the implementation of the Education Reform Act depends upon large-scale, long-term shifts in patterns of behaviour. Five years later, the Conservative reforms seem still to face an uncertain future.

An uncertain future: the dynamics of reform

The Education Reform Act, 1988 transformed the way in which the education service is organised in England and Wales. It brought fundamental alterations to the existing system, involving a large scale redistribution of powers and responsibilities between the several constituents of the educational community, but chiefly away from the local education authorities. Enhanced powers and greater managerial responsibility were thus gained by those at the apex and by those at the base of the educational system - central government, and the managers and consumers of local educational service. The intermediate level of the education services - the local education authorities - lost executive authority and were compelled to develop a new role.

In the Conservative government's strategy of reducing the extent of local authority intervention in education, an important feature was the emphasis placed on extending the role of key consumer groups. The promotion of LMS, by enhancing the powers and choices of parents, governors and schools, inescapably undermines the role of local authority in educational policy making.

The aim was to make local educational provision more responsive to the wishes of parents, by opening up a greater range of options to them, both within the maintained sector and outside it. Within the maintained sector parents gained a notional freedom to select the school of their choice for their children through the lifting of some capacity constraints on individual schools. The evidence in mid-1993, however, was that the reality of parental choice, as measured by success in getting children into the school of first choice, was more elusive than expected due to the intensification of competition.[61]

The effects of the Education Reform Act on the governance of education were in two contrary directions, with a movement towards centralisation in some respects, and towards decentralisation in others. Both national control of the curriculum and school-based management have long antecedents as well as prototypes elsewhere in the world. Neither were actually distinctively Conservative reforms. This cannot be said of the opting-out provisions, which lie at the heart of the Conservative assault upon the LEAs.

At the very least the Act sidelined the local education authorities, since they looked likely to lose any meaningful role in the education service of the future. John Patten clearly identified himself with this projection. His white paper, *Choice and Diversity: A New Framework for Schools* and the subsequent Education Act, 1993, signalled the intention to consolidate and extend the reforms of the Thatcher period.[62] For Patten, all schools should become free of LEA control and attain the status of grant maintained schools (or, in the new terminology, *self-governing* schools) and to this end, the Act facilitated opting out and speeded up the process.[63]

Other protagonists on the Conservative Right felt the 1988 and 1993 Acts did not go far enough; for them the abolition of ILEA should have been taken as a dummy run for the abolition of all LEAs.[64] Yet others imagined that so drastic a step was unnecessary. While the Education Reform Act left LEAs formally intact, it set in train a new dynamic that could lead to their withering away. Abolition, then, would be a superfluous act.

How persuasive is this scenario? The unknown factor is the extent to which LMS and the other provisions of the ERA might work to steadily erode the LEA role, by empowering and making more demanding the parent body, so leading to the progressive exercise of the parental right to opt out. It seems, however, that the dynamic of delegation to schools is not working to promote opting out and the withering away of the LEA.

Far from LMS leading inexorably to opting-out ballots, the response to the new opportunity to escape from LEA control has been muted, at least in comparison with the wilder aspirations. By February 1994, 928 schools had achieved grant maintained status with another 115 in the pipeline. The frequency of ballots on opting out, although still running at a high level, appeared to be falling relative to the previous year, while a slightly smaller proportion had voted in favour of opting-out in 1994 than in the corresponding period twelve months before.[65]

For some observers, GMS was already a 'flagship on the rocks'.[66] In their own terms, perhaps grant maintained schools have been something of a success. A number of studies purport to show the benefits, even for small primary schools, of being free of LEA control.[67] Separate Ofsted and National Audit Office investigations into the running of the GMS schools were similarly positive.[68] Conservative ministers, then, could feel justified in their upbeat verdict on the grant maintained schools:

> With self-governing schools we are seeing an increase in morale, a greater sense of achievement, greater value for money and, above all, more popularity with parents, as will be seen [next] September when in the main those schools are again overfull.[69]

The claim to success celebrates the effects of competition and choice. That effect has been to bring about higher quality education for the relatively few while failing to address the larger question of access and equity. As such, it provides a suitable epitaph for Conservative education policy under Mrs Thatcher and her successor.

Notes

1. V. Bogdanor, 'Power and Participation', *Oxford Review of Education*, 5(2), 1979.
2. S. Maclure, 'Forty Years On', *British Journal of Education Studies*, 33(2), June 1985.
3. S. Maclure, 'The Endless Agenda: Matters Arising', *Oxford Review of Education*, 5(2), 1979; see also L. Bash and D. Coulby, *The Education Reform Act: Competition and Control*, London, Cassell, 1989.
4. For an account of the shifts in Conservative thinking during the years of the Thatcher leadership, see D. Lawton, *The Tory Mind on Education, 1979-94*, Lewes, Falmer Press, 1994, pp. 33-50; and C. Knight, *The Making of Tory Education Policy in Britain, 1950-86*, Lewes, Falmer Press, 1990.
5. The Education Act, 1980 also established local appeals committees to hear the complaints of parents who had failed to secure a place for their children in a school of their choice. For a discussion of the development of the Parent's charter and its prospects for increasing parental choice see J. Robinson, 'Reforming the Reforms', *New Law Journal*, 142(6552), 15 May 1992, pp. 685-686. For a full account of parental choice see R. Morris, *School Choice in England and Wales: An Exploration of the Legal and Administrative Background*, Slough, National Foundation for Educational Research, 1995.
6. S. Ranson and H. Thomas, 'Education Reform: Consumer Democracy or Social Democracy?' in J. Stewart and G. Stoker (editors) *The Future of Local Government*, London, Macmillan, 1989, pp. 55-77.
7. R. Morris, '1944 to 1988', in *Central and Local Control of Education After the Education Reform Act, 1988*, (editor R. Morris), Harlow, Longman, 1990, pp. 5-20.
8. In 1977, the Department of Education and Science (DES) made its first move towards the notion of a core curriculum, designed to ensure that every child enjoyed a guaranteed minimum of teaching in key areas.
9. Boyson, like his fellow Black Paper contributors Cox and Dyson, had earlier been a Labour supporter.
10. Lawton, *Tory Mind on Education*, p. 49.
11. Department of Education and Science, *The Taylor Report*, London, HMSO, 1978.
12. Hillgate Group, *Whose Schools? A Radical Manifesto*, London, The Hillgate Group, 1986; S. Sexton, *Our Schools - A Radical Policy*, Institute of Economic Affairs Education Unit, 1987.

13. For a succinct review of the gathering attack on the education 'establishment', see Morris, *'1944 to 1988'*, pp. 9-14.

14. Adam Smith Institute, *The Omega File on Education*, London, 1984.

15. S. Sexton, *Our Schools*, pp. 8-9.

16. The Thatcher government's first Education Act was that passed immediately in 1979, to repeal the statutory obligation on LEAs to promote comprehensive schools.

17. Research reveals the advantages of involving parents and public to improve the quality of education. Back in 1967 the Plowden report inquiry into primary schools devoted a full chapter to the importance of parents. The value of parents having an understanding of what happens in school has also been recognised by papers published by Her Majesty's Inspectorate and the Department of Education and Science: Her Majesty's Inspectorate, *Good Teachers - Education Observed*, London, Department of Education and Science, 1985, p. 13; *Parental Influence at Schools*, London, Department of Education and Science, 1984; *Better Schools*, London, Department of Education and Science, 1985.

18. Department of Education and Science, *Teaching Quality*, London, HMSO, 1983; Education (Grants and Awards) Act, 1984.

19. See Knight, *The Making of Tory Education Policy*.

20. A phrase used in a Conservative Research Department briefing paper quoted in Lawton, *The Tory Mind on Education*, p. 91.

21. K. Baker, *The Turbulent Years: My Life in Politics*, London, Faber, 1993, p. 164.

22. S. Maclure, *Education Re-formed: A Guide to the Education Reform Act 1988*, London, Hodder and Stoughton, 1988.

23. Under the Act the University Grants Committee was replaced by the Universities Funding Council. Polytechnics and higher education colleges were removed from local authority control, and incorporated as independent charitable bodies. These changes were soon overtaken by the Further and Higher Education Act of 1992, which replaced the UFC and PCFC with three Higher Education Funding Councils and elevated all the Polytechnics and some of the higher education colleges to University status.

24. Strictly speaking, the powers to declare CTCs already existed under Section 100 of the Education Act, 1944, and indeed this initiative had been officially announced as early as 1986. However, the ERA package looked the stronger and more radical for the inclusion of this additional provision.

25. S. Ranson, 'Education', in N. Deakin and A. Wright (editors), *Consuming Public Services*, London, Routledge, 1990, p. 193.

26. ibid.

27. G. Whitty and I. Menter, 'Lessons of Thatcherism: Education Policy in England and Wales 1979-88', *Journal of Law and Society*, 16(1), 1989, p. 48.

28. M. Thatcher, *The Downing Street Years*, London, HarperCollins, 1993, p. 593.

29. The Act spells out the ways in which the standard number may be varied. A proposal may be made by a local authority to increase or reduce a school's standard number. Such proposals are subject to procedures set out in the Act to include the publication of notices, and the consideration of objections made by local electors, or the governing body of any school affected by the proposals or by any local education authority concerned.

30. By January 1994, more than 200 enquiries had been made to the DfE about establishing CTCs, and just 15 had been established.

31. Originally, only those schools with more than 300 pupils could apply for GMS, but a policy change to remove this minimum size threshold was announced in October 1990.

32. All parents of registered pupils at the school are eligible to make a written request to the governors to hold a ballot, and to vote in any such a ballot. The result of the ballot will be determined by a simple majority of those voting, unless the total number of those voting is less than 50 per cent of those eligible to do so. Under such circumstances the governors are required to arrange for a second ballot to be held within 14 days of the first ballot. The result of any second ballot is to be determined by a simple majority of those voting, irrespective of the number of parents who do so.

33. D. Halpin, J. Fitz and S. Power, *The Early Impact and Long-term Implications of the Grant-Maintained School Policy*, University of Warwick, Department of Education, March 1992; 'Local Education Authorities and the Grant-Maintained Schools Policy', *Educational Management and Administration*, 19(4), October 1991, pp. 233-242.

34. D. Halpin, S. Power and J. Fitz, 'Opting into State Control? Headteachers and the Paradoxes of Grant-Maintained Status', *International Studies in the Sociology of Education*, 3(1), 1993, pp. 3-23.

35. For an account of UK government interest in delegated authority for school-site management, culminating in the Education Reform Act, 1988, see B. Davies and L. Ellison, 'Delegated School Finance in the English Education System: an Era of Radical Change', *Journal of Educational Administration*, 30(1), 1992, pp. 70-80.

36. For accounts of what has been described as a 'world-wide movement' to school-based management practices, see L. E. Sackney and D. J. Dibski, 'School-based Management: a Critical Perspective', *Educational Management and Administration*, 22(2), April 1994, pp. 104-112; Y.C. Cheng, 'The Theory and Characteristics of School-based Management', *International Journal of Educational Management*, 7(6), 1993, pp. 6-17; P. Sleegers and A. Wesselingh, 'Decentralisation in Education: a Dutch Study', *International Studies in the Sociology of Education*, 3(1), 1993, pp. 49-67; P.C. Cline and P.T. Graham, 'School-based Management: an

Emerging Approach to the Administration of America's Schools', *Local Government Studies*, 17(4) July-August 1991, pp. 43-50.
37. For a survey of the provisions for local management covering planning, budgeting, information and premises, and personnel see *The Times Educational Supplement*, (3842-5), 16 and 23 February, 2 and 9 March 1990. See also Audit Commission, *The Local Management of Schools*, November 1988.
38. For a study of the implications of LMS for schools' patterns of expenditure and of the factors which influenced headteachers and governing bodies when making spending decisions see K. Maychell, *Counting the Cost: The Impact of LMS on Schools' Patterns of Spending*, Slough, National Foundation for Educational Research, 1994.
39. R. Dixon, 'Local Management of Schools', *Public Money and Management*, 11(3), Autumn 1991, pp. 47-52.
40. Coopers and Lybrand, *Local Management of Schools: Report to the Department of Education and Science*, 1988. See also S. Hegarty, 'Taking Steps Towards LMS', *Public Finance and Accounting*, 10 June 1988, pp. 23-29.
41. G. Thomas, 'Setting Up LMS', *Educational Management and Administration*, 19(2), April 1991, pp. 84-88; see also R. Dixon, 'Repercussions of LMS', *Educational Management and Administration*, 19(1), January 1991, pp. 52-61.
42. Department for Education, *Local Management of Schools*, Circular 2/94, para 226.
43. T. Lee, *Carving Out the Cash For Schools: LMS and the New Era of Education*, University of Bath, Centre for the Analysis of Social Policy, Social Policy Paper, No. 17, November 1990.
44. An important consequence of the funding formula is that, as the resource allocation formula is heavily weighted by pupil numbers, the more pupils a school can attract the greater the resources allocated to it. A study of 7,000 schools carried out by Thomas and Bullock on the impact of local management funding formulae revealed this to result in a distinctive pattern of winners and losers. H. Thomas and A. Bullock, 'School Size and Local Management Funding Formulae', *Educational Management and Administration*, 20(1), January 1992, pp. 30-38. A more detailed study of the impact of formula funding in one LEA can be found in R. Levacic, 'Local Management of Schools: Aims, Scope and Impact', *Educational Management and Administration*, 20(1), January 1992, pp. 16-29.
45. J.A.G. Griffith, *Central Departments and Local Authorities*, London, George Allen and Unwin Ltd., 1966.
46. M. Kogan, D. Johnson, T. Packwood, and T. Whitaker, *School Governing Bodies*, London, Heinemann, 1984.
47. Thatcher, *The Downing Street Years*.

48. Audit Commission, *Losing an Empire, Finding a Role: The LEA of the Future*, Occasional Paper, No. 10, December 1989.

49. Other LEA responsibilities are to provide training and support to head teachers, teachers and governing bodies to equip them for their new management roles; to develop information for developing management information systems, curriculum monitoring and performance indicators; to manage the non-delegated budgets of those schools which do not qualify for delegated budgets; and, prior to the Education Act, 1992, to monitor and evaluate the performance of schools through their inspectorate.

50. A chief education officer's response to the 1992 LGMB survey of organisational change. The CEOs overwhelmingly cited LMS as the principal 'change driver' forcing restructuring upon their LEAs.

51. D. Winkley, 'The LEA and the Primary School: Changing Relationships', *Local Government Policy Making*, 18(1), July 1991, pp. 14-19.

52. T. Bush, M. Kogan and T. Lenney, *Directors of Education: Facing Reform*, London, Jessica Kingsley Publishers, 1989.

53. S. Brown and L. Baker, *About Change: Schools' and LEAs' Perspectives on LEA Reorganisation*, Slough, NFER, 1991.

54. See A. Bullock, H. Thomas and M. Arnott, 'The Impact of Local Management of Schools: a View from Headteachers', *Local Government Policy Making*, 19(5), May 1993, pp. 57-61; J. Halsey, 'The Impact of Local Management on School Management Style', *Local Government Policy Making*, 19(5), May 1993, pp. 49-56. More generally, the HMI carried out a study of 63 schools which piloted LMS in 21 LEAs. *The Implementation of Local Management of Schools*, Her Majesty's Inspectorate, Department for Education, HMSO, 1992.

55. Audit Commission, *Adding the Sums 2: Comparative Information for Schools*, London, HMSO, 1993.

56. E. Marren and R. Levacic, 'Senior Management, Classroom Teacher and Governor Responses to Local Management of Schools', *Educational Management and Administration*, 22(1), January 1994, pp. 39-53.

57. For a general discussion see HM Inspectorate of Schools, *The Quality of Training and Support for Governors in Schools and Colleges: September 1990 - April 1991*, London, DES, 1991.

58. An examination of the progress of implementing LMS and support for the new system undertaken in 1990 concluded that changes were being made too quickly for their impact to be properly assessed. T. Lee, 'Where is LMS Taking Us?', *ACE Bulletin*, 39, January/February 1991, pp. 7-9.

59. Her Majesty's Inspectorate, *The Implementation of the National Curriculum in Primary Schools: a Survey of 100 Schools*, Department of Education and Science, 1990. This and other critical reports by HMI eventually contributed to a government decision to disband the Inspectorate

in its existing form, replacing it with the Office of Standards in Education (Ofsted) and a contracted inspection field-force.

60. M. Golby and R. Appleby (editors), *In Good Faith: School Governors Today*, Tiverton, Fair Way Publications, 1991.

61. R. Morris, *Choice of School: A Survey, 1992-93*, London, Association of Metropolitan Authorities, 1993.

62. For a complete account of the provisions of the Education Act, 1993 and a discussion of its probable consequences see R. Morris, E. Reid and J. Fowler, *The Education Act, 1993: A Critical Guide*, London, Association of Metropolitan Authorities, 1993.

63. P. Meredith, 'The Education Act, 1993: Further Development of the Grant Maintained Schools System', *Education and the Law*, 6(3), 1994, pp. 125-131.

64. S. Lawlor, *Away with LEAs: ILEA Abolition as a Pilot*, London, Centre for Policy Studies, 1988.

65. *House of Commons Debates, 1993/94*, Vol. 244, Col. 506. In the six months to the end of May 1994, 176 schools held ballots on GMS, with parents voting in favour of opting out at 104 of them. The corresponding figures for 1993 were 385 and 302.

66. M. Rogers, 'Opting Out: A Flagship on the Rocks?', *Local Government Policy Making*, 19(5), May 1993, pp. 35-39.

67. T. Bush, M. Coleman and D. Glover, 'Managing Grant Maintained Primary Schools', *Educational Management and Administration*, 21(2), April 1993, pp. 69-78, examines the effects of GMS on the first hundred primary schools to opt out, concluding that well-led schools could thrive without LEA support. See also the same authors' *Managing Autonomous Schools: the Grant-Maintained Experience*, London, Paul Chapman, 1993.

68. Office for Standards in Education, *Grant Maintained Schools, 1989-92*, London, HMSO, 1993; National Audit Office, *Value for Money at Grant-Maintained Schools: A Review of Performance*, London, HMSO, 1994.

69. DfE Minister Robin Squire, MP, *House of Commons Debates, 1993/94*, Vol. 244, Col 506.

3 Public Housing in the Twilight Zone

Historically, housing has been a touchstone of the tensions over the proper role and functions of local government. It has been a particular focus of conflict since 1979. In the last decade, the development of housing legislation and the use of legislative powers by central government to control local government housing activities reflected and amplified the crisis in the relationship between the two.

Until the early 1980s, local government played a central role in the provision of social housing in Britain. Local authorities were expected to provide the bulk of rented housing; they were given the responsibility of repairing, maintaining and modernising their own stock; and they had a major role in dealing with substandard housing. The role of local housing authorities and their relationship with central government was to change dramatically with the election of the Thatcher government in 1979. The aims of government policy in the subsequent years were to curtail the role of local authorities, to increase the contribution of housing associations, and to revive the private rented sector, while continuing to encourage the expansion of owner-occupation. Following Mrs Thatcher's third election victory in 1987, the pace of change began to accelerate.

The Conservative strategy for housing

Housing was the second major area where the policies of Mrs Thatcher's governments were driven by clear political vision. As she recalled in her memoirs:

Of the three major social services - Education, the Health Service and Housing - it was, in my view, over the last of these that the most significant question mark hung. By the mid-1980s everything in housing pointed to the need to roll back the existing activities of government.[1]

As with education, the measures taken during the first two administrations were but a prelude to what was to follow.

Between 1979 and 1987 the emphasis had been on shifting local authority housing into owner occupation. All governments since the 1950s - particularly Conservative governments - have encouraged home ownership, although in Labour's case that encouragement was tempered by the higher political priority given to public sector rented housing.[2] The Conservative government of 1970-74 pursued this aim by giving incentives to council tenants to buy their own homes and move out of the municipal rented sector. That route to home ownership was given far higher priority after Mrs Thatcher's election in 1979, when the Housing Act, 1980 introduced the *right to buy*, so enabling council tenants to purchase their homes more easily. By intensifying existing policy, the 1980 Act enabled more than one million properties to be sold by the end of the decade. The Housing and Planning Act, 1986 gave a further impetus to sales through increased discounts. The impact of the policy was described thus:

> As a result of this legislation, almost 1.5 million local authority and new town tenants bought their homes during the 1980s. Annual sales peaked at 226,000 in 1982, but fell to less than half this level in 1985 and 1986. Between 1986 and 1989 sales increased in each year before falling again in 1990 when only 140,000 dwellings were sold...[3]

Apart from being predominantly concerned with promoting home ownership, the first Thatcher governments were also committed to ensuring the development of public land by the private sector. Under the 'build for sale' policy between 1979 and 1986 more than 16,500 houses on former local authority land were built by private developers for owner-occupation. In June 1985, the Department of the Environment set up the Urban Housing Renewal Unit (later renamed Estate Action) to draw private builders into the renewal of run down housing estates. Brindley and Stoker claim that since the establishment of Estate Action, joint partnerships with the private sector to refurbish empty council dwellings for owner occupation ran at three times the level in previous years.[4] The Housing and Planning Act, 1986 introduced further measures to encourage these initiatives.

Meanwhile important shifts were occurring in the scale and character of the British housing system. Council housing declined from its peak in 1979, when it accounted for 32 per cent of the United Kingdom housing stock, to 26 per cent in 1987.[5] Second, its quality undoubtedly deteriorated, making council tenure increasingly undesirable.[6] Third, while a relatively high proportion of intermediate non-manual and skilled manual workers were council tenants in the 1970s, the 1980s saw a decline in social mix, and an increasing social polarisation between the two main sectors.[7] Council housing was becoming a residual tenure, a trend which, if anything, worsened those conditions the policy was intended to address. Moreover, the early indications from council house sales suggested that 'residualisation' was accelerated by the sale of the better properties on estates where tenants could afford to buy, leaving the more run-down flatted estates as low income islands of municipal housing.

The decline of public housing produced increasing demands from local authorities and independent sources for more investment for new construction and renewal of the social housing stock. However, the Thatcher government was preoccupied with restraining public expenditure, and their investment in housing fell heavily in real terms, a result vividly reflected in the number of housing starts. Public sector house building, which had 173,800 starts in 1975, fell to 80,100 in 1979 and further to about 33,000 in 1986. Figures in the 1989 public expenditure white paper showed that local authority house building programmes were expected to decline from 15,000 in 1988/89 to 12,000 in 1990/91 and 6,000 by 1991/92. In actuality, just 4,100 starts were made that last year.[8]

This then was the setting in which the Conservatives formulated their far-reaching proposals for public housing, published in their 1987 general election manifesto. Lady Thatcher (as she now was) recalled in her memoirs that Nicholas Ridley had already drawn up policy papers proposing a way forward:

> His main ideas - all of which eventually found their way into the manifesto - were to give groups of tenants the right to form tenants' co-operatives and individual tenants right to transfer ownership of their house (or flat) to a housing association or other approved institution - in other words to swap landlords. Housing Action Trusts (HATs), modelled on the highly successful UDCs were to be set up to take over bad estates, renovate them and pass them on to different tenures and ownerships. We would also reform the housing revenue accounts...[9]

Nicholas Ridley's 1987 white paper *Housing: the Government's Proposals*, whilst maintaining a strong commitment to owner-occupation, also placed new emphasis on the role of private renting. The government's objective of revitalising the private rented sector was justified by claims that 'There has been too much preoccupation with controls in the private sector and mass provision in the public sector. This has resulted in substantial numbers of rented houses and flats which are badly designed and maintained and which fail to provide decent homes'.[10] The white paper set out four main objectives of future housing policy in England and Wales. These were: to reverse the decline in rented housing and improve its quality; to give council tenants the right to transfer to other landlords if they chose to do so; to target money more accurately on the most acute problems; and to continue to encourage the growth of home ownership.

What linked these themes together was a new vision of the role of local authorities. This conception of a new *enabling role* was clearly set out in the white paper: 'Local authorities should increasingly see themselves as enablers who ensure that everyone in their area is adequately housed; but not necessarily by them'. Thus, while their function as providers of housing was to be substantially reduced, their role remained 'closely associated' with housing need but as a 'strategic one identifying housing needs and demands'. Accordingly 'there will no longer be the same presumption that the local authority itself should take direct action to meet new and increasing demands'.[11]

Introducing the Local Government and Housing Bill, 1989, Nicholas Ridley described the essence of the legislation as

[completing] the framework whereby local authorities would become enablers and regulators rather than providers of services. Regulation - protecting the public interest in services provided by others, and seeing fair play, is the true function of government, both national and local...our legislation takes political manipulation out of rent policy and gives back to councils the original role of regulating the market to enable people to have a decent choice of accommodation to rent.[12]

The new policies were aimed at 'providing more competition and choice in the housing market', but not just for people in the private sector. Instead, the white paper stated that 'The emphasis must be on greater consumer choice and more say for tenants. This can only be achieved by offering a variety of forms of ownership and management; this will help to break down the monolithic nature of large estates'.[13]

The government's proposals to provide greater choice to the customer and tenant stemmed from its perception that 'In the public sector too little attention has been paid to the wishes of tenants or to their views on how their requirements can best be met; tenants have generally not been allowed to express their choices clearly and have therefore not always found the kind of accommodation they want. In the worst cases this has led to understandable resentment and a consequential lack of commitment to their homes'.[14] As a result,

> There are still too many estates where the quality of life is less than satisfactory. It is not what tenants want, and it is not what the original designers of the estates had in mind. Tenants live there not from choice, but because they have nowhere else to live. Many tenants feel that standards of maintenance are inadequate and that management is too remote.[15]

It was, then, a truly comprehensive scheme. Mrs Thatcher was subsequently to praise its subtlety:

> The beauty of the package which Nick devised was that it combined a judicious mixture of central government intervention, local authority financial discipline, deregulation and wider choice for tenants. In so doing, it achieved a major shift away from the ossified system which had grown up under Socialism.[16]

The legislation to give impetus to most of this package was contained in the Housing Act, 1988, with the financial measures embodied in the Local Government and Housing Act, 1989.

The housing reforms and the Housing Act, 1988

Tenants' choice

The government's legislation on tenants' choice (introduced in Part IV of the Act) was seen as extending the rights and choices already given to council tenants since 1980 through the statutory Tenants' Charter and the right to buy legislation in the Housing Act 1980, later extended in 1984 and 1986. The 1988 Act enabled council tenants to choose to transfer their existing homes to another landlord. The Thatcher government sought to 'open up the closed world of the local authority housing estates to competition and to the influence of the best housing management practices of other landlords'.[17]

To this end, the Housing Corporation was given the central role in servicing the tenants' choice arrangements. The Corporation was to provide objective information and advice to tenants to enable them to use their powers to choose. The Corporation also had a wider role role in selecting and approving landlords ready to take over public housing. It sets out the guidelines on housing management practices to which all new landlords are required to subscribe. Local authorities are to be advised when an approved landlord application is received by the Corporation. The Corporation was positive in its attitudes towards tenants' choice, judging that local authorities could create a better deal for their tenants and give those tenants a greater say in the running of their estates by encouraging them to choose their landlord.

Tenants of houses were given the right to choose individually, but in blocks of flats or maisonettes they could decide to transfer only collectively. Tenants, however, did not have to transfer to a new landlord if they did not wish to do so. New independent landlords who had obtained prior approval as appropriate social landlords, under the conditions laid down by the Housing Corporation, had the right to take over council housing stock if a vote of the existing tenants decided on this. The approval criteria required applicants to show viability and competence, to commit themselves to the long term provision of housing for rent and to subscribe to the 'tenants' guarantee' laid down by the Housing Corporation.

The aim of tenants' choice was to give more choice to tenants who could not, or do not wish to, exercise their right to buy. Even where tenants voted against transfer to another landlord, they were still expected to benefit; the government's argument being that, 'Exposing councils to healthy competition would contribute to a better general standard of services'.

A number of surveys carried out in the late 1980s found majorities of tenants expressing a desire to remain with their councils.[18] Evidence also pointed to many councils making efforts to meet the needs of their tenants, seeking their tenants' views and improving services, so as to forestall any moves to opt out of local authority tenancy. In this respect, the Act may be seen as having acted as a successful catalyst to change in housing management practices.

Voluntary transfers

The Housing Act, 1988 spelt out the ways in which councils could dispose of some or all of their housing stock to housing associations under powers in the Housing and Planning Act 1986. Guidance notes issued by the Department of the Environment and the Housing Corporation set out the conditions for transfers. The interests of existing tenants were to be protected, and authorities were obliged to ensure that they were fully informed about the proposal and its implications for them, should it succeed. The authorities had also to ensure that they remained able to discharge their statutory functions post-transfer. The new landlords were to be viable, responsible and independent bodies. Guidance was also given as to the likely maximum size of the stock which could be transferred. Finally, three quarters of any capital receipts realised as a result of a transfer were to be set aside for debt repayment.[19]

Several councils explored the possibilities of voluntary transfers of their stock, some sponsoring new associations to take over their housing. By early 1990 three authorities had already succeeded in transferring their entire housing stock to housing associations. Three years later the number had risen to 18, with 94,000 tenancies transferred and speculation that up to a hundred further authorities were preparing schemes.[20]

Local authorities proposing the voluntary transfer of their stock needed to demonstrate to the Secretary of State that their proposals had the support of the tenants. The way in which evidence of support was adduced, however, was not clearly specified, and in the absence of early guidance a number of authorities used the balloting arrangements for tenants' choice. The use of this system stirred much controversy. If a majority of eligible tenants voted 'no' under the tenants' choice system, then the application for transfer to another landlord failed. The procedure was not however one of simple majority, in that an abstention was counted in effect as a 'yes' vote. Under tenants' choice, at least 50 per cent of all voters had to vote 'no' to stop a transfer.[21]

The best publicised case of a authority trying this form of ballot was Torbay borough council. With 787 tenants voting in favour of transfer, 2,210 against, and 2,209 abstentions, the council declared that a majority of tenants - 2,996 (787 plus 2,209) against 2,210 - were in favour, and it decided to go ahead with the transfer. However, following protests from tenants' groups, the Secretary of State refused permission for a voluntary transfer and the council was not able to proceed. This difficulty over the balloting system made the initial implementation of the policy difficult for many authorities which took the initial steps towards transfers, or were considering doing so.

Several other authorities subsequently failed to transfer their housing, through clear votes being cast against such transfers. In Rochford, Salisbury, Gloucester and Arun, for example, tenants voted against the proposals to transfer and the councils had to retreat in the face of tenant opposition. In Chiltern, Sevenoaks and Newbury strong votes in favour of opting out enabled the councils to transfer their housing stock to newly created housing associations. In these cases the local authority created new housing associations, to which their housing staff transferred.

Under voluntary transfer, tenants voting 'no' would not escape transfer to the new landlord. The arrangement was thus different from that of tenants' choice. Surveys of tenants showed many tenants to be wary of their new rights and of the other uncertainties involved in such transfers. Some local groups campaigned on the grounds that the policy undermined the rights of tenants and reduced their options. For example, the Tenants Participation Advisory Service (TPAS) commented that where polls were held, 'tenants have been railroaded into a ballot before they can take in all the issues'.[22] Research into the process of voluntary transfers suggests that although most tenants understood the basic elements of the proposals, they were unclear as to the details.

It is uncertain to what extent the future direction of housing will be shaped by tenants' choice or by voluntary transfers if the provisions of the 1988 Act remain in force. Much depends on the relative advantages and disadvantages of the two policies for tenants and for local authorities. The threats to council housing - reductions in housing investment allocations, and the effect of the Local Government and Housing Act, 1989 in further restricting borrowing - ensured that local authorities would find it increasingly difficult to provide new housing and repair their existing stock. The threat of compulsory competitive tendering and further financial restrictions held out little prospect of a future for local housing authorities, while the fear of tenants' choice applications by 'predatory' landlords provided an incentive for them to act pragmatically. It was under these circumstances that some were moved to investigate the possibilities of voluntarily transferring their stock to alternative landlords.

Housing Action Trusts

The Housing Act 1988 provided for the establishment of Housing Action Trusts (HATs). Housing Action Trusts were the government's key weapon in its attempt to improve the most run-down council estates and, ultimately, to give tenants of these estates a choice over whether the estates should be run by local authorities, housing associations or private companies. The government argued that the Trusts, designed to tackle the special problems of concentrations of poor quality local authority housing, offered more hope of improving these estates than if they were left in the control of local councils.

The Trusts, modelled on the Urban Development Corporations (UDCs), were to have the job of drawing up and putting into effect comprehensive programmes of improvement. In deciding on the areas to designate, the government concentrated on those with a predominance of the worst local authority housing. Housing Action Trusts were expected to seek the maximum possible support from the private sector, and to involve private sector resources in the work of refurbishing stock and taking over landlord responsibilities. Thereafter, it was envisaged that, as long as the HAT remained the owner of the property acquired from the local authority, it would assume the functions of a local authority landlord for that property, and also for privately owned housing within the designated area. The local authority was no longer to have a direct landlord role over the property transferred to the trust, although it would continue to have the responsibility for housing homeless people.

The policy raised a number of questions about future rents, security of tenure and the ability of the local authority involved to deal with homelessness. For this reason, the HAT proposals were not well received by the tenants' associations. The government was criticised for avoiding adequate consultation with tenants. Energetic lobbying of Parliament was organised by tenant groups on the estates earmarked by the government for HAT treatment. They contended that the idea of introducing HATs was not in tune with the feelings of tenants, most of whom feared being taken over by a private landlord. While many tenants blamed their local authorities, at least up to a point, for the deteriorating conditions on estates, councils nonetheless appeared to be the safer bet as landlords.

Tenants' opposition was so fierce that the chances of implementing so coercive and confrontational a policy were slim. Accordingly, the Department of the Environment made substantial changes to the terms on which HATs were designated. Tenants were given the opportunity to vote for a return of the ownership and management of their estates to the local authority when the HAT concluded its work. Most significantly, while the government had resisted tenant ballots on the establishment of a HAT, this right was conceded following the government's defeat on a House of Lords amendment in July 1988.[23]

Making the best of a bad job, and hoping to separate the tenants from local authorities, Nicholas Ridley posed the question of ballots in these new terms:

> We have heard wildly exaggerated fears that have been sown in their minds, and the absence of the ballot was the one clear point to unite opposition. I came to the view that real arguments were impossible to get across if the ballot question was obscured. Let there be a ballot. I am proposing that there should be a ballot. There will be only one issue: which is more important - the political opposition of the Labour party, or greatly improved conditions for the people in these areas.[24]

HATs evolved steadily between 1987 and 1992. Granting a ballot did nothing to make the policy more acceptable as it simply legitimised the tenants' opposition. It then became necessary to co-opt the local authorities in to the provision of HATs by offering such greatly improved packages that they themselves would have an incentive to lead tenant opinion. Thus the policy moved from one of coercion, through negotiation, to one of incentive. The effect was to increase the budget for the first six HATs from

£125 million over three years (or around £20 million per area), to £160 in Waltham Forest, and £190 million in Liverpool alone.

Private renting and housing associations

Part I of the Housing Act, 1988 was aimed at transforming the private rented sector, which at that time accounted for less than eight per cent of homes in Britain. The intention was to reverse the long term decline in private renting, to regenerate the sector through deregulation, and to stimulate its growth by removing rent controls and introducing new-style assured tenancies.[25] Assured tenancies enabled landlords and tenants to devise their own rent levels through negotiation, with new tenancies no longer protected by the Rent Act by removing the rent controls that had brought it about. The sector could only be revived, in the government's view, if letting property again became an economic proposition. This was clearly a very long-term aim. It was evident that, even if private renting was made profitable in the short term, private investors, because of the past history of rent controls, were unlikely to risk future investment on any scale in housing for rent. They would avoid it in favour of more secure forms of investment.[26]

The government also sought to bring about a major shift in the housing association sector. The objective was to move them away from quasi-public housing role into which they had developed since 1974 towards a more private sector style 'independent' rental sector.[27] To this end, new housing association tenancies were deregulated to put them in much the same footing as those in the private rented sector. Housing association provision was to be expanded by drawing in private finance to create 'mixed funding' schemes. One predicted effect was a move away from inner city rehabilitation to new building under the new financial regime, as rehabilitation schemes are relatively more risky.[28]

The housing finance reforms

Underlying all these changes were new provisions for housing finance, embodied in the Local Government and Housing Act, 1989. The capital and revenue regimes it introduced set a new agenda for local authority housing. The government claimed the legislation to have three main purposes: to increase the efficiency of local authorities, to increase the efficiency of resource allocation and to 'influence the level of rents to a market-like level'.

The Local Government and Housing Act, 1989 introduced a new system for the regulation of local authority capital finance foreshadowed in the DOE/Welsh Office consultation paper *Capital Expenditure and Finance*.

It also established the new financial regime for local authority housing which had been proposed in an earlier consultation paper.[29]

The capital control system

Central governments have consistently sought to control local authority finances, and since 1919 there has been an underlying conflict over the amount that should be committed to meet housing need. Local authorities faced an increasing dilemma. They recognised the need for greater investment, but they were also aware of the increasing pressure from central government to curtail expenditure. The introduction of 1989 system of capital finance meant that local authorities had to cope with more controls and pressures.

The government's position was that the system of capital controls introduced in the Local Government, Planning and Land Act 1980 had proved deficient. It argued that the system had not been able to deal effectively with high levels of capital receipts from council house sales and had not prevented local authorities from exploiting the loopholes. In addition, the system failed to bring about net capital expenditure consistent with public expenditure plans. The new system laid greater emphasis on borrowing rather than spending. The government's objectives for the new system of capital controls were to control the overall levels of local authority capital expenditure and borrowing; to bring about a distribution of capital expenditure which reflects both national and local needs; to reduce the size of the public sector by encouraging asset sales; and to provide local authorities with a sound basis to plan their capital programmes.

As one of its measures to control borrowing, the government gave most authorities credit approvals which took into account the authority's available capital receipts. This new system enabled central government to direct borrowing ability towards areas of housing need with particularly limited resources, such as inner London authorities. Many authorities with under-average capital receipts but high General Needs Index (GNI) scores could expect higher allocation levels than in the past. The reverse was true for a number of authorities, particularly in the South East, which had amassed their capital receipts.

Secondly, in order to pay off debt or meet known future borrowing commitments, local authorities were required to set aside 75 per cent of the proceeds from council house sales, and 50 per cent from other asset sales. Under the former system central government had only restricted the use of capital receipts to 20 per cent in the year in which they were generated, permitting a carry forward of the unspent 80 per cent for re-use in the following years. By this means councils had been able eventually to spend the whole value of their receipts.

The local authority associations, particularly the Association of Metropolitan Authorities and the Association of London Authorities, whose members represented the urban areas of greatest housing need, criticised the new restriction on the use of capital receipts, arguing that the proposals would discourage new building, and that capital expenditure would have to be significantly reduced. The AMA and the ALA were concerned that their member authorities would be severely restricted in their ability to meet housing needs; and that the proposals implied a worsening housing repair service, deterioration in the maintenance of other council assets, and an inability to make substantial new investments to, for example, house the homeless or meet other urgent needs.

The Institute of Housing predicted that the new capital control system would lead to a significant reduction in investment in major repairs and improvements; very few new dwellings would be built in the public sector, which would imply a poorer service for tenants. According to the Institute, 'The prospect of this bleak future has certainly led many local authorities to consider voluntary transfer of their stock, and will no doubt lead to several others to follow their example'. Providing an incentive to such transfers was part of the logic of the housing reform package.

Housing revenue finance

The Act also introduced major changes in the revenue funding of council housing. The 1987 white paper set out the government's intention to introduce a new financial regime to 'reinforce the present statutory distinction between the provision of housing and other local authority functions and replace the existing housing revenue accounts by arrangements which are more in accord with modern accounting practice'.[30] This was reiterated in the consultation paper of July 1988 which proposed a more tightly defined housing revenue account to 'reinforce the distinction between the provision of housing and other local authority functions'.

At the heart of the Conservatives' housing reforms were the changes dealing with the housing revenue account (HRA) and its constituent parts. The HRA deals exclusively with day to day expenditure and income for the local authority housing stock. The main items of expenditure are loan charges for council house building, management and maintenance costs and surpluses transferred to the general rate fund. The chief sources of income at that time were rents (net of rebate) from council tenants, rent rebate subsidy, income from investments of capital receipts, rate fund contributions and housing subsidy. In addition, rents were henceforth to bear a close relationship to what properties were worth and not to historic costs. Under the earlier system, nearly 50 per cent of the funding of the housing revenue account was in respect of the historical costs of providing, modernising and improving the council stock.

The new system of revenue finance introduced a single housing subsidy, which replaced housing subsidy, rate fund contributions (supported by rate support grant) and the rent rebate element of housing benefit subsidy. In the new HRA the principal sources of income are just gross rents and housing revenue account subsidy; and the main outgoings are loan charges, management and maintenance spending, revenue contributions to capital expenditure on HRA dwellings (as provided for in the new capital system), surpluses transferred to other accounts of the general fund, and other charges including standard community charge (later council tax) on vacant dwellings.

One of the most potent aspects of the new system was the 'ring fencing' of the HRA, whereby discretionary transfers in either direction were not permitted. Authorities continued to have to budget to avoid a deficit on the housing revenue account. The Conservatives' claim was that by limiting the housing revenue account in this way, council landlords would be more accountable to their customers, the tenants. Conservative governments had long sought to tackle subsidies from the rate fund, claiming that they had in the past allowed authorities to cushion their tenants against the effects of local authority inefficiency, and kept rents artificially low for political reasons. The Act removed local authority discretion over subsidisation by combining existing schemes into a single subsidy controlled by central government. Prior to the introduction of this new system only 70-80 local authorities had received housing subsidy, but henceforth virtually all authorities were brought into subsidy.[31]

Local authorities continued to retain local discretion in running their housing operations, for instance in balancing the rents they set against the standards of management they provided. The intention was, once again, to sharpen and clarify choice:

Well run housing departments will be able to provide a good standard of service at a modest rent; on the other hand, inefficient landlords will be unable to conceal their poor standards or their extravagant costs. Tenants will thus be given clear signals about the performance of their council's housing operation. They will be able to take better informed decisions about the alternatives the government's housing policy is placing before them, and to decide whether to exercise the options that government is giving them through the right to buy and tenants' choice.[32]

Implications of the proposed changes

Such a fundamental change in policy was to have important consequences for local authorities. In the first place, central government gained greater control over rent levels and the management and maintenance expenditure of councils. Under the previous system only a quarter of all councils actually received subsidy; the new system meant that all authorities were brought into central government subsidy entitlement thereby falling under central control. Central guidelines over rent levels were to have a major impact. Where authorities' housing revenue accounts were in surplus without any housing revenue subsidy, councils were required to transfer a specified surplus to the general fund so that no financial cushion could remain on the housing revenue account to protect tenants from future rent rises. Central government was thereby able to influence rent levels even in those councils which required no further subsidy.

The exclusion of rate fund contributions reduced the ability of councils to switch money from ratepayers to the housing revenue account and to hold rents down by switching. In the past some authorities (mainly Labour) held down rents by such transfers. They could no longer do so. However, in the first year of the scheme from April 1990 there were no major average increases in rents, as the initial housing revenue account subsidy was based on the average of previous subsidies including rate fund contributions. The switch to rents based on a return on the current values of the housing stock implied that council tenants were likely to be the losers. The new changes were intended to encourage tenants to move into the private housing market, despite the claim that 'rents should not exceed levels within the reach of people in low-paid-employment and in practice will be below market levels'.

The inclusion of rent rebate subsidy within the housing revenue account marked a fundamental change in the financing of housing benefit. It meant that local authorities with surpluses on their HRA would receive a proportionately reduced government contribution to the rebates given to their tenants in the form of housing benefit. As a result of this, council tenants not in receipt of housing benefit would be helping to meet the costs of financial help to poorer tenants via housing benefit. This was seen to represent a 'shift of welfare responsibilities not just from central government to local government but from central government to particular council tenants in areas where the housing revenue account is in surplus'.[33]

This detailed analysis of the housing finance proposals demonstrates that the government's intention in introducing the new financial reforms was to take tighter control of local authority housing financial decisions, and so promote the sought-for shifts in tenure and ownership. Where rents rose steeply it became harder for local authorities to compete with other agencies seeking to take over their stock. At the same time, large increases in rents might make tenants keener than they otherwise would have been to transfer to alternative landlords.

Such was the package of measures contained within the third Thatcher government's two major housing Acts. It was clear that the changes set out in the Housing Act, 1988 could only take effect over the long term, when they might pose a major challenge to the traditional housing roles of both local authorities and housing associations. If the measures proved as effective as the government hoped, then only two possible futures for local housing authorities were conceivable, both of them highly restricted. Either local authorities would continue to maintain their traditional role within the constraints of a tight financial environment, or they would collapse under the weight of the combination of increasing central intervention and demands for change from tenants. Either outcome was likely to reduce the role of the local housing authority to that of a residuary welfare housing agency.[34]

A change of government aside, the overall impact of these housing and financial reforms will depend on a number of factors. These include the way in which housing associations respond as well as how strongly central government manipulates grants, subsidies and expenditure controls, and how strenuously local authorities seek to protect their tenants. Much is bound to depend ultimately on the responses of the tenants themselves, and it is noticeable that the much-vaunted tenants' choice proposals give them no tangible incentives to opt for an alternative landlord.

How these reforms worked in practice in the initial stages of the housing policy is the subject of the remainder of this chapter. It looks first at voluntary transfers, one area in which the local authorities themselves held the initiative. It then examines the HAT programme as a contrasting example of central direction. The working of both of these aspects of the Conservatives' housing reforms is illustrated by the on-the-ground experience of early implementation.

Local authorities as initiators: voluntary transfers

Voluntary transfers allowed local authorities themselves to initiate the change of tenure. On the face of it there seemed to be significant financial and managerial advantages to authorities if they made such transfers. Transfers enabled local authorities to escape direct government financial controls. With voluntary transfers authorities were able to ensure the retention of the existing stock of rented accommodation, as new lettings were not subject to the right to buy. Finally the transfers made possible the provision of a locally based housing administration, which might be more sensitive and efficient than council management. On the other hand, tenants could see several disadvantages to such transfers in terms of loss of local political accountability and financial risk. In particular, transfers offered no satisfactory future for those dissenting individuals who sought to maintain their *status quo* as municipal tenants.

The balance of advantage was such that local authorities of all political persuasions were initially, if reluctantly, attracted to the transfer option by two opportunities it gave them. Government restrictions on borrowing by local authorities had in recent years starved them of resources, but with voluntary transfers they could generate capital resources for new construction and for modernisation of the remaining housing stock. Transfers also allowed authorities to preserve the stock of rented accommodation in their areas, which had been substantially eroded by the right to buy. Even as a second-best solution, it had to be carefully considered.

By the end of 1991, as many as 63 authorities in England and Wales had undertaken an initial assessment of whether they should consider a voluntary transfer of their stock into other hands. Thirty authorities had gone so far as balloting their tenants on a firm proposal for a voluntary transfer, either to an existing housing association or, as in the great majority of cases, to an association specifically created for this purpose.[35] The outcomes had varied from a positive vote of eight per cent to one of 91 per cent, on turnouts which fell on only one occasion below 70 per cent.[36] Twenty-one authorities had dropped their proposals prior to balloting.

Table 3.1
Attitudes to voluntary transfer by size of housing stock

	committed to retention %	positively favours voluntary transfer %
Size of housing stock:		
less then 5,000 dwellings	62	21
5,000-9,999 dwellings	64	16
10,000 and more dwellings	77	3

Source: LGMB, unpublished data.

Authorities considering transfer had one feature in common - a relatively small housing stock. The larger the stock, the less likely an authority was to even consider transferring it. The 1992 LGMB survey of 292 housing authorities confirmed just this. As Table 3.1 shows, authorities with large housing stock show a greater commitment to retaining and managing housing and express less support for voluntary transfer than authorities with small housing stock. However, while the initiatives for transfers were largely from Conservative councils, a few Labour councils such as Swansea also attempted transfers, albeit unsuccessfully. Just 16 authorities had successfully transferred all their stock by the end of 1993. The first of these were Chiltern in Buckinghamshire, Sevenoaks in Kent and Newbury in Berkshire: all, significantly, in the south-east.

In the forefront of transfers

Conservative-controlled Chiltern district council was the first authority to transfer its council homes, in this case to the newly sponsored Chiltern Hundreds Housing Association. The association was set up to take on the responsibility for the council stock and to build new homes for rent and sale. In common with most other authorities, Chiltern had seen its Housing Investment Programme (HIP) cut back and its stock reduced through the right to buy, and the council was uncertain about its freedom to use its future capital receipts. Transfer to an association seemed the most attractive option, and this was successfully completed with a decisive tenants' vote in favour. All-party political support and the absence of opposition from tenants' groups and associations were crucial factors in the council's success in transferring its property.

The Chiltern success was soon followed by Sevenoaks district council. Sevenoaks responded to the new legislative provisions by setting up the West Kent Housing Association to receive the transfer of its entire housing stock. As a registered housing association, legally and financially independent of the council, West Kent Housing Association owned about 6,300 dwellings after taking over the council's housing stock in March 1989. The way in which this was achieved well illustrates the transfer process under the Housing Act, 1988.

Sevenoaks is a green belt area in West Kent within easy reach of London and the coast. Housing is expensive, with Victorian terraced houses valued at £100,000 in 1988, and three bedroom semi-detached houses at £120,000 and flats for £70,000 or more. For people on modest incomes, housing in Sevenoaks is not within easy access either for rent or for purchase. In 1988 the council owned 16 per cent of the total dwellings in the district (about 6,600 out of a total of 42,956) comprising around 4,000 houses, 2,000 flats and nearly 600 sheltered units. The great majority of the dwellings in the area were owner-occupied (81 per cent) while private rented dwellings and housing association dwellings accounted for only two per cent and one per cent respectively.

Since 1976, the council had sold about 2,500 dwellings to its tenants. In 1984/85, the council sold 216 properties which increased to 338 in 1985/86. It sold a further 400 units in 1988/89. The council envisaged that, if such sales continued, its housing stock would reduce to below 3,000 within ten years. The process was bound to reduce the stock of rented housing locally, and would have severely limited the opportunities of those on lower incomes. Increasing demand for housing was adding to the council's waiting lists, which in 1989 contained about 1,800 applicants. In 1986/87 about 200 applicants were housed from the council's waiting lists; in 1987/88 only 80 waiting list applicants could be housed. There is a growing housing problem for single people as well as for families seeking two or three bedroom houses.

With increasing homelessness on the one hand and the housing stock diminishing through right to buy on the other, the options facing Sevenoaks were to decide either to do nothing, or to look for a way to safeguard its tenants and the future supply of local rented housing. Transferring the council's housing stock to a housing association formed for that purpose was seen as the best option. New tenants would not then have a right to buy and this would check the decline in available rented housing. The association would also be able to develop new housing in future to meet the increasing housing needs, something which would not have been possible for the council under the government's financial reforms.

The changes in the HIP allocation and the constraints of the new financial reforms were among the factors that prompted the council to decide in favour of the transfer. Sevenoaks' allocations had been reducing each year and were likely to reduce further. In 1982/83 its HIP allocation was £2.7 million, which decreased to £2.2 million in 1985/86. In 1988/89, this figure came down further to £1.3 million and in 1989/90 it was about £1 million. Against this background of declining investment, the council would find itself unable to build more housing for local people, and would have little or no influence on local housing provision or management in the future. Its role as a major landlord would thereby lapse.

Yet the requirement for affordable housing to meet local needs - starter homes for young couples, family homes at affordable prices or sheltered accommodation for the elderly - would still remain. Under these circumstances, and in the light of the positive encouragement given by the government to housing associations under the Act, the council concluded that by transferring its properties to an association it could continue to ensure efficient and sensitive housing management to meet local housing needs.

The transfer option offered the possibility of creating a non-profit housing organisation operating outside local government financial controls. As a housing association, it would not be constrained by government controls and it would be able to gain access to funds from the Housing Corporation, as well as the council and the private sector. The housing association's rents would be based on long term fixed rate building society loans and, therefore, would not be subject to the higher rents and charges which the new local government financial provisions would compel.

Both the council and the West Kent Housing Association recognised that, to ensure the success of the policy, it was important to consult the tenants and inform them fully about the legal consequences, likely rents, policies on waiting lists and transfers, and other aspects of housing management. The council undertook discussions with its tenants, explaining why the proposals were being put forward and how they would work. From July to September 1988 it distributed free newspapers, leaflets and notes. It also organised a mobile exhibition, a programme of public meetings in every ward and on every estate, and seminars for tenant groups, wardens and other interested people.

The proposals guaranteed tenants that they would keep their rights to buy, transfer and exchange, and would enjoy rents initially held to a low rate of increase. New tenants would not have a right to buy, but their rents, although higher than those of existing tenants, would still be at affordable levels. Making clear to tenants its commitment to long term housing and to the provision of rented accommodation, Sevenoaks council assured tenants that, on transfer to the new association, they would not have rent increases in the first three years exceeding four per cent a year plus inflation. Tenants were also told that rents would be adjusted as necessary after that at the association's discretion, but in such a way that rents would remain 'within the reach of those in low paid employment'. This increase was expected to be between five per cent and 10 per cent plus inflation after the first three years.

Aware of the disastrous consequences of the much publicised voting method adopted by Torbay borough council, Sevenoaks decided that the ballot should be on a straightforward majority of those voting in favour of the transfer. A formal ballot took place under the scrutiny of the Electoral Reform Society in November 1988, in which 80 per cent of all tenants voted, as many as 85 per cent of them in support of a transfer to the housing association.

The stated role of West Kent Housing Association, set up in March 1989, was to provide and manage housing at reasonable or affordable costs for local people by its acquisition of council stock and by new building. Much of the capital required for future building was to be from private finance sources, possibly supplemented by housing association grants or assistance from the council. The association maintains the housing waiting list on the council's behalf, provides direct allocations to housing association dwellings wherever possible and runs an advisory service for homeless families.

The contract governing the relationship between Sevenoaks council and the West Kent Housing Association also provides for the council's homeless persons' hostels to remain in the ownership of the council, but with day to day control of those hostels managed in collaboration with the association. The council continued to employ two homeless persons officers to work within the offices of the housing association, investigating homelessness cases and allocating accommodation within either the council's hostels or the association's housing stock.

The association adopted virtually unchanged the council's policies on transfers and exchanges. The district council remains responsible for the ownership and control of sites for future development, providing some of the finance for the new association and other local housing associations for new development, the annual review of the housing investment programme strategy, and supervision and monitoring of all sectors of housing within the district.

Tenant veto: the Rochford case

Bordered by the River Crouch, the North Sea, the Essex borough of Southend-on-Sea, and the districts of Castle Point and Basildon, Rochford district council covers a large rural area together with two main towns - Rochford and Rayleigh - and 14 villages. The expanding population in the late 1980s pushed house prices up beyond the reach of many people. For those with low incomes the only hope of a decent home was to find one to rent. Yet of the district's 28,000 dwellings, roughly 80 per cent were owner occupied, with the district council owning nine per cent, and housing associations two per cent.

Rochford had three main reasons for deciding to transfer its stock to a housing association: the progressive erosion of houses available for rent (as a result of right to buy policy), the reduction in housing investment and fear of a fragmentation of the management of housing stock. Council sales had been increasing in Rochford under the right to buy policy, and a total of 101 dwellings had been sold by 1987/88. Such sales were effectively reducing the number of houses available to rent, and at the same time investment in housing had been declining, so that it was becoming increasingly difficult for the council to meet housing needs. The Housing Investment Programme allocation in 1989/90 was £2.2 million and this was expected to reduce to £1.95 million in 1990/91 and £1.92 million in 1991/92.

In these circumstances, the council recognised the advantages of transferring the stock to a socially responsible landlord. In the absence of an existing local housing association with the capacity to absorb the local authority stock, the council decided to create a new locally-based association. Crouch Valley Housing Association was therefore established, with the aims of preserving and enhancing the stock of houses available for rent, and of 'meeting the needs of its tenants in a sympathetic, efficient and cost-effective manner'. The association was set up with the objectives to provide good homes at rents appropriate for people in need, with a full range of housing services; to develop a sound relationship between landlord and tenant; to ensure that all available accommodation would be used to the best advantage and let to those in greatest need; and to promote schemes to build new homes for rent. It was to take on 2,343 units of council stock, including 14 sheltered schemes.

One of the conditions of the transfer was that existing tenants would not lose any of their rights. Existing tenants were to retain their right to buy, to continue to get the same discounts and to secure a mortgage. The council also gave an undertaking that, if the stock were transferred to the association, there would be no dramatic increases in rents: in the first year after transfer the association's rent increases would not exceed seven per cent, whereas if the stock stayed in council ownership the increase was likely to be around eight per cent. Tenants were also told that 'no new policies which directly affected the management or the conditions of tenancy would be implemented without taking tenants' views into consideration'.

The association was to undertake all the requirements to house homeless people referred to Rochford council. It was the council's intention to provide homes for local people who would not be able to buy. In partnership with the housing association, the council, in its enabling role, was to use its land and the money allocated to it by central government under the HIP to enable the association to build more accommodation. As for the local authority staff, the association would employ them on the same conditions and terms. Despite the council's attempts to inform and persuade tenants, representatives of tenants' groups said that they were not made aware of the implications of the decision to transfer, and that they were, to a large extent, left in the dark. Tenants were unclear about the future rent levels and tenancy agreements. They were also suspicious about the level of service they would receive on repairs and maintenance, and were concerned about how far, and by what means, their rights would be maintained. In addition, they were worried whether the new association would be able to offer houses at affordable rents to future tenants.

Tenants' suspicions were reinforced when a consultant's report commissioned by the council concluded that, although transfer would 'provide a degree of certainty for tenants in terms of future rent increases', the long term financial effects were difficult to predict. This raised doubts in the minds of the tenants about the financial viability of the new association. Most tenants therefore came to oppose the policy. They forwarded a petition opposing it to the Department of the Environment, and a group of tenants formed an action committee (the Rochford Housing Action Group) to protest about the way in which the consultation was being conducted. Members of the opposition parties who were opposed to the transfer were said to have joined the Rochford Housing Action Group and carried out door to door canvassing to vote against the proposals. When the ballot was finally conducted, only eight per cent of those who voted did so in favour of the transfer.

Rochford's experience showed that tenants were unlikely to support a transfer where there was organised local opposition to the proposal. With all party support implementation of the transfer policy was more likely to be a smooth process. The successes in Sevenoaks and Chiltern can primarily be attributed to these two factors. In contrast, the failure of Rochford to implement the policy was largely the result of tenant and political opposition.

The difficulty of winning consent for whole stock transfer led some authorities, for example, Glasgow and Waltham Forest, to consider selective disposals of their stock. Waltham Forest had considerable problems with several of its estates and had for many years been trying to explore ways of improving and redeveloping them. The council realised that neither an HIP allocation nor capital receipts adequate to meet the cost of redevelopment could realistically be expected. It therefore considered disposing of four of its estates, with a valuation that reflected the outstanding repair requirements: this would result in a 'dowry' being paid by the council to the new landlord, which would be a tenant-controlled body. Such selective transfers offered some scope for local authorities proposing to transfer their stock while still seeking to maintain their tenant services. Such schemes had an important advantage, in that they did not risk the same large-scale rejection as may occur with proposals for general transfers. Disposals of areas could be done in such a way so as to suit the particular problems of the estates concerned and the aspirations of the local tenants.

Central government as initiator: Housing Action Trusts

The Housing Act, 1988 sets up a framework within which the Secretary of State will be able to appoint Housing Action Trusts to take over council housing in designated areas. The 1987 white paper and the consultation paper suggested that HATs would be established in inner city areas with serious housing and other social problems and in areas with a predominance of council housing. The government proposed to allocate £125 million to HATs for the years 1988/89 to 1990/91.

The objectives of the Housing Action Trusts were to take over local authority housing within the designated area; to repair, modernise and improve the stock; to improve the living conditions and general environment of the area; and to secure diversity of tenure. The government argued that Housing Action Trusts could do much to help local authorities. Where a trust was established, the local authorities were to be relieved of some of their most difficult housing stock. This was justified as enabling them to concentrate their efforts and resources on the stock that remained.

Local authorities required to transfer their housing stock to the HAT, which would be expected to remain in existence for five years. At the end of the Trust's life, the tenants would be free to choose whether they wanted their estate to go back to the local authority, to a housing association or to a private landlord. Brief sketches of the development of the HATs proposal in face of its reception at the grass-roots level illustrate the ways in which local authorities and tenants approached the risks and opportunities the programme offered. The cases of Lambeth and Sunderland show the difficulties of imposing a particular solution from the centre. The case of Waltham Forest shows how high the price of gaining acceptance could be.

HATs off in Lambeth

The London Borough of Lambeth extends from the south bank of the river Thames at Waterloo through the densely built-up areas of Vauxhall, Stockwell and Brixton to the suburbs of Streatham and Norwood. The borough is cosmopolitan in make-up - about a third of the population is black, the largest ethnic groups being of West Indian origin, and there is a sizeable Irish community. Lambeth has all the characteristics of an inner city area - high levels of unemployment, poverty and overcrowding, a declining industrial base, and large numbers of elderly people and of people dependent on social security. On Department of the Environment indices, the borough ranks as the fourth most deprived in the country.

The council's HIP statement for 1989/90 showed that of the housing stock in the borough, 43 per cent was council owned, eight per cent with housing associations, 24 per cent in owner-occupation, and 23 per cent privately-rented (with the remaining two per cent being 'other public sector' housing). Lambeth has an acute housing shortage, illustrated by its high level of priority homeless admissions. In 1987/88, two-fifths of all lettings of council property went to priority homeless families. Other such families had to be placed in various forms of temporary accommodation and bed and breakfast hotels. Overcrowding is another aspect of the housing shortage. The council's Housing Needs Survey in 1986 showed that about one in seven households were overcrowded.

Much of the housing stock in the borough is in an unsatisfactory condition. The Greater London House Condition Survey showed that about 70 per cent of the stock in the council sector was in need of major renovation. Council estimates show that around 35 per cent of its stock was hard to let. Many council estates are high density and multi-storey and have high child densities, poor environment, design faults and high levels of vandalism. Lambeth, then, suffers a classic combination of poor physical environment and high levels of social deprivation.

In July 1988 the government proposed two estates in Lambeth - Angell Town and Loughborough - for transfer to Housing Action Trusts. Consultants were appointed for the estates by the government with the objectives of putting the case for a Housing Action Trust to the people and assessing the extent of tenant opposition or support for the proposals. If the consultants advised the government that there were good prospects of support for HATs in Lambeth, then the tenants would be balloted for their views.

Lambeth had been trying to tackle the problems of Angell Town, working closely with the tenants in improving the estate and the surrounding area. Most of the capital finance for those initiatives came from the Housing Investment Programme, supplemented in earlier years by Inner City Partnership money. With continuous reductions in HIP allocations, the council faced increasing difficulties in finding adequate capital to carry out such work. The council was concerned that establishing a Housing Action Trust for Angell Town - as for Loughborough - would redirect resources to private developers which could instead be allocated to the council for refurbishment.

The council was opposed to the Housing Action Trust policy, both in general (it responded critically to the government's consultation paper on the idea in 1987, before any estates were identified) and in respect of the two Lambeth estates in particular. In the council's view HATs would focus attention on a limited number of areas, syphoning off finance which would otherwise be available to the local authority to tackle its wider housing problems. It feared that areas in Lambeth without Trust status would suffer.

The council argued that the imposition of the Housing Action Trust on the Angell Town estate would disrupt its own programme of work there. It also predicted that rent levels would increase, that new lettings in the borough would fall, and that the renovated properties were unlikely to go to people in the borough in the greatest housing need, including members of ethnic minority communities.

A council officer was given special responsibility to oversee and coordinate the responses of all council departments within the HATs areas, including measures to improve service delivery. At the same time the council supported tenants' campaigns against HATs. A tenant liaison team was established to operate on the estates, establishing close working relationships with tenant groups, acting as intermediaries for the council and tenants, and providing tenants with information about HATs.

Partly as a result of these interventions, concern about HATs increased throughout both of the proposed Housing Action Trust areas. Since July 1988, when the government indicated its intention of creating the Trusts, tenants in the two estates campaigned to stop them being set up. Tenants are worried that the trusts will redevelop the estates in a manner disadvantageous to them. Supported by the tenants, the council decided not to co-operate with the consultants and denied them access to information, premises and other material which would be of use to them.

The tenants had several anxieties. Many were worried that homes would be sold off to developers to provide owner-occupied housing for people with high incomes, as there appeared to be no guarantee that refurbished properties would not be sold on the open market. They believed that demolitions and the construction of new homes would leave fewer homes at the end of the day. They feared that the property retained for rented housing would be relet at unaffordable rents, and they were uncertain about future changes in their conditions of tenure and other rights. The roots of these uncertainties lay in the nature of the HATs scheme itself, as no plan could be made for future disposals until after the Trust was established. Tenants were being asked to take a leap in the dark.

The tenants' campaigns grew steadily, through public meetings and campaign planning meetings. Posters and leaflets had been distributed throughout the estates, highlighting the disadvantages of the new proposal. Tenants in both the estates formed a joint campaign coordinating committee to pool their efforts, and worked closely with associations in other areas in Sandwell, Southwark, Sunderland and Leeds, where HATs were also proposed.

The intensity of the opposition in Lambeth and elsewhere made a deep impression on the consultants appointed to evaluate the several schemes. It became clear that tenant opposition could block the implementation of the HATs programme. In March 1989, virtually on the eve of the planned HAT declarations, the government announced that it would proceed more cautiously towards a round of consultations, leading up to the ballots which the House of Lords had forced upon them.

Although the consultant's report made a strong case for HATs in Angell Town and Loughborough, such was the opposition of the tenants there that the Lambeth schemes had little chance of surviving any opinion-sounding. A MORI poll in September showed that almost three quarters of the affected tenants rejected the HAT proposals. Recognising defeat, the government withdrew the Lambeth proposals in the spring of 1990.

Losing the argument in Sunderland

Sunderland is a large urban centre in the north-east of England, close to Newcastle upon Tyne. Its population has been declining since the early 1970s. The local shipbuilding industry, formerly the biggest local employer, has declined dramatically, but the economy has benefited from some growth of employment in light manufacturing industries.

The council owns about 42 per cent of the total stock in the borough of Sunderland. Three per cent of the dwellings are in the housing association sector. The largest tenure is owner-occupation, comprising 53 per cent of the total stock. Four of the council's estates were proposed for Housing Action Trusts, at Downhill, Hylton Castle, Town End Farm and parts of Red House. These proposed HAT areas contained 10 per cent of the council stock. Within the HAT areas council ownership was the predominant tenure, although recent years had seen the proportion of non-local authority dwellings in these areas increase, from five per cent in 1981 to 16 per cent in 1989, mainly because of the right to buy policy. A late upsurge in the number of right to buy applications was believed to have been stimulated by concern about the HAT proposal.

The estates in the proposed Housing Action Trust area, comprising 6,500 dwellings, were built between 1953 and 1967 to cater for the rapid population growth that occurred during this period. The council's existing policies in these areas aimed at modernising and improving the stock. To this end, the council invested some £13 million in the six years up to 1989/90, completely upgrading around a third of the dwellings. It was initially estimated that a little under £30 million more was required to complete the modernisation programme together with associated schemes of environmental improvement in the HAT area, although a consultants' report subsequently revised this to between £55 and £71 million.

The government's view was that the target estates suffered from the problems which Housing Action Trusts were designed to treat. The Trusts would institute modernisation and development programmes aimed at transforming the physical fabric of the estates and the economic and social welfare of their residents. The government's own consultants, however, were less sanguine, and expressed reservations about designating HATs in

Sunderland, whose problems were of a lower order of magnitude than those further south.

Sunderland borough council did not reject the Government's approach outright. It could see advantages in establishing HATs for its estates. The improvement and modernisation work already carried out on some of the estates proposed for HATs had been made possible under the government's estate action programme; a lot of work still needed to be done, and the council itself could hardly expect to find the resources needed if the government would not increase the HIP allocation to the borough. One of the attractions of the HAT proposal, then, was that it offered easier access to financial resources.

The council had some serious concerns, however. It was unhappy that the resources being made available to the HATs required a change of ownership. It was far from convinced that the stock would return to municipal ownership after the HATs had completed their work, and sought an assurance from the government that it would be able to buy back the estates and would be given the resources to do so. Given these assurances, the council cooperated fully with the government's consultants, providing them with detailed information on housing conditions, socio-economic characteristics and future improvement programmes in the HAT areas.

The council consistently maintained that the ultimate decision over the HATs was for tenants to make. As in Lambeth, the initial government decision to implement HATs without consulting tenants aroused local anger. The report by the consultants commissioned by the government showed that the tenants were primarily concerned about future rents and security of tenure and feared not being able to return to local authority tenancies at a later stage. Most tenants felt that, despite the financial problems, the council was doing a satisfactory job in running the estates. Many said that they would ideally like more money to be given to the council without the introduction of HATs. But, like the council, they recognised that HATs were likely to generate more resources for investment than could be available from any other source.

Despite a rather weak claim to HAT eligibility in terms of housing need, Sunderland looked like a good prospect for the government's plans. The neutrality and pragmatism of the council was underpinned by the main tenant campaign body STAND - Sunderland Tenants Against No Democracy - whose main aims were conceded by the government and who thereafter did not oppose the proposed HAT. Yet the tenants themselves were evidently less convinced, for the outcome of the eventual ballot was little different from the MORI poll in Lambeth: 80 per cent of Sunderland's tenants voted to reject the HAT, and the government withdrew the proposal. Once it had departed from its initial stance of confrontation and coercion, the government was forced to argue its case for HATs, and to win the support of the local authorities and their tenants. In Sunderland, despite the pragmatic stance of both bodies, that argument was lost.

Lowering the targets

Between them, rising costs and tenant opposition to HATs forced the government to drastically revise their position. It became clear that a HAT could only be established by consent, a fact which placed the local authorities in an immensely strong bargaining position. The unexpected rejection of the HAT proposals in Southwark seemed for a while to sound the death-knell of the programme. As it limped along, and proposals were rejected or shelved, the political premium placed on success in the remaining areas became all the greater. To that extent, the government was forced to pay the price that the local authorities, acting in concert with their tenants, chose to exact. And its willingness to do so ensured that something - at whatever price - would come out of the HATs scheme.

Salvation was to be found in the north-east London borough of Waltham Forest. Waltham Forest owned four estates of post-war concrete panel construction, which represented a seemingly insoluble problem of renovation, due to the very high costs involved. The estates had already been subject to consultants' studies. A proposal to swap landlords under the tenants' choice provisions collapsed when the government refused to allow the estates to be transferred to a tenant-controlled housing association at a negative value. The publicity engendered by these abortive attempts was a considerable embarassment to the government, and it was with relief that ministers greeted a Waltham Forest application for HAT designation.

With the council standing aside, the key negotiations were between the government and the tenants' associations, who were virtually able to set their own terms for representation on the management committee and for the eventual ownership of the post-HAT estates. A tenant ballot in July 1991 produced an 81 per cent vote in favour of the HAT, in striking contrast to the overwhelming rejections registered elsewhere by that time.

A second scheme in Hull, initiated by the local authority, similarly produced a large majority vote in favour, and actually beat Waltham Forest to the dubious distinction of being the first scheme launched under the now-battered HAT programme. The dominance of the local authority interest in the Hull arrangements, and the high cost relative to the undeniably modest nature of the housing need involved, underlined how far the eventual outcome has drifted from Nicholas Ridley's original vision. With the political climate transformed by Mrs Thatcher's departure, Conservative ministers were now portraying HATs as a form of partnership between central and local government.

This change of approach, and the increasingly opportunistic stance of the local authorities involved in Hull's scheme - presented by the council as the 'North Hull *Voluntary* HAT' - opened the door for a wider take-up of the programme. At the same time, the unanticipated increase in the scale of the investment required undermined the claim to deliver value for money and ensured that very few schemes would be introduced. In so far as the Housing Act, 1988 proposals represented an attempt to break with the past, the fate of HATs clearly demonstrated just how difficult such breaks could be in practice.

Dilemmas and contradictions in housing policy

The Housing Act, 1988 and the Local Government and Housing Act, 1989 introduced a series of measures designed to radically restructure social housing during the 1990s. While continuing the incentives to buy rather than rent, they aimed to open up the prospect of a social housing system in which an increasingly diverse group of landlords could become ever more responsive to the needs and wishes of their tenants. The move towards a greater plurality of tenures in the social rented sector was also intended to bring about greater efficiency, and better value for money, in a sector of housing which was perceived by the government as wasteful in its use of public funds. The extent to which this vision becomes a reality remains uncertain, although the preliminary steps which have been made towards it suggest a considerable shortfall on the initial, ambitious, expectation.

The main policies to facilitate the transition to this new and more diverse world of social housing were embodied in the legislation creating tenants' choice and Housing Action Trusts as well as in the enhanced role given to voluntary transfers. These policies were intended to encourage tenants and local authorities to seek out alternative landlords for housing currently owned and managed by local authorities themselves. Even if an appropriate new landlord cannot be identified, it was argued that the right to seek one would force existing local authority landlords to become more concerned with service standards, with tenant involvement and with participation. In this way Mrs Thatcher's government hoped that pressure for improvements in the quality of service delivery, and for the efficient use of resources, would become as commonplace in the social rented sector as in other sectors, more directly responsive to market forces and customer preferences.

Council tenants prior to the 1988 Act - unless they were prepared to buy - had a virtually indissoluble tie to a landlord who in many cases owned all the suitable and affordable rental housing in the area. Tenants' choice provided for the first time a framework in which council tenants could consider whether their local authority was the most appropriate landlord for them, or whether they should opt for a change of tenure. Voluntary transfers supplemented this tenant-led choice by allowing a local authority landlord itself to consider whether it was preferable to divest itself of housing management responsibilities, in favour of an alternative which might offer a comparable or better level of service or management. The tenants were able collectively to make their own evaluation of the alternatives and come to their own decision. Finally Housing Action Trusts were intended to offer the tenants of run-down and poorly maintained estates the opportunity to receive major new investment while (at least temporarily) opting out of local authority control.

Taken together, these policies represented a major effort by central government to provide local authority tenants with the opportunity to make choices and play a more active part in meeting their own housing needs. At the same time they placed powerful pressures on local authorities to become more 'customer-oriented' if they wish to retain the loyalty of their tenants.

Incentives to change

The political background to the 1988 Act, and the influence of Secretary of State Nicholas Ridley in particular, show that the motivation behind these government policies was not based entirely upon an altruistic desire to liberate council tenants from dependency upon inept or overbearing landlords. They were rooted also in detestation of the power of local government, and a desire to break the grip of the Labour party upon the political allegiances of council tenants. For Mrs Thatcher, it was imperative 'to get local authorities out of managing and owning housing'.[37]

The success of the Conservative housing reforms was bound to depend upon the strengths of the incentives they embodied to encourage their take-up by tenants, local authorities and alternative landlords respectively. Incentives intended to give tenants greater leverage over the local authority and to enable them to take the initiative to leave local authority landlords were financial discounts, legal rights, the provision of information and, most controversially, voting procedures which favour those wishing to exit.

Incentives intended to encourage local authorities to divest themselves of their stock were reinforced by financial constraints upon the use of capital and revenue which make it difficult for councils to continue as substantial landlords. Incentives intended to allow competing landlords - especially housing associations - to offer a similar or better level of service aimed to ensure that local authorities were not seen as the only acceptable landlords in the social housing sector, and to maintain pressure on them to improve their own services at a time when the financial resources to do so were declining. These changes are likely to alter the expectations of current and prospective tenants, thereby making alternative landlords seem more acceptable, both in comparison to local authorities and as landlords on their own merits.

Alongside efforts to restructure the social housing sector by diversifying tenure, the Thatcher government introduced measures to limit local authorities' financial autonomy in housing. The 1989 Act required local authorities to redirect capital receipts from council house sales away from housing, and required surpluses from rental income to be used to pay for the housing benefits of council tenants. These may be seen as complementary pressures, intended to encourage competition between landlords and to oblige local authorities to become more efficient or to propel them into relinquishing their landlord role.

Controls of this sort appeared to have been designed to reinforce the incentives offered to tenants and local authorities. They were intended first to bring local authorities' financial resources more into line with their intended role as 'enablers' and strategic planners rather than direct providers. Secondly, they sought to reduce the advantage of an existing, usually self-supporting, stock of property that local authorities currently hold over alternative landlords such as housing associations or tenant co-operatives, creating thereby a 'level playing field' for freer competition. Thirdly, they increased the pressure on local authorities to maximise cost-effectiveness in the use of public funds.

In seeking to bring about sectoral shifts within social housing, the government greatly increased the level of financial support to the housing association movement, increasing the funds it obtains through the Housing Corporation from about £815 million in 1989/90 to £1,736 million in 1992/93. Additional provisions of the Housing Act 1988 also brought pressure to bear upon housing associations to charge rents closer to market levels and so to increase their financial strength and independence. These two measures combined were intended to enable the housing association movement to take its place alongside the local authority sector as a major alternative supplier of social housing in the 1990s.

Problems of implementation

The continuing attempts to constrain local authority powers and discretion had not gone unopposed by the local authorities themselves. An instance of local authority resistance to central government control was the attempt by some to circumvent the reduction in local authority spending on new construction. Some authorities developed a variety of leaseback arrangements and other financial devices which exploited, albeit temporarily, loopholes in the government's structure of control and which allowed them to maintain modest building programmes.

These moves by local authorities to thwart central government intentions led the government to adopt new measures. Some such measures, designed to close existing loopholes and to tighten financial controls, were embodied in the Local Government and Housing Act, 1989. A second approach was to use institutions other than local authorities. This was done, for instance, by encouraging the expansion of housing associations, by looking to tenants as the main agents for institutional changes and by taking Urban Development Corporations as a model for the large scale improvement of run-down housing areas.

Similarly, from the early 1980s local authorities developed a variety of responses to limit council house sales - a policy central to the government's attempt to increase the level of owner-occupation and to reduce the role of councils as landlords. Their efforts had the initial effect of markedly reducing both the uptake and the speed with which sales progressed. In Norwich the local authority had opposed the government's policies by appointing an officer to provide financial counselling, and refused to appoint staff to give council sales priority over other housing policies and duties, forcing central government to intervene directly to stamp this resistance.[38] Thereafter, sales to council tenants increased rapidly nationwide.[39]

The right to buy policy was a success, to the extent that it enabled a million and a half tenants to buy their homes by 1992. This increase in owner occupation was of course gained at the expense of a decrease in the rented stock, as homes sold were removed from the rental sector. While this did not in itself detract from the overall success of the policy, it had an important consequence which ran counter to the government's aspirations to renew the worst of the run-down inner city housing estates. For it was not on these estates that tenants exercised their 'right to buy'; they were generally too poor to do so, and their homes an unattractive, unsaleable proposition. Thus, the impact of the policy has been to undermine the intention to revitalise these estates, for which HATs remained the only proffered solution.[40]

Despite the 'clarity' and undoubted vigour of Nicholas Ridley's vision for housing, it was never likely that central government would find it easy to achieve its ambitious aims. In particular, it faced a major task in persuading sceptical tenants, who have the decisive control over implementation, that their interests would indeed be better served by leaving local authority tenure. Yet unless they shared the government's view that municipal tenancy is a yoke from which they should yearn to be liberated, few of the reforms were likely to be seen as providing tempting opportunities. Given the key role of tenants, it was obviously in the interest of local authorities opposed to the reforms to ensure that their tenants believe that their future was best safeguarded by remaining under the local authority umbrella. And, by and large, it was the local, and not the central authorities, that won the battle for tenants' loyalties.

The future of local authorities in housing provision was made increasingly uncertain by the 1988 Act. If those policies were continued, and implemented with greater effectiveness, they would gradually lose much of their role as direct housing providers and public landlords. By the end of 1992, it had become clear that HATs, tenants' choice and voluntary transfers were making less headway than had been hoped. While it had proved possible to promote HATs through greater financial incentives, something different was required to encourage large-scale voluntary transfers. Ministers did not conceal their disappointment: large scale voluntary transfers

> have made a valuable contribution to the government's objective of diversification of tenure of rented housing, although they have not brought about the break-up of social housing ownership into the smaller units that ministers had hoped to see.[41]

The way forward was to encourage other forms of transfers, and to limit the proportion of municipal housing stock transferred to any single recipient. A new emphasis on greater diversity and the avoidance of local monopolies was proposed.[42] But early in 1996, this too was abandoned.[43]

Even had the 1988 Act reforms - the enhanced right to buy, tenants' choice, voluntary transfers and HATs - been widely adopted, a major statutory role in housing for local authorities would remain: to house the homeless. Evidently, the general thrust of the housing reforms reviewed in this chapter conflicts with the local authorities' requirement to face up to the pressing social issue of homelessness. In particular, the statutory obligation, which is placed upon local authorities alone, conflicts with their intended reduced role as landlords. That obligation cannot be delegated or transferred, leaving authorities with the options of retaining some temporary accommodation, or entering into agreements with the housing association to whom their housing stock has been transferred.[44]

Change would in any event have come slowly, and the transition would have been painful. In the longer term, the changes will be viewed in different ways, depending upon the balance the measures appear to have struck between consumer choice and equity. Among local authorities in particular the policies may be seen by some as offering the possibility of achieving genuine improvements for their tenants, while others - undoubtedly the majority - will regard them as having come close to destroying the virtues that public housing has displayed over the past century. Although Mrs Thatcher's successor has adopted some of her rhetoric in recent attacks on large scale municipal housing estates, he fails to carry conviction. The fundamentalism of the Thatcher/Ridley period expired with the withering away of the more flamboyant expectations that tenants' choice, voluntary transfers and HATs would between them, rewrite the history of social housing in Britain.

Notes

1. M. Thatcher, *The Downing Street Years*, London, HarperCollins, 1993, p. 599.
2. J.A.G. Griffith, *Central Departments and Local Authorities*, London, Allen and Unwin, 1966.
3. *Social Trends*, 22, 1992, p. 147.
4. Central Office of Information, *Britain 1989: An Official Handbook*, London, HMSO, 1989, p. 196.
5. See P. Willmott and A. Murie, *Polarisation and Social Housing*, London, Policy Studies Institute, 1988.
6. *Audit Commission, Managing the Crisis in Council Housing*, London, HMSO, 1986.
7. T. Brindley and G. Stoker, 'Housing Renewal Policy in the 1980s: the Scope and Limitations of Privatisation', *Local Government Studies*, 8(3), 1988, p. 53.
8. J. Doling, 'British Housing Policy: 1984-1993', *Regional Studies*, 27(6), 1993, p. 585.
9. Thatcher, *Downing Street Years*, p. 571.
10. Secretaries of State for the Environment and Wales, *Housing: the Government's Proposals*, Cm 214, London, HMSO, 1987, para 1.3.
11. ibid., para 5.1.
12. 'Local Government Bill: Last Major Legislation', *Municipal Review*, April 1989, p. 9.
13. *Housing: the Government's Proposals*, para 1.4.
14. ibid., para 1.3.
15. ibid., para 5.3.
16. Thatcher, *Downing Street Years*, p. 600.
17. *Housing: the Government's Proposals*, para 1.16.
18. London Research Centre, *Housing in Kensington and Chelsea: Living in the Royal Borough*, London, LRC, 1988; London Research Centre, *London*

Housing Survey 1986-87: Full Report of Results, London, LRC, 1989; Market Opinion and Research International (MORI) surveys among council tenants found the following proportions voting to remain with their council as landlord: Luton, 1989, 85 per cent; Horsham, 1989, 81 per cent; England and Wales, 1988, 73 per cent.
19. See also S. Randall, F. Birch and R. Pugh, *Large Scale Voluntary Transfer of Housing: Key Legal and Practical Issues*, London, Lawrence Graham, 1992.
20. D. Mullins, P. Niner and M. Riseborough, 'Large-scale Voluntary Transfers', in P. Malpass and R. Means (editors) *Implementing Housing Policy*, Buckingham, Open University Press, 1993, p. 169.
21. Only three authorities used the tenants' choice form of ballot in which abstentions were counted in favour of the proposition, the remaining adopting a straight majority system. D. Mullins, P. Niner and M. Riseborough, *Evaluating Large Scale Voluntary Transfers of Local Authority Housing: An Interim Report*, London, HMSO, 1992.
22. 'Tenants pushed into transfers, says TPAS', *Housing Associations Weekly*, 5 May 1989, p. 3.
23. V. Karn, 'Remodelling a HAT', in Malpass and Means, *Implementing Housing Policy*, pp. 74-90.
24. Quoted in Karn, 'Remodelling a HAT', p. 79.
25. Virtually all new private lettings, including housing association tenancies, was to be either 'assured' or 'assured shorthold' tenancies. An assured shorthold tenancy must be for a period of a least six months and the tenant must be notified at the outset that it is a shorthold tenancy.
26. C.M.E. Whitehead and M.P. Kleinman, *Private Rented Housing in the 1980s and 1990s*, Cambridge, Granta Editions for the University of Cambridge, Department of Land Economy, 1986; Willmott and Murie, *Polarisation and Social Housing*, pp. 84-85. An assessment of the short-term effects of these provisions showed about a 10 per cent increase in the number of tenancies to have occurred as a result of the Act by as early as 1990. Average rents rose by 43 per cent in the same period. I. Rauta and A. Pickering, *Private Renting in England 1990*, London, HMSO, 1992.
27. B. Randolph, 'The Re-privatisation of Housing Associations', in Malpass and Means, *Implementing Housing Policy*, pp. 39-58.
28. Part II of the Act further extends the activities of housing associations to include activities which are incidental or ancillary to their main housing activity. For instance, they will be able to create or rehabilitate commercial or industrial premises. The Act also sets up a new body 'Housing for Wales' (Tai Cymru) to take over the functions of the Housing Corporation in Wales, and 'Scottish Homes' in Scotland.

29. Department of the Environment/Welsh Office, *A New Financial Regime For Local Authority Housing in England and Wales: A Consultation Paper*, Welsh Office, 27 July 1988.

30. *Housing: the Government's Proposals*, para 5.7.

31. 'Paying for Council Housing', *Inside Housing*, 10(1), 1993, pp. 10-11.

32. *New Financial Regime for Local Authority Housing in England and Wales*, p. 7.

33. 'Making tenants foot the Bill', *Roof*, September/October, 1988.

34. P. Malpass, *Reshaping Housing Policy*, London, Routledge and Kegan Paul, 1989.

35. Only three of the 30 proposals on which tenants were balloted involved a transfer to an existing housing association. Among the reasons for preferring a new creation was the need to overcome any opposition from among the council's housing staff, who would be reluctant to join an existing body, although it was often the case that no existing association would have had the capacity to absorb a large-scale transfer.

36. Mullins, Niner and Riseborough, *Evaluating Large Scale Voluntary Transfers*, p. 9.

37. Thatcher, *Downing Street Years*, p. 606.

38. A. Murie and R. Forrest, *An Unreasonable Act?*, University of Bristol School for Advanced Urban Studies, 1985; A. Murie and P. Malpass, *Housing Policy: Theory and Practice*, London, Macmillan, 1987, pp. 233-234.

39. Doling, 'British Housing Policy', p. 583.

40. N.J. Williams and F.E. Twine, 'Increasing Access or Widening Choice: the Role of Re-sold Public Sector Dwellings in the Housing Market', *Environment and Planning*, 24(11), November 1992, pp. 1585-1598.

41. Department of the Environment, *Local Authority Housing in England: Voluntary Transfers Consultation Paper*, November 1992, para 3.

42. ibid., para 13.

43. The Housing Bill, 1996, sought to repeal the 1988 Tenants' Choice reforms.

44. The government's review of the homelessness legislation confirmed local authorities as the main agents responsible for coordinating a response to homelessness, while also recognising that it would be unreasonable to restrict further the criteria by which homelessness is defined. It also implicitly accepted the view that, in the short term at least, the deregulation of the private rented sector is unlikely to bring about the end of the homelessness problem.

4 Competition, Contracts and Change

The late 1980s saw the introduction of compulsory competitive tendering (CCT) for local authority services. The Conservative government's espousal of contractual relationships presupposed that distinct managerial benefits were to be gained from separating out client and contractor functions and by introducing commercial disciplines into public services. It was argued that CCT is part of the process of liberating managers from the constraint of the democratic and bureaucratic structures of local government. Councillors can confine themselves to setting objectives and determining service standards, while taking a neutral stance over service delivery, which is left to be determined by the tendering and contract processes. This approach has been called the 'new orthodoxy' of government by contract.

The Labour Party and Labour local authorities opposed these changes, ridiculing the oft-repeated claims that a new 'enabling' role had been defined by the adoption of competition and contracting-out.[1] As a result, Labour-controlled authorities were often slow to adapt to the new requirements, their very reluctance making it less likely that their in-house services would survive. Yet the actual experience of competition has visibly shifted the debate on to more pragmatic ground, and the 'new Labour Party' has come to show signs of appreciating the dowry which Conservative regimes have bestowed upon Labour local authorities. Enforced competition has brought about the depression of pay and conditions, the slimming down of operations, and the adoption of new management practices. It has forced them to separate client and contractor roles and establish internal markets in the place of bureaucratic allocative mechanisms. The significance of the Conservatives' CCT regime is that managing client/contractor splits and operating effective internal markets lie at the heart of the new-style public management.

A final judgement has yet to be made, but by mid-1995, the implementation of CCT in a number of areas had become shrouded in uncertainty and clouded with ambiguity. Responding to the legislation had from the beginning been problematic, especially for authorities whose approach was one of reluctant compliance, but two additional uncertainties bedevilled the implementation of CCT from 1992 onwards. The first of these was occasioned by the requirements of European Community law regarding the protection of the employment rights of staff transferred when responsibility for an 'undertaking' - that is, an economic function - changes hands through privatisation. The second was the long-heralded extension of compulsory competitive tendering to white collar services within many of the local authorities' 'core' functions, an initiative that threatened to transform the nature of local government itself.

The policy framework

Compulsory competitive tendering is rooted in the broader principles of privatisation, embraced by Conservative governments since 1979, and discussed in chapter 1. Resort to competition as an alternative means of securing public sector service delivery increased dramatically during the 1980s and 1990s, when it spread progressively within local and central government and the National Health Service.[2] In local government the strategy for winning value for money and better service for the public sector by exposing providers of public services to competition was first manifested in the Local Government, Planning and Land Act, 1980. The Act introduced limited CCT in local authority building construction and maintenance and highways maintenance work. It required these services to be subject to competitive tender, and local authorities were only allowed to carry out the work themselves, through their Direct Labour Organisations (DLOs), if they won the right to do so through successful competition. Subsequent regulations lowered the thresholds at which items of work had to be exposed to competition.[3]

If ministers expected much from this initial foray into the world of competition they were to be disappointed. According to Wood, by 1987 only 350 contracts had been awarded to the private sector, while the Act failed to encourage voluntary exposure of other core services to the tendering process.[4] The lack of enthusiasm to extend competition on the part of local authorities led to progressive tightening of government regulation of the competitive process, culminating in the Local

Government Act, 1988. This Act extended the competition requirement to such services as building cleaning, grounds maintenance, schools and welfare catering, street cleaning, vehicle maintenance and refuse collection. The legislation permitted the Secretary of State to add to the list of defined activities and in 1989 sport and leisure management was included.

In 1991 a further consultation paper, *Competing for Quality*, put forward proposals to extend compulsory competitive tendering beyond manual work into professional and technical activities. The Green Paper estimated the market for these activities to be worth between £5-£6 billion. The proposals were substantially enacted by the Local Government Act, 1992, which not only extended CCT to finance, computing, personnel and architectural, library and construction services, but in addition required local councils to publish information about the standards of performance of their services. By summer 1992 housing management was also in the frame with the publication of *Competing for Quality in Housing*, the government's consultation paper on the introduction of CCT into the management of council housing, on which modified proposals were incorporated in the 1992 Act.

The Major government, then, continued to view contracting out as an integral part of the new management of local government. Indeed, it pushed the competition regime forward, far beyond the limits seriously envisaged in Mrs Thatcher's time. Mr Major's ministers have been surprising y radical in this regard, and apparently inured to the sometimes conflicting evidence as to the effects of CCT. This is probably because they saw other, non cost-related advantages from shaking up the management of local government through CCT; benefits that far outweigh any disadvantages in promising fundamental change in the organisation and working of public services.

Claims and counter-claims

While the legislation in part reflected an ideological belief in the benefits of competition and privatisation, its introduction was also based on a perception that those local services which had introduced the policy of tendering-out services in the early 1980s had significantly reduced costs. In 1984 the Audit Commission undertook a comprehensive examination of the refuse collection industry. The Commission's findings, published in *Securing Further Improvements in Refuse Collection*, estimated potential savings of £30 million per annum in England and Wales through contracting out. The report claimed that contractors performed better than the average DSO, and that councils which contracted out refuse collection activities provided the most cost effective service.[5] This was followed by other publications purporting to show that where a service had been subject to the tendering procedure it resulted in a significant improvement in the efficiency with which the service was provided.[6]

Supporters of compulsory competitive tendering also pointed to the inefficiencies of public sector 'in-house' monopolies, with their restrictive labour practices and low productivity. The view was that regular recontracting would allow for a review of both the quality and cost of the service on offer. Such arguments in favour of CCT predicted efficiency gains associated with service provision in terms of improved management, better value for money, and greater accountability for public spending. It should be recognised that the coalitions for and against contracting out are, to a large extent, drawn along political lines. The debates have been polemical in tone, with claims and counter claims not always firmly anchored in evidence. What does that evidence suggest?

The first studies of the impact of CCT focused on refuse collection services. In 1986, Domberger and his associates examined refuse collection data from over 300 local authorities for a two year period. Their study showed that authorities which had contracted out refuse collection services to private firms enjoyed costs about 22 per cent lower. Those authorities which held a competitive tender and then awarded the contract to the existing in-house workforce also appeared to have lower costs, but in their case 17 per cent lower than the non-tendering average. The authors concluded that 'it is the introduction of competition, rather than awarding contracts to private firms, which is the critical factor in achieving lower costs'.[7] Similarly a study by the London Business School in 1993 reported that direct unit costs for refuse collection had fallen since the introduction of CCT by 27 per cent, with total savings of £40-80 million.[8]

In 1991 the Department of the Environment commissioned a major research project to evaluate the effects of the 1988 Act. The study, carried out by the Institute of Local Government Studies, examined the experience of a cross-section of 40 local authorities in England and found that competitive tendering had produced average savings of six to seven per cent in the annual cost of providing services. Wide disparities were also reported ranging from one authority saving 49 per cent to another with increased costs of 26 per cent. The study also showed the cost of tendering to be 2.5 per cent of total contract value.[9] However, other findings purport to show that where services are retained in-house, reductions in staffing, earnings and conditions of employment have often been achieved by abolishing bonus systems or through other adjustments to the pattern of work.[10]

Cost factors aside, the success rates of local authorities in competing to provide public services have also been investigated. The LGMB's sixth CCT survey report showed that local authority DSOs had won 69 per cent of all contracts put out to tender up to 1992. This constituted a total market share in cash terms of 84 per cent (worth some £1.6bn a year). The survey, based on 3,900 contracts in England and Wales, showed that DSOs' share of contracts after seven rounds of CCT ranged between 54 per cent (building cleaning) and 92 per cent (school catering).[11] The LGMB's more recent study revealed that Direct Service Organisations are continuing to maintain a two-thirds share of contracts under CCT.[12]

Notwithstanding this initial success on the part of DSOs, a follow up survey carried out by the LGMB in 1993 revealed growing competition from the private sector. The study showed that whilst the in-house share of virtually all contracts under CCT dropped in the period 1992-93, the worst hit were contracts relating to building cleaning and school catering. Private sector contractors, the report identified, were stepping up their share in the lower paid services, which exposed DSOs' vulnerability in areas of low wage and unskilled work.

CCT's opponents have fastened upon its impact on just such areas. Pointing out that private sector provision is solely inspired by profit motives, they argue that the cost savings by private contractors are achieved through a reduction in wages and worsening of conditions of service, usually amongst lower paid workers. They also emphasise falling standards, problems with the fulfilment of contracts, increases in costs associated with tendering and management processes, and fragmented internal relationships. A report by the Local Government Information Unit, *CCT on the Record*, maintained that CCT has led to a decline in standards and that improvements in quality have not yet materialised. 'Given the financial constraints under which local government is operating', the report argued, 'there is inevitably a conflict between cost and quality in tender evaluation and a tendency for any savings to be achieved at the expense of front-line services and jobs'.[13]

Aside from reservations about the extent to which the cost savings achieved under CCT have been at the expense of the lowest-paid and least secure workers, the critics also argue that the savings are modest in comparison with the exaggerated estimates made by the advocates of competition, and may even be illusory. While conceding that *initial* cost reductions may be obtainable, their benefits may be limited in time by the practice of loss-leading and qualified by reduced standards of service provision. Opponents of CCT claimed that while savings initially appear to rise, the trend may be reversed as early as four years after the award of the original contract. As contracts were normally let for a period of five years, they concluded that underbidding was taking place with a view to obtaining a long term relationship with the local authority.

Even the Audit Commission has admitted that in some services the supposed savings of CCT have not been realised.[14] Furthermore, the initial cost of setting up market processes could be substantial. The Coopers and

Lybrand consultancy reports for the Department of the Environment, on the scope of CCT for legal and construction related services, identified a potential increase in client costs of around five per cent of current costs for legal services, and three per cent for construction-related services.

Overall, then, the available evidence on compulsory competitive tendering suggests several points. First, that competition has resulted in tangible cost savings, although these have varied widely. Secondly, that the majority of the contracts have been retained in-house, with reduced staff levels and lower conditions of service. Other evidence suggests that problems with termination of contracts tend to be higher amongst private contractors, while tighter specification and monitoring is likely to reduce allegations of lower quality service provision by private contractors. Only more recently has evidence on the effectiveness of competition management emerged, with the Audit Commission identifying over-bureaucratic administration and poor financial management as resulting in widespread variations in the cost of managing contracted services and a large number of public complaints in some service areas.[15]

The road to competition

The Local Government Act, 1988, with its provisions to compel local authorities to put services out to compulsory competitive tender, required all authorities to respond by defining their objectives and adopting appropriate organisational arrangements. New structures and procedures suited to the changing environment included the setting up of Direct Labour/Service Organisations (DLO/DSO). For senior management this meant developing broad planning timescales, drawing up specifications, identifying areas of future involvement of councillors and officers, and assessing the implications for central and other support services. A change was called for, and this challenge produced very different responses from different authorities. It prompted a number of councils to develop radical and imaginative approaches to service delivery, management style and internal organisation, while others sought to cushion or evade the impact of the legislation.

Initial approaches

The government's 1984 announcement of its intention to secure more competition in refuse collection, street and building cleaning, vehicle and grounds maintenance and catering services had provoked no marked reactions among most local authorities. Labour councils in particular reacted cautiously, and apart from occasional reports to committees most did little. Their thinking was that compulsory competitive tendering would go away, whilst still others took the view that 'the government would not win the next election to see it through anyway'. Much of their declared resistance was to the *compulsory* nature of the legislation, a useful tactical argument. With the passage of the 1988 Act, many Labour councils regrouped around a traditional anti-privatisation stance, typically declaring it to be 'the clear policy of this authority to support in-house service provision'. This implied that they would take all possible steps to retain jobs in their own DLOs.

The more favourable responses generally came from Conservative controlled authorities. Many saw the legislation as having given them the opportunity to tackle their unions, to behave commercially and enhance their efficiency, in ways which were not open to them in the past. Some Conservative authorities went further, and sought to set the pace on the introduction of competition by exceeding or anticipating the statutory requirements. A senior officer in a Conservative county council recalled the determination with which competition policy was prosecuted:

> Whatever the legislation said we exceeded. On highways 50 per cent was required, we did 75 per cent. We did it for Conservative dogma... There was also pressure on finance, seeking to get savings through competition and redeploy resources to front line services. Policy was to subject everything possible to voluntary competition, providing it, in the round, showed a profit. To the mid-80s we were working step by step through the council's administration. We began by attacking the soft underbelly: cleaning went external well before 1988. There was a tremendous fuss at the time, first due to the number of cleaners made redundant and second, due to allegations that the successful tenderers were paying lower rates and conditions.

Political outlook, then, had a marked effect on authorities' initial responses to competition. By the same token, a subsequent change of political control could entirely re-orient an authority's approach. Typically, though, it would fall short of a reversion to the pre 1988 situation:

> The May 1993 election stopped the expansion of competition. We are on a political tight rope. Both [Labour and Liberal Democrat] parties agree that value for money is not to be rejected. They won't featherbed in-house providers at the expense of the tax payers. This enables us still to do some competition. They are prepared to allow previously competed-for contracts to continue, they don't want to get back to in-house provision.

Externalisation: two cases

While local authorities have been drawn into the competitive tendering process - however reluctantly or enthusiastically - some authorities have sought to circumvent the requirements altogether. The principal escape route involved the prior transfer of the entire service-providing capability to a consortium of former service managers - *management buy-out* - or to a private company - *externalisation*. Both represent pre-emptive strikes to remove a service from the scope of CCT.

Few authorities have succeeded in selling a service to an MBO - a group of managers previously employed by the authority.[16] While the close - and possibly exclusive - tie of an MBO to the parent authority is attractive, enthusiasm for this mode of external provision may be tempered by doubts as to the viability of the new enterprise. The MBO record of protecting jobs and conditions of employment is also equivocal, although there is evidence that new owner-managers may choose to trade-off pay increases against pension and sickness benefits.

In contrast, externalisation involves the transfer of staff and associated work to a host company which then contracts to manage and deliver services to a specified level and standard using the staff transferred. Authorities which have considered externalisation have generally done so on the grounds that it would safeguard the services and the interests of staff while avoiding the uncertainties of CCT. But the quality of the service delivered, the views of the staff and unions, the state of the market place, and the corporate implications of the option have all to be taken into account. Two instances of externalisation attempts - one unsuccessful, the other succeeding - will serve to illustrate these considerations.

The first concerns a northern metropolitan district council which explored externalisation as a means of circumventing the CCT requirements, which it feared it would be unable to meet with success. The authority sought advice on externalisation from consultants before embarking upon detailed internal discussions and briefings. The consultants examined each area and advised the council 'you will lose the lot'. Externalisation was the response to this bleak prospect. The plan was to anticipate the CCT timetable by transferring a wide-ranging package of services and their associated staff and plant to a host company. Discussion in the authority was dominated by the protection of terms and conditions through entrenchment. Externalisation looked an attractive option, and an initial trawl for expressions of interest produced more than 50 applications, which were whittled down to six or seven serious contenders over a period of months.

Other benefits were adduced here in favour of externalisation: it would widen the scope for career development of staff, by offering the opportunity for exposure to other fields of activity and other locations. It was also envisaged that the expertise and resources available from other parts of the host company group would facilitate an improved response to workload fluctuations. Warmly supported by managers - who stood to gain from such a move - these preparations nevertheless eventually failed in this politically balanced authority. A councillor recalled that: 'externalisation would have saved pay and conditions. But the unions withdrew because they believed they could win under CCT. The Labour Party changed under trade union pressure'.

The process proved more of a success for the second authority, crucially because there was all-party support for the policy. In this authority a number of small, time-limited policy development panels explored the principle of transferring work and staff, and ultimately directed the externalisation itself:

> We spent 18 months on a review of support services. We set up trading agencies - which were not popular - in some areas like finance, property etc. This resulted in externalisation of financial services and highways and planning. With regard to the latter, we felt that integrated services were under threat; the environment budget was always in difficulty; redundancies were increasing as the department was shrinking...

When the council made public its intention to externalise its highways and planning there were 148 expressions of interest, confirming the existence of a strong, lively market. Specifications were drawn incorporating service-based performance indicators, setting out the levels of service and quality required. The council's response was to be highly selective: 'we went out to look for the market leaders and big firms. We needed to be sure our partner could sustain the necessary investment and not collapse or lose overnight'.

This authority decided that a planned response was necessary. The council sought to maintain or increase standards, preserve local knowledge, and ensure the continued availability of services. Externalisation appeared to do this but also to offer other, indirect, benefits:

> It takes a significant load off central services such as payroll, income and accounts payable so that the future strategy for these can be reassessed... As well as reducing costs at the centre, externalisation has tightened our grip on management and has resulted in a clearer focus on important functions...each time a service or function is externalised, it forces a reappraisal of who is doing what and why.

Although the authority experienced a change in its political control during the elections of May 1992, it neither altered the externalisation policy nor interrupted its development.

Despite the all-party support for externalisation, staff in this authority were reported to have expressed concerns about its effects. And whilst they were anxious that this development might lead to a deterioration in their terms and conditions of employment, the issue of pensions predominated in discussions with management. Whilst staff were allowed to retain the statutory rights to freeze or transfer their local government entitlements and choose personal or company pension schemes, the council additionally looked at splitting the pension fund to cover any shortfalls in the future pensions of transferred staff.

It is clear from the foregoing account that local authorities embarking upon this route face several difficulties and uncertainties. Externalisation inevitably means a loss of control over the management of the service. To attempt to compensate for that by tight agreements with a company could fall foul of the restrictions on local authority companies under the Local Government and Housing Act, 1989, which are designed to prevent councils from evading the accountability regime by setting up 'arm's length' operations.

Companies taking over local authority work, on the other hand, are not entirely free of constraints. The potential risk for them arises from the possibility that the flow of work might not hold up, or the contract might not be repeated, and that replacement work might not be secured. In such an event, a company would have to make staff redundant under terms that reflected all the accumulated benefits and entitlements from their previous local government service. These uncertainties have been amplified by recent developments affecting the transferred rights of workers, and discussed later in this chapter.

Client/contractor relations within the authority

The advent of competition has led to a separation of the client and contractor roles. Required under the legislation, the detailed regulations follow the principle that those with responsibilities for the conduct of the competition process should have no direct interest in the result of that process. Regulations made under the 1992 Act aim to provide a clearer framework, but fall short of specifying how authorities should structure themselves to meet the requirements. Accordingly, authorities have made a variety of responses, with more or less rigid client/contractor splits being established within the authority.

Two models

To some extent, the arrangements councils made reflected their different circumstances as well as the degree to which competition and conflict was regarded as politically tolerable. The basic distinction is between the adoption of *twin-hatted* arrangements, in which client and contractor roles are co-managed within the same department, and a more arm's length approach with a clear distinction in lines of responsibility for separately managed functions.[17] One variant of this latter arrangement is to group services together in a multi-purpose DSO, typically entitled 'Contract Services Department'.

While the central government has sought a clearer distinction between client and contractor roles, the local authority experience illuminates both the advantages and the disadvantages of separation. On the one hand, responsibilities are clarified, service standards established, monitoring improved and management strengthened. On the other hand, splitting functions itself incurs costs. Moreover, instituting a clear demarcation of responsibilities can lead to ruthless competitiveness or even antagonism and outright conflict.[18]

Those authorities which had initially opted for greater distance between the client and contractor roles saw this as a way to end potential confusions and conflicts of interests, allowing the client/purchaser to become the advocate of the consumer, rather than the defender of the producer. Additionally such a separation also forced both sides to define the nature of the service and the standards of quality to be provided. As one officer explained:

> If the client and the contractor are one it is very difficult to see how the business ethos can survive without the client, or the contractor, suffering in respect of their very proper and divergent aims. The in-house contractor needs to be maintained at arm's length from the client and proper procedures laid down to ensure that the client receives value for money.

The more complete form of separation expressed in the multi-purpose DSO appears at first sight to foster commercial awareness and a sharper competitive edge. By the same token, it promotes inter-departmental rivalry and inhibits the development of co-operation and partnership. Thus, in one large district council visited, the development of conflict was widely remarked, with officers pointing to the loss of colleague relationships, and their replacement by open jealousies and suspicion. These coloured personal relationships and extended, on one account, to those between the wives of former friends who now found themselves on opposing sides of the client/contractor divide.

At the other end of the scale, twin-hatted arrangements generally have a more collaborative style. The officers responsible for contractor and client roles in the Technical Services Department of one metropolitan district visited were perfectly comfortable being interviewed together, giving an agreed account of their experiences. Twin-hatted arrangements facilitate the retention of common purpose and promote a more co-operative relationship between client and contractor; they enable shorter lines of communication to be maintained and provide for ready access to the full range of departmental support services. For these reasons, they are often suspected of being too 'cosy' for efficient operation. It seems likely, though, that neither form of organisation can overcome basic weaknesses in competitive position, nor, in itself, elevate the quality of management. Twin-hatted and arm's-length arrangements are structural solutions to what is essentially a problem of process, and may for that reason fall well short of expectation, as the following example shows.

A cautionary tale

In this authority consultants were asked to identify strengths and weaknesses within the organisation, and their recommendations led to the creation of a Contracts Services Division (CSD) and the appointment of the director of contract services. The CSD comprised building and highways services, environmental services and cleaning and catering services, with a business support unit designed to support the operating services and give contract services a degree of independence from the council's central finance and personal services.

For two years, building works experienced financial problems and subsequent investigations showed that it suffered from lack of financial awareness, weak management and lack of control over labour costs. Furthermore, the absence of commercial budgeting and poor documentation were leading to declining productivity, high costs of supervision and increasing indirect costs. A subsequent consultant's report concluded that building work was not a viable activity and would clearly be unable to produce a break even or even an adequate rate of return. Serious errors of judgement with regard to estimated costs and income were found, together with a continual failure to provide timely and accurate information. 'In a contracting/trading environment managers can only be judged by results' reported the Chief Executive:

> Therefore it must be concluded that the new management structure set up in 1989 has failed. Perhaps the most worrying aspect for

members has been the unrealistic nature of the projected performance of the division given in committee reports and business plans. In my view this has been caused by the over-optimistic assumptions used by managers, the lack of clear information at the right time from the business support unit and a failure to persuade the workforce to adapt and change to become more productive. It has also been due to a strategy based on winning the award of tenders rather than the delivery of the trading returns subsequently.

As with building works, highways also reported losses for four years between 1989 and 1993. Although there were opportunities to tender, the DLO failed to win any of the significant contracts and came to be increasingly dependent on 'as of right work' awarded by the council's department of engineering and surveying. Again some of the problems identified were not dissimilar to those faced by building works: incompetence within the estimating section, loss in productivity, poor tendering performance and heavy losses on single schemes. The cost to the council of continuing to use the DLO for this work became substantial and the council soon found it difficult to justify meeting the cost differential in addition to the trading losses it incurred.

One underlying problem, common to this type of arrangement, was that the personnel and finance functions within the CSD were not influential enough to achieve the change in working practices. The Division had created its own business support unit with personnel and finance functions. But with only one personnel officer for more than 2000 people there was no possibility of doing more than routine personnel administration. Following the abolition of the CSD and the absorption of its functions into operating departments under 'twin-hatted' arrangements the functions fell within the purview of central personnel and are under new pressures to reduce costs and find more efficient ways of working.

This experience is far from unique, and illustrates the limits of a simplistic, structural approach to competition. Something more is required for a local authority to achieve competitiveness. Although a requirement, splitting client and contractor roles is a means to that end, not an end in itself. However incorporated in the organisation, a confidently-managed client-contractor separation prescribes the relationship between the purchaser and the provider, and thus paves the way to the development of an internal market for services.

Internal markets

Many councils operate internal trading accounts for central services, having been prompted to do so by the 1988 Audit Commission report. In doing so, they anticipated the requirements of the 1992 Act, which requires the corporate services of local authorities such as legal, financial and personnel services to introduce a consistent internal accounting regime as a preliminary stage before competitive tendering. The introduction of internal trading accounts, leading ultimately to the creation of an internal market, fundamentally changes the relationship between service departments and central services within the organisation.[19]

Internal markets operate through quasi-contractual arrangements, either on a full trading account basis or through service level agreements (SLAs). These arrangements contrast with the more traditional practice of providing central services on an 'as needed' basis, or recharging against devolved budgets. The concept of the SLA emerged from the initial experience of competition in a competitive environment. DSO/DLOs found difficulty in carrying the charges for financial, computer, legal, personnel, and architectural services, while their allocation was so imperfect that recharging scarcely reflected either the value or the use of such services.

Faced with such pressures, DSO/DLO managers sought to find a mechanism to control central costs and to relate them to value for money criteria. As a county council officer recalled:

> There were new pressures around the 1988 Act. Various parts of the council said, 'It's not fair - we can get competitive but we are being loaded on by central services and support [e.g. transport] services'. This was answered by restructuring. It was virtually a complete separation between service providers and purchasers - or as it then was, clients and contractors - this structure still remains.

The extension of internal trading accounts gives service departments a clear picture of the cost of the corporate professional services for which they are being charged. The government's intention is that service managers, as customers, should be able to assess the cost of using internal professional services and consider whether alternative suppliers might offer a better bargain. Since a proportion of all these services will be exposed to competitive tendering, it will be possible to identify whether internal prices have been pitched at a higher level than can be obtained externally.

Competition at the crossroads: the effects of TUPE

TUPE - the Transfer of Undertakings (Protection of Employment) Regulations - were enacted by the UK government in 1981 in order to implement the European Commission's Acquired Rights Directive of 1977. The purpose of the Directive is to protect in law the rights of employees when the organisation which they work for is transferred from one employer to another. Where there is held to be a transfer for the purposes of the regulations, the main consequences are first, that the new employer has to take over the contracts of employment of the employees on the existing terms and conditions; secondly, that employees have the benefit of continuity of employment; thirdly, that any dismissal connected with the transfer is automatically unfair, unless the employer can show an economic, technical or organisational reason entailing changes to the workforce; fourthly, that collective agreements with recognised trade unions are transferred to the new employer; fifthly, that there is a duty to inform and consult with recognised trade unions prior to any transfer; and finally, that unless employees are actually dismissed, there will be no redundancy payments.

The 1981 UK regulations did not adequately implement the 1977 directive. In particular, they purported to restrict the application of the regulations to undertakings 'in the nature of a commercial venture'. The European Commission, however, decided that the acquired rights directive would be revised to cover transfers by contract. The UK government has since issued guidance on the relevance of the regulations to 'market testing of public services', which includes compulsory competitive tendering by local authorities.

The principal uncertainty relates to whether or not an *undertaking* is transferred when the provision of a service is contracted out. In a statement to the Commons Standing Committee on the Trade Union Reform and Employment Rights Bill, the Attorney General set out the principles regarding the 'transfer of an undertaking' as follows:

> The contracting out of a service is not a transfer of an undertaking unless it involves enough of the elements of the original operation such as premises, staff, goodwill or customer base to constitute the transfer of a going concern... But no single one of these [elements] is essential for there to be a transfer. The case law makes clear that it is the overall sum of what is transferred which determines whether there has been a transfer of an undertaking.[20]

However, the Employment Appeal Tribunal ruled late in 1993 that all the circumstances had to be taken into account in determining where there was 'a recognisable economic entity, a going concern' which, having been run by the local authority, was to be continued by a contractor.

The substance, not the form, was important; while in most cases premises, equipment, existing contracts or goodwill might be transferred, it was not necessary for this to be the case for the transfer of the economic function - and hence of the undertaking - to have occurred.[21] Local authorities soon discovered that it was not easy to reach a conclusion at the outset of the tendering process as to whether the contracting out of a particular service under CCT would involve the transfer of an undertaking for the purposes of the regulations. If the council were to stipulate or indicate at an early stage that the regulations would apply, and at a later stage the courts determined otherwise or the council itself changed its mind in the light of further information, the earlier stipulation or indication would have several disadvantages.

First, the council might be considered to have acted anti-competitively. Additionally, external tenderers may, accepting that they are required to tender on the basis of the existing terms and conditions of the council's staff, ask the council to provide details of current staff numbers, their terms and conditions of employment, their ages and length of service, on the grounds that only then are they able to formulate a bid. If the council were to accede to such a request, firms would gain a significant advantage in formulating their bids, through information on much of the content of the council's own (DSO) bid, and information on the longer-term costs to the tenderer of gradually achieving a reduction in their own costs through turnover of staff, retirement and dismissal, followed by the recruitment of new staff on less advantageous terms and conditions.

Moreover, if the council were to determine at the outset that the regulations apply, it could not then take redundancy costs into account in evaluating the tenders, because it is already committed to the proposition that no redundancies will occur. If the council were to change its mind, decide that the regulations did not in fact apply, and wished to take redundancy costs into account in the evaluation, this might be regarded as anti-competitive. If the council were to award the contract to an external contractor, and the courts subsequently found that the regulations did not apply, the council would have to meet redundancy payments but would have missed the opportunity to take them into account in the tender evaluation.

Finally, if the council is unsuccessful in the tendering process, it will not be entitled to make staff redundant and make redundancy payments to them. If the successful tenderer disputed that the regulations applied, some employees might find themselves in the position of neither being employed by the tenderer nor receiving a redundancy payment, and would have to undertake court proceedings either to establish that the regulations applied and their contracts of employment continued in force with the new employer, or to establish the right to redundancy payments. This may also have another disadvantage for the council in terms of the loss of morale which this potential outcome might produce among staff.

Preparing for white collar CCT

In November 1991 the government published the consultation paper *Competing for Quality in the Provision of Local Services*. Twelve months later it announced a decision to extend significantly the competition requirements to a group of central or corporate white collar functions which it considered to share common characteristics. Embodied in the Local Government Act, 1992, this extension covers corporate and administrative services, financial, personnel, legal and computer services, as well as housing management, construction-related services, some leisure services and some further manual services.

Competition for central services

Under the 1992 Act, all authorities are to provide full statements of the gross costs of their operations in a *Statement of Support Services Costs* so as to enhance the transparency of central service provision. In November 1993 the government announced proposals defining the activities to be exposed to competition, the timetable for implementation and the sizes of contracts. The separate timetable for authorities affected by the Local Government Review was announced soon afterwards.[22] Draft statutory instruments and guidance on the avoidance of anti-competitive behaviour were issued in January 1994. The guidance stressed that authorities should describe the service to be delivered, not the process by which it is to be delivered, so as to allow scope for contractors to propose better ways of delivering services. Each service identified by the government is to be described as a defined activity, and (except in the case of small authorities) the total cost of that activity within an authority is the base on which a proportionate requirement to expose to competition is imposed. The initial proportions were:

corporate and administrative services	15 per cent
financial services	25 per cent
personnel services	25 per cent
legal services	45 per cent
computer services	80 per cent

Although the requirement to submit these services to competitive tender is new, the practice of doing so is already familiar. Councils have in many cases already voluntarily contracted out parts of this work, for example in payroll administration or job advertising, while figures as high as 60 per cent for legal and IT work have been quoted. Where this is the case, the value of the contracted-out work can be 'scored' against the total percentage requirement for that activity.[23]

Competition for housing management

The government foreshadowed its proposals for the extension of CCT to housing management in the *Citizen's Charter* white papers, and spelt them out in its 1992 document *Competing for Quality in Housing*. The aim of CCT in housing is to be 'a further stimulus to efficiency, as a means of ensuring that councils examine their performance and seek maximum value for money. It offers the prospect of breaking down entrenched monopolies and generating large gains in efficiency through competition'.

According to the proposals set out in the consultation paper all housing management has to be tendered within five years, with the first contracts intended to be let from 1 April 1996. In the case of district councils faced with local government reorganisation, an exemption until 18 months after the new authority starts functioning was proposed.

Tenants had meanwhile gained the right to be consulted on housing management issues under the *Tenant Involvement and the Right to Manage* proposals announced in December 1992, gaining thereby an involvement in the CCT process. However, although tenants in some circumstances have a right to take over the management of their housing, they have no clear standing on the award of contracts for others to manage their estates.[24] Tenant involvement and consultation thus remain difficult concepts. Although tenant consultations and forums have been set up in many authorities, there is still a lack of clarification about what involving tenants means. What exactly are they being involved in? If they are being involved in decisions, how final are their decisions? Until now tenant involvement has only been advisory, but there are signs that CCT can act as a catalyst to encourage greater participation in areas where it has been low or non-existent.

The housing requirements provided for the stock to be parcelled up on an area (typically on an estate) basis, rather than on a function basis. This is intended to preserve the ethos of the comprehensive housing service and to retain developments in decentralised management and tenant participation. Housing management, however, remains difficult to define in view of the complex nature of the comprehensive housing service. While the consultation paper envisaged housing management as comprising essentially those estate management services that are funded through the Housing Revenue Account, the DoE has suggested the inclusion in the designated service list of housing-related services not funded from the HRA. The government did not wish to see CCT impeding the exercise of the central policy function of housing authorities. Unlike the largely manual services that have been subject to CCT to date, there is in housing management a less clear split between the client and contractor roles. That said, the key areas of client responsibilities include tenant participation; policy on rents and rent arrears; preparations for capital schemes and maintenance contracts; policy on allocations and nominations to housing associations; policy on monitoring of voids and homelessness; assessment of housing supply and demand; provision of neighbourhood offices; co-ordination of IT systems development; HRA budgeting and monitoring; and repairs and maintenance policies.

Similarly, on the contractor side proposed responsibilities include day-to-day allocations; collection of rents and rent arrears; implementation of tenancy agreements; information to tenants; repairs reporting; controlling voids; staff training; administration of housing lists; transfer applications; administration of exchanges; leasehold management; right to repairs schemes; managing capital programmes on a day to day basis; and warden services for sheltered schemes. Councils have several choices in determining the nature of the client/contractor split. The basic choices lie between having the split at area level or centrally; having non-CCT operations linked to the contractor unit, the client unit or standing alone; and having staff working across CCT and non-CCT activities or fully separated.

Many of the affected authorities embarked upon re-organising their departments, and moved promptly towards establishing the framework for competition management. They set up financial management structures, assessed costs, sought to engender cultural change, to improve service levels, and slim down their staffing. The need to improve financial awareness throughout housing departments was quickly recognised. Wages are by far the largest component of a housing department's outgoings and so became a prime target for reducing costs. Yet few members and officers in any such authorities would have been under any illusions as to the size of the task involved in making the improvements in housing management required to meet the CCT challenge.

The price of change

What has been the impact of the local authorities' exposure to competition? Their experience appears to have been conditioned by three factors: their initial approach to competition; their pre-existing competitiveness in terms of service costs, labour practices (in turn a reflection to some extent of political factors) and management capability; and the intensity of private companies' competition for contracts. In each of these respects, adaptation has often been painful. Job losses, lower rates of pay, reduced benefits and a general drop in conditions of employment have been required in order to sharpen competitiveness, while management structures and processes adopted at the outset have in some cases been wholly recast subsequently.

There is clear evidence on the extent of the competitiveness of local authorities as service providers in the success rates of private contractors in winning tenders against them. The surveys quoted earlier show that private contractors were most successful when competing for the smaller contracts in building cleaning, while London has proved a favourable market for refuse collection and street cleaning contractors. There is a general trend towards greater competitiveness and, in consequence, more successful private sector tenders.

To a considerable extent, the potential impact of CCT was foreseeable. The main thrust of the pre-CCT debate in the area of building cleaning revolved around the impact competition would have on the pay and general conditions of the cleaning workforce. The concern for local authorities who opposed CCT was that private contractors would win contracts simply by employing fewer staff at lower rates of pay than the DSO. They feared that CCT would lead to low morale among the workforce and ultimately to a reduction in the quality of service provision. It was however also evident that there would be extensive rationalisation in the lead up to the tendering process. In order to compete local authorities would either have to reduce rates of pay, shed jobs or do both. Similar forecasts as to the impact of the CCT in refuse collection on the quality of service provision and the pay and employment conditions were made.

Most of the cost predictions made during the run-up to competition have been borne out, at least in part. A report by the Institute of Local Government Studies indicated that CCT has led to decreasing employment, worsened staff conditions and a reduction in wage rates. A survey undertaken for the LGMB, reporting the impressions of 285 chief executives, confirmed this broad view, with 60 per cent reporting reduced costs, and 55 per cent reduced pay, but with no clear adverse effects on staff morale.

To the extent that local authorities have achieved productivity gains, depressed pay and trimmed back on benefits, they have competed with more success. To the extent that they have not done so, they have lost contracts, and thus incurred redundancies. While authorities did adapt to a remarkable extent, the magnitude of the task involved in achieving so much change quickly enough to make a difference proved to be beyond some of them.

The key issue is the disparity between in-house productivity rates and the rates found in the private sector. Local government manning levels tend to be more generous, while private contractors are in addition freer to engage and release workers on a seasonal basis as the demands of the work dictate. However, co-operative unions and a willing workforce can help to achieve productivity gains through reduced manning levels, better work planning, and the eradication of feather-bedding. Restrictive practices were relinquished as realism dawned, often sooner among the workforce than among their representatives. The limiting factor was however so often the universality of nationally agreed conditions. Councils found it difficult to be competitive. They are locked into national agreements on pay and allowances, under which their terms and conditions are more expensive to maintain than those of the private sector.

Some authorities sought to respond to the price advantages of private contractors by instituting a margin within which a more expensive in-house bid could be accepted, justifying their decision in terms of the need to meet the costs of failing to win a tender. A good example comes from this metropolitan district council:

> The council sought to ensure that the in-house bid would win. We had a two per cent rule: if the in-house bid was within two per cent of the lowest bidder it would get preference. There were big changes in the management of departments overnight. Then inevitably we started to get pushed on tenders and lost some. Then the full effect was seen. Labour started to refuse to accept competitive tenders from successful companies. Some tenders came within the two per cent rule. The real crunch was coming slowly. The two per cent rule was miles adrift. External companies were much cheaper, our working practices and prices were not moving. Contract services were losing more than a million annually.

In part, the problems councils faced were those of outlook and attitude. Moving towards a true competitive environment demanded that they relinquished many long-established practices and habits of mind. They began to realise that officers had been too concerned with protecting themselves and their employees and insufficiently concerned about their customers. 'Many of us have had wrong priorities and it now shows up' confessed one contrite officer.

If some began to face up to the magnitude of the changes confronting them, more DSOs were led by sheer desperation to severe under-pricing, winning contracts only to fail to deliver the work to standard and price. Building cleaning is a prime example of a service exposed to such sharp competition from the private sector as to have the inescapable effect of forcing costs down. In the early stages of CCT this intense competition led to some unrealistic tender prices and a number of failures and defaults have been seen to follow.

As experience of competition accumulated it has become clear that the loss of a few key contracts could start a spiral of declining competitiveness, leading in turn to further losses. Thus, the consequence of losing services gradually to outside contractors could prove cumulative, as the loss of contracts in one area of DSO operations leads to the loss of economies of scale in another. For example, in one authority, a vehicle maintenance section adopted, on workforce initiative, sweeping changes in manning levels, working practices and pay to achieve a high degree of competitiveness. These improvements were appreciated and the initiative of the workers applauded. Yet it proved to have been in vain. The loss of grounds maintenance contracts by one of the other DSOs so reduced the maintenance throughput of vehicles and machinery that the section lost economies of scale and was pushed back into a non-competitive condition.

The loss of major contracts requires the charging of the common services overhead upon a smaller trading base. Local authority overhead costs may be virtually fixed in the short run, and not susceptible to immediate reductions in response to a smaller range of service provision operations. The surviving DSO services are thus forced to carry a disproportionately high overhead, which may even offset their hard-won reductions in operating costs. One county council which lost its cleaning and 50 per cent of its ground and highway maintenance found it very difficult to maintain existing services due to lower capacity and higher overheads. A senior officer spelled out the realities: 'There are about 10 job contracts weekly and if you lose a term contract and succession of job contracts you are dead'.

How then did authorities feel about these sometimes dramatic effects? 'In terms of the cost/VFM equation we have ended up with cheaper, better service and achieved higher standards' remarked one officer. Others concurred:

> The benefits were that we saved money and the services were no worse. Broadly it is the same service at less cost. We would never have done it without compulsion. It was done with a lot of pain and human costs.

Yet in some cases the more rosy expectations were disappointed:

> We expected major cost reductions... We expected to sharpen up and win everything in-house. It was a discipline to make us more sensitive to costs and sharpen accountability. It wouldn't aggravate industrial relations in the authority because it is a government requirement to become more cost-efficient. But we hadn't saved nearly as much as we thought we would. It has been a very difficult procedure to run with.

A level playing field?

Perhaps the most variable aspect of local authorities' experiences of CCT concerns the degree of market interest and the intensity of competition for contracts. Experience has shown the degree of competition to vary between different services as well as between different parts of the country. There is evidence that the realities of competition are spreading as the private sector gains experience with each round of tendering. Research undertaken for the Department of the Environment shows that with the exception of sports and leisure management there exists a considerable pool of private contractors with the potential to bid for contracts.[25] If the size of the contracts offered was smaller, there is no doubt that the degree of competition would be still more intense. At present, too many small firms are of insufficient size to handle many of the contracts currently on offer. By way of contrast, local authorities face less of a challenge in sports and leisure management, as private competitors are relatively few, are highly specialised, and many of them have bid unsuccessfully in the past. The same research study also showed a growing trend towards facilities management, where companies promise to show increasing interest in the larger local authority contracts in future.

Table 4.1
Regional variations in contracting with the private sector:
sports and leisure management

	contracts won by private contractors %
Northern	-
Yorkshire and Humberside	3
North West	5
East Midlands	10
West Midlands	12
Wales	-
East Anglia	18
South East	21
South West	25
London	31

Source: Ernst and Young, *Analysis of Local Authority CCT Markets*, DoE, 1995.

Local factors have had great importance in shaping the challenge to in-house provision. Evidence from the LGMB's CCT information service shows pronounced regional variations in the success rates of private contractors in sports and leisure management in particular. As Table 4.1 shows, competition in that sector has been more intense, and private contractors more successful, in southern England than in the north. Another research study undertaken for the Department of the Environment shows private contractors to be generally confident that their future share of local authority contracts will increase, and to have found local authorities' attitudes to competition in 1994 more favourable than five years or so before. In particular, the political complexion of the authority has had little bearing on a firm's likelihood of competing for a contract. geographical location, size of contract and the mix of work have proved the more important factors in determining a company's level of interest in submitting a tender.[26]

Table 4.2
Contractors' attitudes to CCT

	strongly agree %
CCT is a great business opportunity for my firm	35
CCT has given firms like ours a chance to expand into new markets	37
We are interested in working for local authorities, regardless of political persuasion	58
We would only want to work for a local authority which was genuinely interested in using private contractors	49
Most local authorities try to discourage private contractors from bidding	16
Most local authority contracts are just awarded on price - quality is not important	58
When you tender for local government work, the probability of winning the contract is much lower	42
Generally speaking, CCT contracts are less profitable than other business	35

Source: CCT: the Private Sector View, DoE, 1995.

This optimistic pragmatism has not been dimmed by the actual experience of competing for contracts, a process which very many firms have found to be riddled with uncertainty, suspicion, and bureaucracy. On balance, the prospect of new business - albeit at a lower rate of profit - seems to outweigh a scepticism about the process by which it might be gained. Table 4.2 summarises the views of some 220 firms on their experiences of tendering for local authority contracts.

These figures of course show the experience of competing for contracts under the 1988 Act, and may prove a poor guide to the future, where the impact of successive waves of CCT on housing management and central services remains a matter of conjecture. In respect of housing management, the number of potential contractors is at the present time small, and they are relatively inexperienced in comparison with local authorities. But this is unlikely to last. In contrast with the manual services where the initial private sector bidding was subdued, companies preferring to use the first round to learn how in-house teams would tender, there is expected to be sharper competition from a well-prepared private sector by the time housing management comes on stream.

While private contractors are more experienced than their in-house rivals in the practices of competition, they also enjoy the advantages of greater freedom in pricing, and in picking which contracts to bid for, and they have greater employment flexibility. As to price, private companies have the ability to submit loss-leader bids for municipal contracts and can cross-subsidise contracts or areas of work. Local authorities were aware of the experience of the early rounds of NHS tendering when contractors, eager to gain a foothold in the market and justify a great deal of investment, were submitting artificially low prices for cleaning contracts. While the actualities of 'loss leader' bids are difficult to define, the DoE appears to sanction the practice. The DoE circular on anti-competitive behaviour states: 'an assessment that a contractor will make a loss on a particular project cannot by itself be a significant reason to reject a contractors' bid.'

While a private contractor can be selective about the work (both public and private) for which he decides to tender, the DSO can only bid for the public sector contracts. This gives the private contractor a sizeable advantage over its in-house rival. DSOs cannot bid for work in the private sector, whereas private firms have the choice of which work to bid for, thus obtaining greater variety, continuity and spread of work. The private contractor can use one successful contract to keep costs down in another, and when two contracts are in adjacent authorities then the contractor can further reduce costs by sharing facilities and depots. Thus each contract won by a private contractor helps to keep costs down for the next tender.

DSOs also work under the constraints of local authority capital control systems in obtaining capital for investment, whereas private firms have the scope to raise capital from any source under the best conditions they can get and are subject only to company law. Local authorities' DSOs are also generally required to secure an annual rate of return on capital employed of five per cent, and are not allowed to use surpluses from one trading account to subsidise another. These are national restrictions, and fall with equal weight upon all authorities. Additionally, locally-determined policies may set still higher thresholds for DSO operations. A senior officer in an enthusiastic Conservative authority recollected that:

> The unions...argued that the council's rules worked against success. For example, the council demanded that business units made a rate of return even when not required. The profits were drawn into the centre and redistributed by the leader on the grounds that profit was generated from another spending department. This rule reduced competitiveness. We make business units pay interest on capital employed charged at the going rate. This also loaded their prices. It was also argued that client side demands were too great and favoured the private sector in terms of specifications. The unions deplored the 'us' and 'them' attitudes.

It must be acknowledged that seeking to run a commercial operation from beneath the local authority umbrella has a number of inherent difficulties. While profit is the prime motive for commercial organisations, local authorities traditionally have been driven by public service values and good employment practices. In a political context, local authority decision-making can be slow, restricting the ability to react quickly to market forces while commercial considerations do not always align with political ones. Local authority conditions are better and basic pay generally higher than for the private sector, which directly affects competitiveness. DSOs operate in a restricted market place with one single customer, and when that market shrinks there are very few opportunities to find work elsewhere.

These problems now promise to be extended by the 1993 legislation. The overall impression is that authorities have learned from their experience under the earlier rounds of competition and are planning ahead to achieve change:

> White collar CCT is compelling local authorities to look very carefully at in-house support services. It is forcing support services into trading units. We are already working on a notional trading account basis focusing on profitability and working methods. It is

forcing officers' minds in the first instance on getting organisations into proper shape and on the specification of services.

Through these measures, a clear picture of the competitive council is beginning to emerge.

Accountability and the competitive council

The effects of competition upon local authorities are both direct and indirect. The direct effects can be seen in the adaptations they have made to their style and practices in relation to DSO and client side organisation. Some of the indirect effects may be seen in the adoption of approaches in areas apparently unrelated to the competition process, but attributed to that process by the officers and members. It is difficult to identify these indirect and more subtle effects with certainty. Although competition may be pre-eminent among the host of powerful influences which have borne upon local authorities in recent years, it is not the sole influence. What follows is an account of those recent changes that do seem to be clearly attributable to competition.

It is evident that one of the effects of CCT is to disengage councillors from direct involvement in the services provided by private contractors. It makes councillors formally responsible for awarding contracts, but takes away from them influence on how a service is delivered, particularly where a private contractor has won the contract (except when conditions laid down in the contract have been broken). Once the contract is agreed, elected members are unable to have any direct say in how a private contractor operates a service. They can specify the service, describe the tasks to be done, the quality and quantity to be delivered, but they cannot (by and large) say how these objects are to be achieved. They can hold a contractor to account for the standard of the service, identify shortfalls, issue notices to require remedial action, and impose penalties in cases of non-compliance. But they cannot attempt to steer the delivery of the service by *ad hoc* interventions. Nor can they build-in the facility to do so in the contract, as authorities are bound by tendering rules and by government regulations which prohibit anything which central government might consider to be anti-competitive behaviour.

Certainly, the complexity and technical character of competition can make CCT difficult to grasp for many councillors. Some complain that the more fragmented structures developed for managing competition make it more difficult for them to take a corporate, strategic, view. Bodies such as the Association of Direct Labour Organisations argue for a clear member view and close control of the process, but do so against current trends. At one time, it was expected that the government would impose a prohibition on members having both client and contractor side involvements, although ministers have now decided that to prevent an individual member from being involved on both sides of the fence would be inappropriate. Nevertheless, the member role is expected to shift under the impact of competition from direct involvement to the setting of standards and service evaluation. How far was this found to be the case in practice?

First, the national evidence. The study carried out by Inlogov for the DoE concluded that 'member involvement in the continuing management of competition was limited, and member involvement, therefore, declining'.[27] The 1992 LGMB survey of organisational change also asked about the extent of the involvement of elected members in the management of competition. The results from 285 authorities confirmed that members are 'closely involved' in developing policy (43 per cent) and setting standards (47 per cent), but play a negligible role in specifying contracts (only 15 per cent 'closely involved') and in monitoring them (14 per cent), and are not greatly involved in tender evaluation (Table 4.3). This overall pattern however masks considerable differences between types of authority, with councillors most fully engaged in the contracting process itself in the London boroughs, and the least engaged in the district councils.[28]

Table 4.3
Members' overall involvement in competition issues

	closely involved/ in direct control %	not very involved %	not involved/ left to officers %	N/A %
Developing policy	43	39	17	2
Setting standards	47	42	10	1
Specifying contracts	15	45	39	1
Evaluating tender bids	26	39	33	2
Letting contracts	43	35	20	2
Monitoring contracts	14	48	37	2
Management of DSOs	38	34	25	3

Source: LGMB unpublished information.

Where an authority has successfully bid for contracts, in-house provision through a DSO gives councillors some scope for a more direct say in how the service is managed and operated. Too close an involvement may create management problems through the confusion of responsibilities, but this is an area in which authorities essentially make their own choices and establish their own norms. The 38 per cent of authorities reporting that members were 'closely involved/in direct control' of DSO management in the 1992 LGMB survey once again mask considerable variations, with London borough councillors the most, and county councillors the least, involved.

A number of factors appear to drive councillors' desire to be involved in the management of competition. The first is a general wish to feel 'in control' of service provision, made immediately manifest in one authority whose arm's length relationships, established by a Conservative majority, had little appeal for the incoming majority group.

> The new members didn't find the reporting conventions comfortable. General managers were only required to report twice a year; they delivered a business plan and made an annual report. They would be questioned by the committee. Under the Conservatives we had 'specialist' members, one for each trading unit to be a 'bit of a friend'... no responsibility but show an interest. [Moreover] there was no joint meeting of these members to take an overview.

Labour members in particular tend to seek this closer accountability in which they can actually hold officers to account for service delivery rather than merely hear an account of what they have done. The second factor is a sense of vulnerability to public criticism leading to more intervention in DSO management. In one council, members struggled to find a structure in which they could 'get hands-on'. 'Two things bother them', explained a chief officer: 'they don't want to manage the business units but they hate and detest being found wanting over things they don't know about'.

A councillor's own connection with the people he or she represents is rooted in the complaints process, as the registering of a complaint about a service is often cited as the primary reason for contacting a councillor. So the contracting out of a service can seem to many apprehensive members to threaten responsibility without power. Typically, in one city council members anticipated a problem of reduced service levels when the refuse collection contract was lost to the private sector. Yet the expected complaints did not materialise. 'Members thought their phones would be red hot but it was not so' observed an officer, who concluded: 'I am not sure all our members would [now] die in a ditch to keep services in-house'. Indeed, relieved surprise seemed to be a general reaction in that authority:

Street cleaning and refuse collection services used to be a disaster with members getting a lot of complaints. Since it has gone out to external contractors members are delighted with the service.

There are however deeper problems when, for example, the option of externalisation is considered. Members in one authority sensed that using private consultants to inform the council on key issues could raise potential conflicts of interest. Moreover, they suspected external providers would not have the same loyalty and commitment to member priorities. These concerns raise questions about how far an authority can go in contracting out a service without risking loss of control over the strategic advice that guides local developments. This question raises in turn the issue of the definition of core corporate services, considered further below.

Thus, while some local authorities have relished the experience of being released from responsibility for directly providing and managing services and have readily adopted a concept of 'enabling only', others have opposed this shift since it gives elected members even less control over the services for which they are ultimately held responsible by their constituents.[29] But whatever their approach, few have been able to construct a new and more appropriate version of the councillor's role. Many councillors react with perplexity as past orthodoxies are by-passed by events. They find yesterday's panaceas - for example more extensive delegation to officers to give them enhanced freedom of action - already inadequate to the new situation. 'Delegation requires a lot to be reported back. It is difficult to reconcile with operating on a commercial basis' observed a metropolitan district officer. Apart from coping with the shift to commercial operation, some deeper questions of strategic management in the new contracting mode remain unresolved. Overall, however, the pattern of accountabilities has been changed, rather than destroyed, by the need to manage competition. So too has the pattern of management.

The effects on management

Compulsory competitive tendering spells enforced change in local authority practices. Its most immediate impact is upon terms and conditions, whether established nationally, enshrined in local agreements, or simply tolerated as 'custom and practice'.

Working practices have had to change dramatically. They didn't at first due to hope of general election rescue. The big bang was the realisation that you are going to have to win. The unions moved more than the Labour party. They moved on hours and rates but they didn't change enough. The grounds maintenance bid was lost on standard terms and conditions.

The magnitude of the task of achieving substantial change in pay, practices and conditions in a short space of time can hardly be overestimated. But the changes required to become truly competitive range far beyond labour practices to the basic tenets of local authority management.

DLOs and DSOs operate under a different set of financial regulations from other parts of the authority. Their management has more freedom, with greater flexibility in staffing and the virement of expenditure. This greater freedom encourages a more commercial outlook, a shift in approach which may come to be reciprocated by the client side. To that extent, a set of mutually dependent quasi-commercial relationships can grow up within the authority, marking off the competition-driven parts of the operation from those conducted on more traditional lines: 'Under the old regime departments got a service that was deemed good for them. Now purchasers have the power, they get what they are prepared to pay for and what they want' said one senior county officer. 'We are breaking down traditional bureaucratic structures' claimed another.

Competitive tendering looks set to breed a new style of public sector manager. DSO managers have had to grapple with competence in financial management and forecasting, and the need to be innovative and capable of meeting the demands for effectiveness and efficiency. The skills demanded of them have been considerable: to negotiate successfully with trade unions to change local government conditions of employment; to turn departments into profitable business units; and to keep their fingers on the pulse of market trends and know what competitors are doing.

However, it was equally clear that the process of change triggered by CCT is more far-reaching than the DSO operation. DSO managers generate pressure for greater cost control and lobby for accountability in the provision of central services, thus spreading the pressure for change wider. 'Greater devolution means more pressure on the central services. The centre has to become more accountable' insisted one officer. In the light of these pressures, it is a natural further development to establish quasi-contractual arrangements in the form of service level agreements between the DSO and central departments, in which the DSO becomes the client, and the central department the contractor.

In some authorities the approach had been extended further with central support services being set up as trading or business units conducting their own relations with service departments and with one another. 'There is no doubt that the [business] units are more efficient than they ever were' reflected a county officer. 'For example, personnel services, now under the director of operations, provides a better service, more cheaply... it is more innovative and now has greater freedom'.

It follows that the change process triggered by CCT may in time run throughout the local authority, bringing about changes in management processes, manager behaviour, and even in the outlook, attitudes or 'culture' of the authority. Indeed, the 1992 LGMB survey suggests that this has already occurred (Table 4.4).

Table 4.4
Chief executives' views on the impact of
compulsory competition on management

	Agree %	Neither Agree nor Disagree %	Disagree %
The impact of competition has been limited to those services subject to CCT	32	4	63
Responding to competition has changed management processes across the authority	93	4	4
Responding to competition has changed the culture of this authority	80	12	7

Source: LGMB, unpublished information.

Operational processes apart, these changes require a transformation of management skills and conduct. For some, this was a matter of recognising what was required: 'there are three issues for councils to face up to if they are to succeed in competition - the right attitudes, aims and accountability' said one chief executive. He continued:

What it requires is radical change to reflect the major change in ethos and emphasis which tendering heralds - the need to face up to the fact they are now running businesses to provide services. Clients need to specify the service they want correctly.

This authority's attitude was a latter-day conversion, and others had already gone further. There, responsibilities have been devolved down, accountability expected from officers, and an element of performance related pay introduced. Specification, control of work and cost attribution have reportedly become far more sophisticated than before.

These were not costless changes. Just as many manual workers found themselves casualties of rapid change, so too did managers. The contrast between an adaptable workforce and slow-to-learn managers could be acute. 'In workforce practices there were blatant abuses, but the workforce recognised they needed to behave differently and they became willing to accept changes in practices' recalled a metropolitan district officer. In contrast:

> We didn't address the old issues of management style and culture. We needed to find new ways of doing things. Managers were being required for the first time to manage accountability... We have been into it six years or more now. Initially senior management could not cope with being competitive. Some learned fast, some left. We had to do a lot of retraining.

Other, very different, authorities experienced the problems differently. In one county council which had sought to pioneer competitive processes in advance of the legislation, managers seemed to have lost their bearings, responding to what a corporate services officer disparagingly characterised as the 'sweetshop mentality' - that is, an excited over-reaction to the novelty of operating on a commercial basis:

> People had become very silly. Clients and contractors tended to act as they *thought* business acted. It got very fraught. We are now seeking more of a spirit of partnership based on recognition and mutual interest. It's taken a lot to get back to some sort of partnership after years of cut-throat stuff. The majority party encouraged the contractors to demonstrate their independence. They were encouraged to be a business, with the county councillors the major client.

Competition is an area in which attitudes and assumptions are central to the way in which the authority operates. Its success ultimately stands or falls on that issue. And there can be no doubt that change at this level of significance has occurred. CCT is widely reported as having changed people's attitudes and changed the culture of authorities. Councillors sought change to inward-looking organisations. Officers have become more financially aware, and a new breed of managers appears to have emerged.

Overall, CCT has challenged local authorities in a beneficial way. It has made them more economically aware, more competitive and has sharpened their management. As a result, local government is fitter, leaner and clearer about what it is. One officer neatly summarised the impact of CCT in his authority: 'The process has been beneficial. It's had a once and for all change. [Managers] wouldn't want to drop the ethos, the culture'. He concluded triumphantly: 'today they value the hour'.

It is noticeable, however, that much of this change has occurred on the contractor side, among DSO or business unit managements. Managers on the contractor side feel more independent; have the freedom to spend their devolved budgets as they think right. The effects on the client side are less apparent and yet may be more far-reaching in the long run.

The client side and the strategic centre

The tenets of commercial management are not inherently difficult to grasp, even if they have come rather suddenly to the world of local government. Not so the client side, where perspectives do not come ready-made, skills take time to develop, and models for emulation are thin on the ground. The client side is in consequence often weak, and contract-writing, specifying and supervision poor, even in councils where DSO management is well-honed.

This tendency to weakness in the client or purchaser function can be attributed to the local government officer's bias to practical action. An experienced county officer reflected:

> We had difficulty getting people to join the client side. It was difficult to recruit people to frame specifications etc. Most local government people, for example, are 'doers' - this is where most local government officers want to be... The freedom on the contractor's side is also very attractive. The rewards like performance related pay are better but they like the self managing organisations - it gets the best out of people. Most people would not want to go back to former structures and processes. They like the small scale self containment. They like the autonomy. We'd get as much trouble getting back as we did splitting the functions...

There are signs that DSO managers are beginning to see other futures for themselves than the local government service they had joined years before, futures in which their developing commercial skills could be used to good effect.

There are also indications that regrouping the authority around a set of trading units weakens the centre and exposes the lacunae in the overall strategic management of authorities. The externalisation of parts of technical services, or the loss of a competitive bid by an in-house team under CCT, could have an impact on the authorities' central departments as it reduces the customer base. White collar CCT has proved critical in this regard. While certain aspects of central service provision such as payroll, accountancy, legal and personnel advice and personnel records can be carried out externally, a minimum base of central support services is required to enable the client and regulatory services to carry out their statutory, democratic and strategic functions. Following restructuring for competition, the client side needs to be redesigned to ensure policy generation and advise members appropriately.

The question here concerns the role of the centre of the authority. The concern to establish the competitive authority could lead to a narrow view of the totality as no more than a bundle of trading units. But a major local authority has to face wider issues than the effective management of competition, even where - perhaps especially where - it is more concerned with strategies for service delivery than the retention of the in-house functions. In the past, chief officers directed service-providing departments and gave strategic advice to members. The pressure of CCT is to develop capacities which may be at odds with these traditional roles. But councillors in particular may feel dissatisfied with the quality of advice tendered by the heads of client functions as too narrow in scope, for the skills and requirements of contract management and strategic oversight are quite different. The question of the location and form of the strategic role in the competitive local authority has yet to be fully thought-through, and councils are likely to grapple with these second-order effects of competition to the end of the century.

Competition: an overall assessment

The early 1990s have seen a remarkable process of transformation in public service management. Local authorities have shaped up, reluctantly or otherwise, into a competitive mode. New skills and working practices have placed officers on a steep learning curve. Those on the client side have had to change from 'doers' to advisers, controllers and forward thinkers. Similarly DSO managers have had to acquire a whole new range of competences while developing greater commercial acumen. Where contracts have been won in-house, DSOs have slimmed down, become more cost-conscious and responsive and have improved productivity and quality of service. But change has spread more widely as commercial approaches have come to be applied to the authority at large, and to the relations between its parts. This is, without doubt, the most dramatic set of changes in the history of British local government.

The key questions that follow are obvious. First, would these changes have come about without compulsion? Secondly, would the abandonment of compulsion enable local government to revert to its pre-CCT condition? The answer to the first of these is emphatically negative. A few authorities might have continued to experiment with new models of organisation, but the great sea change would most certainly not have come about had local authorities not been compelled by law to submit defined services to compulsory competition under conditions where the loopholes were, year after year, inexorably closed.

The second question is more interesting, and admits an only slightly less emphatic answer. The new disciplines which CCT imposed are valued, even where the compulsion that produced them is not. The spread of the influence of these disciplines throughout the local authority organisation appears to have pushed beyond the threshold at which change could be reversed. By the end of the century, when white collar CCT has settled in, the removal of the competition requirements by a Labour government would in all probability leave the competitive council intact. Even were the change to come before then, it would be fanciful to suppose that any kind of reversion to the pre-CCT era is possible.

True, some authorities still see the process of competition as disruptive and unsettling. Others - those who regard themselves as at the cutting edge of change - are encountering new problems and raising new issues as they explore the further reaches of the competitive environment. Most, however, including some of the most hostile and reluctant entrants into the service marketplace, have begun to realise the more immediate benefits. It is now more openly admitted that competition has introduced essential disciplines into management practice. The gains have been greater clarity in lines of responsibility, the removal of confusion between service commissioning and service provision, explicitness in service specifications, heightened client awareness of performance, greater precision in performance measurement and the identification of hidden costs.

In all authorities, separating purchaser and provider roles and giving the customer the power to purchase services elsewhere when dissatisfied has concentrated the minds of both parties. Whether a contract is with a private sector or a in-house provider the result is a contractual relationship between the local authority and its supplier, governed by detailed contract specifications. The successful tenderer is required to meet specified performance targets and quality standards. If these targets and quality standards are not met after representations have been made, the purchasing authority has no option but to either withhold payment for work not completed satisfactorily or to terminate the contract, re-tender, and appoint another contractor.

These are potentially powerful instruments in the pursuit of quality in public services. Yet their power can only be realised in a thriving competitive market. In practice, the experience of the market appears highly variable as between services, as between different parts of the country, and over time. The trends, however, are in one direction, towards greater competitiveness. DSO managers must anticipate competing against large, experienced and well-resourced firms, increasingly from Continental Europe, which are gearing up for the UK market. And already white collar CCT is presenting a substantial and attractive market to private sector.

This is not to say that private sector firms feel entirely at ease with the local authorities' version of competition. A common response on their part is that tendering documents are too long and complex (regarded by some as a tactic to discourage their interest). Performance conditions may sometimes be regarded as unacceptable and quality levels as unrealistic. Potential competitors are anxious to know what TUPE would mean for them. Some can live with a requirement to take on all previously employed local authority staff. But many would not be prepared to bid for work under such conditions. This much has been clearly established by research undertaken for the Department of the Environment, which identified a range of disincentive factors in the tendering process, including the complexity of tender documents, the difficulties of obtaining information, and excessive paperwork.[30]

Nor are contractors inclined to put a great deal of trust in local authorities' decision processes. As many as four out of five interviewed in that same study expressed a lack of faith in the fairness of the process, in particular citing what they perceived as favouritism in the allocation of contracts in-house. Other reasons for a coolness towards local authorities included fears about TUPE, low profit margins, and a belief that price was the sole determining factor in the award of contracts. These were no caricatures, for the overall views were shared by successful and unsuccessful firms alike.[31]

Nevertheless, it seems clear that in the absence of changes to existing terms and conditions of service, the prospects of many in-house services attaining commercial viability are remote. Such difficulties have impelled some councils to explore the externalisation option, which was seen as a way of maintaining job security of staff at least in the medium term, and effectively removing the current encumbrance of the cross-boundary tendering rules. Externalising services by negotiation effectively places them outside the CCT arena. A range of considerations - legal, service, political, market and organisational - underpin the moves towards externalisation. While organisational considerations imply a well thought-out philosophy which distinguishes between control/strategic functions and service/support functions, in practice market and political conditions are likely to determine whether a service can be externalised.

At root, local authorities are primarily political, not commercial, entities. The pace of change is limited by this fact, even if there is some suggestion that the effect of CCT has been to enhance officer power at the expense of that of the councillors. Some councillors had worked within the old system for so long that they did not want change, could not respond to it, and found themselves sidelined. Others, having recently sought and won election for quite other reasons, found themselves confronted with an experience which was unexpected and totally alien to them. It seems likely that many councillors, finding it hard to get to grips with the CCT regime, have fallen in with officer plans.

Some councillors continue to wish CCT away. Some openly expect it to disappear within five years, reasoning not just in terms of an expected change in government but in terms of a redirection of policies. They believe that the emerging interpretation of TUPE radically shifts the odds back in favour of the internal bidder. Some claim to detect a groundswell of opinion against price being the determining factor in the award of contracts. Others go further and argue that private sector management is swinging away from price based considerations towards the development of a quality product and that 'the new public management' is following yesterday's commercial conventions. In these matters, as elsewhere, people will believe what they find it comfortable to believe. Speculation aside, the hard realities of CCT, stressed throughout this chapter, remain. The dynamics of competition have proved powerful beyond all expectation, and we shall not see the old familiar patterns of public service management again.

Notes

1. Claims made most vigorously, if least convincingly, in N. Ridley's *The Local Right: Enabling Not Providing,* London, Centre for Policy Studies, 1988.
2. K. Hartley and M. Huby, 'Contracting Out Policy: Theory and Evidence' in J. Kay, C. Mayer and D. Thompson (editors), *Contracting Out Policy: Theory and Evidence in Privatisation and Regulation - The UK Experience,* Oxford University Press, 1986; K. Ascher, *The Politics of*

Privatisation: Contracting out Public Services, Basingstoke, Macmillan, 1987.
3. N. Flynn, 'Direct Labour Organisations', in S. Ranson, G. Jones and K. Walsh (editors), *Between Centre and Locality: The Politics of Public Policy*, London, Allen and Unwin, 1985, pp. 119-134.
4. B. Wood, 'Privatisation: Local Government and the Health Service', in C. Graham and T. Prosser (editors), *Waiving the Rules: The Constitution under Thatcherism*, Oxford University Press, 1988, p. 124.
5. Audit Commission, *Securing Further Improvements in Refuse Collection: A Review by the Audit Commission*, HMSO, 1984.
6. Institute of Public Finance, *Competitive Tendering and Efficiency: The Case of Refuse Collection*, IPF, 1986.
7. S. Domberger, S. Meadowcroft, and D. Thompson, 'Competitive Tendering and Efficiency: The Case of Refuse Collection', *Fiscal Studies*, Vol. 7(4), 1986, pp. 69-87.
8. The study was based on 302 contracts drawn from a handbook of 3,500 in 540 authorities. S. Szymanski and T. Jones, *The Cost Savings from CCT of Refuse Collection Services*, London Business School, 1993.
9. Department of the Environment, *Competitive Tendering for Local Government Services: Initial Experiences*, HMSO, 1991.
10. Local Government Information Unit, *CCT on the Record: A Review of the Experiences of CCT under the Local Government Act, 1988*. An as yet unpublished study by the Equal Opportunities Commission is reported as claiming that while employment in building cleaning, school meals and catering, sport and leisure management and refuse collection has fallen 21 per cent since 1988, the great majority of the job losses have been to women workers. *Guardian*, 11 February 1995.
11. Local Government Management Board, *CCT Information Service Survey Report No 6*, November 1992.
12. Local Government Management Board, *CCT Information Service Survey Report No 8*, 1993.
13. Local Government Information Unit, *CCT on the Record: A Review of the Experiences of CCT under the Local Government Act, 1988*, London, LGIU, 1994.
14. Audit Commission, *Realising the Benefits of Competition*, London, HMSO, 1993.
15. Audit Commission, *Realising the Benefits of Competition*.
16. M. Paddon, 'Management Buy-outs and Compulsory Competition in Local Government', *Local Government Studies*, 17(3), May/June 1991, pp. 27-52. For an assessment of the critical success factors in local authority MBOs, see *Management and Employee Buy-outs in Local Government: a Brief Introduction*, Price Waterhouse, not dated.

17. For a general discussion based on a study of 23 authorities in Northern England, see K. Shaw, J. Fenwick and A. Foreman, 'Client and Contractor Roles in Local Government: Some Observations on Managing the Split', *Local Government Policy Making*, 20 (2), October 1993, pp. 22-27.
18. K. Walsh, *Competitive Tendering for Local Authority Services: Initial Experiences*, London, HMSO, 1991.
19. For an appraisal of the effects of internal markets, and the need to weigh organisation costs against transaction costs, see *Municipal Journal*, 11-17 February 1994.
20. Municipal Journal, *Compulsory Competitive Tendering in '93*, London, 1994, pp. 182-183.
21. ibid.
22. Legal services CCT was scheduled for implementation in October 1995, and the remaining services twelve months later, although the timetable has been varied to take account of local government reorganisation. London boroughs and the Metropolitan districts expect legal CCT to be in place by 1 October 1995 with the shire districts and counties currently facing the structure review having a separate timetable. Legal services and the rest of the white collar CCT would be phased in for new authorities as they start on either 1 April 1995, 1996 or 1997. In Scotland the extension of compulsory competitive tendering to professional and technical services is not to take place until after local government reform. Implementation is planned to be phased in such a way that one third of contracts should be let by October 1997, a further third by January, 1998 and the full value by April, 1998. In Wales too the implementation of CCT has been suspended due to local government reorganisation.
23. Special requirements however operate where the in-house bid was successful following the exposure of white collar services to voluntary competitive tendering.
24. It is proposed that Section 105 of the Housing Act 1985 (covering tenants' rights to be consulted on changes in management) will be amended to make this clear. Section 27 of the Act will also be amended to remove the need for the Secretary of State to approve individual agreements for tenant management organisations to take over the estates.
25. Ernst and Young, *Analysis of Local Authority CCT Markets*, London, Department of the Environment, 1995.
26. BMRB Ltd, *CCT: the Private Sector View*, London, Department of the Environment, 1995, p. 6.
27. K. Walsh and H. Davies, *Competition and Service: the Impact of the Local Government Act, 1988*, London, HMSO, 1993.

28. Local Government Management Board, *A Survey of Internal Organisation Change, 1992: Report of the Corporate Survey*, unpublished, 1993.
29. N. Rao, *Managing Change: Councillors and the New Local Government*, York, Joseph Rowntree Foundation, 1993.
30. BMRB Ltd., *CCT: the Private Sector View*, pp. 91-96.
31. ibid., pp. 32-33.

5 Social Services in a Culture of Choice

The idea of the enabling authority ran through the policies of the third Thatcher administration. That local authorities should relinquish their role as direct service providers is the central tenet of the new public management. Rather than provide in their own right, local authorities are expected to concentrate on ensuring that services are provided, using their financial and statutory power to set standards and monitor their achievement. This new philosophy accepts that welfare pluralism will be the consequence: a wide range of providers working within the parameters set by the local authority, acting as the lead agency.

Although evident in the fields of education, housing, and competitive tendering, it is in community care that this notion of enabling finds its clearest expression. Unlike these other three areas, however, the growth of the enabling role in social services provision was not driven by any ideological impulse. Rather, it followed from the development of practice over a period of years and, to that extent, the concept was by no means a novel one. Community care, in the sense of a planned shift away from institutional care, was promoted during the 1960s, but in its current form originated in a series of papers and speeches in the mid-1980s. The Barclay report and Secretary of State Norman Fowler's 1984 Buxton speech proposed a more strategic role for social services departments (SSDs), in which they would identify, mobilise and promote the fullest range of care services within all sectors on behalf of the local community.

The Griffiths report, *Community Care: Agenda for Action,* built upon this concept and went beyond it to introduce SSDs as *purchasers* of social care from within this complex of providers. According to Griffiths, SSDs would become 'designers, organisers and purchasers of non-health care services and not primarily direct providers, making the maximum possible use of voluntary and private sector bodies to widen consumer choice, stimulate innovation and encourage efficiency'.[1]

In the interval between the publication of Griffiths and the government's response in the white paper *Caring for People,* the distinction between purchasing and providing had been thought through and more fully developed in the context of the NHS. The white paper *Working for Patients* aimed to create an internal market in which health authorities were to purchase services from provider units, NHS trusts and the independent sector. These developments were to profoundly affect the management of social services through the 1990s.

The role of the social services as set out in *Caring for People* was conceived as

> determining clear specifications of service requirements, and arrangements for tenders and contracts; taking steps to stimulate the setting up of 'not-for profit' agencies; identifying areas of their own work which are sufficiently self-contained to be suitable for 'floating-off' as self-managing units; [and] stimulating the development of new voluntary sector activity.[2]

This shift in emphasis from mobilising care provision to purchasing it, had important implications for local authorities in the achievement of welfare pluralism. But the responses accorded to these new ideas by the social services authorities themselves turned on some unrecognised ambiguities in the term 'enabling'.

Enabling was a many sided concept, in which traditional concepts of enabling the personal development of service clients, more radical concepts of enabling 'community development', and the new priority of enabling the market processes sat uneasily together.[3] While each implied different roles, tasks and targets, they were neither mutually exclusive nor mutually reinforcing. The tendency of social services directors, elected members and some managers to perceive these multiple realities of enabling resulted in wide variations in the ways in which implementing community care was approached.

The importance of community care, then, is that it provides the focus for the development of an enabling role in social services. Its essence is the assumption of a lead role by a single agency, in this case the local authority social services department. The SSD is required to assess needs and arrange the provision of suitable packages of care. In doing so it is required to define a clear split between its purchaser and provider functions, and to manage the consolidated budget for social care, spending the greater part of the new funds in the independent sector. The SSD's powers to monitor and inspect the quality of care provided has become very much more important in this enabling role.

The context of community care

The purpose of community care is to meet the needs of client groups in a more appropriate fashion, and to that end a three-pronged policy has been pursued. The first element has been a move from institutions to community facilities. The second, a shift in resources from health and income support to social services. And finally, the development of a fuller partnership between the various agencies providing services.[4]

Out of the institutions

At the level of the client or service user, community care aims to give people the opportunity to live as independently as possible in their own homes, or in 'homely' settings in the community. The focus of this concern has been upon particular groups: elderly, mentally ill, mentally disabled and physically handicapped people. Official reports made increasingly explicit the need to develop more balanced service systems and to extend services 'in the community' in order to reduce dependence on long-stay hospitals.

A general shift from institutional to community care had begun in the early 1960s. Faced with the rising costs of institutional care, ministers had responded by closing down long-stay mental hospitals and encouraging the development of smaller, community-based facilities. A similar approach was taken across the social care sector, for example by promoting fostering as an alternative to residential homes for children in care. The 1971 white paper *Better Services for the Mentally Handicapped* and the 1975 white paper *Better Services for the Mentally Ill,* marked the recognition of the social needs, as well as the clinical needs, of mentally ill and mentally handicapped people. In 1980 the value of care in the community for old people was officially recognised.[5]

Making better use of resources

The second element in community care was the more careful orchestration of the full range of involved services, so as to ensure the co-ordinated use of funding. But by the mid-1980s, it had become clear from a series of independent reports from the Audit Commission, the House of Commons

Social Services Select Committee, and the National Audit Office that the shift to care in the community was developing slowly.[6]

The Audit Commission examined community care in 1986 and reported that the slow and uneven progress made to date was attributable to inadequate finance and contradictory policies. The Commission claimed that the allocation of resources did not match needs, and that there was a failure to adapt systems and structures to accommodate the shift in policy. The report put forward a number of options for organising and funding community care. First, that local authorities should be made responsible for the long-term care of mentally and physically handicapped people in the community. The resources necessary for this could be identified and where appropriate transferred from the NHS.

Secondly, for the care of elderly people in the community, a single budget in an area should be established by contributions from the NHS and local authorities. For mentally ill people in the community, there should be similar arrangements, or the NHS should be given responsibility for all services, purchasing services from local authorities as required. In addition, for all client groups, care funded by supplementary benefit (later replaced by income support) in the private or voluntary sector should be better co-ordinated with the care provided by the relevant local social services department or NHS authority. The report concluded that unless radical changes of this kind were made, community care would remain a distant prospect for many of the very people it was intended to help. Similarly, the National Audit Office found in 1987 that joint finance was not being used as intended, and that progress towards the development of fully integrated local joint plans was very slow.

Acting together

Thus, by the late 1980s, there was a broad consensus about the need for reform of the delivery of community care services. It was clear that the better use of resources depended upon sorting out the institutional arrangements through which a range of agencies were required to act together. In 1988 Sir Roy Griffiths was invited to review the way in which public funds were being used to support community care policy and to advise on the options for actions that would improve the use of these funds as a contribution to more effective community care.[7]

Griffiths' approach was to go beyond leaving matters to the vagaries of joint action, and to clarify some lead responsibilities. His main recommendations accordingly included the appointment of a minister for community care to act as a focus for the new policy, and for the primary responsibility to lie with local authorities.

The report also recommended that a proper planning process should be instituted. Collaboration between local authorities and the health service already existed through the joint planning mechanism and should be developed to the point where plans could be presented to the minister for community care. Griffiths grasped the challenge of the newly-fashionable concept of the enabling authority, and proposed that local authority social services departments should be 'reoriented' towards the design and co-ordination of 'packages of care' largely bought on the care 'market' rather than provided by local authorities themselves.

Caring for People and the NHS and Community Care Act

The white paper *Caring for People*, published in 1989, endorsed much of the Griffiths model, while resisting the recommendation to introduce a specific grant for funding community care, except in the case of mental illness.[8] It set out the government's proposals for the provision of community care. The National Health Service and Community Care Act, 1990 subsequently gave legislative effect to these proposals.

The Act's provisions ranged from strategic objectives to the practical arrangements for providing information to the public and setting up purchasing systems. The key objectives for service delivery were first to promote the development of domiciliary, day and respite services to enable people needing care to live in their own homes wherever feasible and sensible. Secondly, to ensure that service providers make practical support for carers a high priority. Thirdly, to make the proper assessment of need and good case management the cornerstones of high quality care provision. Fourthly, to promote the development of a flourishing independent sector alongside high quality public services. Fifthly, to clarify the responsibilities of agencies and so make it easier to hold them to account for their performance. Finally, the new arrangements were to secure better value for money by introducing a new funding structure for social care.

In order to achieve these objectives, the government proposed a number of changes in the ways in which social care was to be delivered and funded. Local authorities were to be given major responsibility for providing and/or organising social care for the elderly and for people who are mentally ill or have physical or learning disabilities. Responsibility for the funding of residential care for elderly people and others was to be transferred from the social security department (DSS) to local government. A case management and assessment system was to be introduced to determine eligibility for publicly-financed services.

Of crucial importance, a comprehensive planning system for community care was to be built up with the active involvement of health and housing authorities and voluntary organisations. The Act also proposed the introduction of an 'arm's length' inspectorate to monitor standards in local authority residential care and the independent residential care sector. Finally, the emphasis for local authorities was to be on purchasing rather than directly providing services.

All the above elements were to have been introduced in April 1991. There was much that all political parties and interested groups welcomed in the government's proposals. Many lent support to the objective of community care, to provide the right level of intervention and support to 'enable people to achieve maximum independence and control over their own lives'. In early 1990, social services departments received unprecedented levels of draft guidance from the Department of Health. Many departments were already preparing to implement the legislation in April 1991, but on 18 July 1990 the government announced its decision to phase implementation in three stages over two years from April 1991.

The phased timetable defined April 1991 as the target date for the establishment of inspection units, the introduction of the specific grants for people with mental health problems and for people who abuse drugs or alcohol, and the introduction of comprehensive complaints procedures. By April 1992, the SSDs were to publish their community care plans, complete the preparatory work to introduce a unified assessment procedure, and be prepared to introduce a case management scheme for people whose service needs are complex. By April 1993 a unified assessment procedure was to be in place, and case management schemes fully introduced. By that date a start was also to be made on transferring funds from the DSS to the local authorities. For this to work, arrangements needed to be in place to administer the transferred funds, make financial assessments of individuals in need of community care services, supply appropriate departmental services, and purchase the necessary services from other sectors.

The government's main explanation for the postponement was its lack of confidence in the capacity of local authorities to carry out the reforms in a single stage within reasonable cost limits. This was a period in which the Thatcher government's onslaught on the local authorities was at full strength. Ministers claimed that many local authorities were unable to manage their services and to constrain their expenditure within the limits set by the Standard Spending Assessments (SSA). The prime minister was known to be particularly reluctant to accept local government - an institution for which she had so little regard - in the lead role for so important a service. Phasing was chosen instead on the grounds that:

> It is only sensible for any additional new burdens on local government in 1991/92 to be kept to an absolute minimum. Local authorities have made it clear that the changes that we propose in community care would lead to many authorities increasing their

expenditure and their levels of community charge. This would place a further unacceptable burden on charge payers.[9]

The new timetable was to ensure that 'local authorities had longer to come to terms with the need to discharge their duties efficiently and at a cost which their community charge payers could afford'.

The government's decision to postpone full implementation raised concern in many quarters and sowed doubts as to whether local government would ever claim its inheritance. In 1990, the then president of Association of Directors of Social Services, John Rea Price, expressed regret at the prospect of delay and stated that, 'local authorities are geared up to at least deliver the basic minimum that will be required next April'.[10] Peter Westland, deputy secretary for social services at the Association of Metropolitan Authorities, warned:

> The estimated 140,000 who would have been offered assessment of their needs will not now have that, and will only have resources to go straight in to residential care at government expense. The government is opening the door to uncontrolled expenditure on residential care for which it was rightly criticised by Sir Roy Griffiths.[11]

A King's Fund paper pointed out that the continued use of social security funds to finance residential care implied that resources would not be transferred to support the government's primary objective of extending care at home; and that the charge on the social security budget would continue to rise, defeating the government's intention to curtail a rise in income support spending.[12] Some hard-pressed social services authorities were nevertheless grateful for the unexpected breathing space. The phasing-in of the changes provided an opportunity to ensure that the transition would be planned and managed with more care to achieve better results for clients and staff.

In November 1990, the Department issued its final policy guidance based on the drafts put out for consultation in June 1990. The guidance set out the framework within which authorities would need to develop new arrangements in order to implement community care policy fully by April 1993. A series of more detailed publications produced by the Social Services Inspectorate, and by individual organisations specially commissioned for this purpose, offered information about good practice and advice on how to implement the policy.

The changing role of social services: the enabling authority

The government's white paper *Caring for People* proclaimed a period of major change for the social services. It developed the now-familiar concept of an 'enabling authority': initiating, contracting and monitoring appropriate packages of care rather than directly administering provision.[13] It sought to expand the range and nature of service suppliers. The basic premise of the white paper was that social and health care can be acquired from four sectors: statutory, voluntary, commercial and informal, and that it was desirable to have a mix of these under a regime of welfare pluralism.

Local authorities were to have the key responsibility for organising community care services, acting as the agents of people needing care, ensuring that proper needs assessments are carried out and purchasing the appropriate services from a range of service providers. They were required to alter their administrative structures along more managerial lines, delegating authority and revising information systems.

Social services departments were required to make strategic decisions about the nature of and mix of service provision most appropriate for their community. 'Welfare pluralism' offered several alternatives in the design of community care services, and it was therefore imperative for departments to plan and make positive decisions about service design at a strategic level. Collaboration between the relevant statutory authorities was considered fundamental to the implementation of community care policy. The main proposal was for joint planning agreements between health and social services authorities covering common goals, funding arrangements, operational strategies and contract specifications.

The white paper also emphasised that local authorities were expected to 'take all reasonable steps to secure diversity of provision'. One of the government's objectives was to 'promote the development of a flourishing independent sector', by which was meant both voluntary (non-profit) and private (for-profit), providers. The SSDs were to retain their ability to act as direct service providers only if other forms of service provision were 'unforthcoming or unsuitable'. Furthermore, they were also under an obligation to make use of private providers 'wherever possible' and to 'stimulate such activity' where available. The government argued that greater use of the independent sector would lead to an increase in the range of services on offer, create more flexibility and consumer choice, and stimulate competition, resulting in better value for money and more cost-effective services.

Changing roles: purchaser/provider

In line with the promotion of greater diversity in service provision, local authority social services departments were expected to change from being direct service providers to being purchasers of services. The white paper stressed that the statutory sector would continue to play an important role in providing care, though it was essential for authorities to separate their purchaser and provider functions at an early stage. In order to gear up for this split, social services departments would have to find ways of achieving organisational separation of the two functions. The planning of overall service strategy, the development of contracts and service specifications, and the necessary arrangements for regulating and monitoring, were to be dealt with by a separate division. In the new mixed economy of care, with its emphasis on quality, consumer choice and value for money, authorities would be required to treat their own units no differently from others with whom they contract, much as had the client divisions under CCT. The requirement for separating-out the assessment of need and the purchasing process, from the provision of services to meet those needs, was spelt out in the Social Services Inspectorate's *Purchase of Service Practice Guidance*, published in April 1991; Price Waterhouse were commissioned at that time to work up detailed guidance on the organisational implications of such a split.

Under this new regime, a new role for the voluntary sector providers was envisaged. They were to have a greater role in drawing up contracts and developing their contractual relationships with local authorities. The policy base on which contracts were to be drawn up was to be clearly specified. Such measures were designed to clarify the role of voluntary agencies, to give them a sounder financial base and allow them a greater degree of certainty in planning for the future. This, in the government's view, would enhance the development of more flexible and cost-effective forms of non-statutory provision.

Changing styles: service-led to needs-led

The proposals in the white paper introduced formal assessment of clients' needs for community care services upon which the provision of such services was to be based. Concepts of case management and assessment were central to the government's plans for restructuring community care. Case management was 'the lynch-pin of an individual client needs-led assessment'. It involved selecting specific individuals, on the basis of clearly established criteria, for a comprehensive assessment of need. A single point of entry for those seeking help was proposed together with a single point of contact and accountability. Moreover there were to be devolved budgets to enable co-ordination of local solutions for individuals' needs, and development of 'care packages' to suit individual circumstances.

Local authorities' duties to assess individual needs were restricted to those needing community care services, as judged by the authorities themselves. They were required to publish their criteria for deciding whether an assessment was necessary. They had to consult service users when drawing up their community care plans. These requirements would make explicit the demand-led pattern of care services envisaged.

The white paper thus accepted Griffiths' proposal that the provision of care should be preceded by a proper assessment of the individual's needs. However, in describing local authority responsibilities, it made clear that while the assessment 'should take account of the wishes of the individual and his or her carer', decisions on what services to offer 'will have to take into account what is available and affordable'. The aim, then, was to enable those requiring help to have a greater say in what should be done to meet their needs and provide them with a limited degree of choice.

Monitoring the quality of social care

The white paper proposed two new mechanisms for monitoring the quality of care: each local authority was required to set up a monitoring and inspection unit to set standards of care for residential homes, and to establish a complaints procedure to allow users to make formal complaints about the services they were receiving.

Inspection units were to have the key responsibilities of monitoring and promoting quality throughout social services; to register and inspect all residential care homes, provided by both the independent sector and the local authority sector; and develop operational management of quality assurance policies and procedures. In the establishment of the complaints procedures, local authorities were required to consult with staff associations, voluntary organisations and trade unions, and to incorporate staff and users' views into their procedures. The objective was to address the unequal power relationships between clients, users and carers on the one hand, and the decision-makers and providers on the other, and to rectify these imbalances.

Yet the government's notion of 'quality' did not go uncontested. Critics argued that the proposals in *Caring for People* were addressed more to how social services were to carry out their functions than to issues of users' access and rights to services. The white paper was also criticised on the grounds that it failed to acknowledge the high levels of unmet demand, and contained no proposals as to how any shortfalls in provision would be met. More importantly, Griffiths' proposal for the ring-fencing of funds allocated to local authorities for community care was not incorporated into the legislation. Social services expenditure in many authorities at that time was well in excess of their SSA. The introduction of the community charge was already forcing many authorities to reduce their expenditure, and they anticipated great difficulties in finding the additional money to improve their services.

Planning and collaboration

The issues of planning agreements and relationships dominated the community care agenda. They set an organisational framework which brought together the key players in service provision. It was envisaged in the white paper that a new spirit of partnership would shape developments at two levels: through the inter-professional production of individual care packages, and through the inter-organisational production of community care plans. At the inter-professional level, it was expected that an individual client would receive a package of care, based on the outcome of a comprehensive, multidisciplinary assessment of needs. This partnership on assessment was then to be extended to service delivery.

At the inter-organisational level, the new system emphasised co-operation in drawing up community care plans. Section 46 of the NHS and Community Care Act required local authorities, District Health Authorities and Family Health Services Authorities (FHSAs) to prepare and publish their plans for community care. Together they were required to show how the plans would be realised, taking account of local needs and resources. Thus planning agreements were to provide the basis for the future national policy on community care. They were to cover a range of key requirements - common goals for particular client groups, funding agreements, agreed policies on key operational areas and agreed contract specifications for securing joint working between service providers. In this respect these planning requirements were a marked departure from the values of public sector reform expressed in other areas of social policy.

The FHSAs (who oversee primary health care) occupied a distinctive position under the community care plans. They were required to collaborate closely with the District Health Authorities in assessing community health services, in drawing up community care plans, providing the specification, and ensuring the delivery of these plans. In collaboration with social services departments it was envisaged that FHSAs should find the means to engage more general practitioners in the processes of effective social care.

In acting - apparently uncharacteristically - to promote co-operation between local government and health authorities, Mrs Thatcher's government was seeking to solve three long-standing problems. The first to co-ordinate health and social services; the second was to reconcile local decision-making and central control; and the third was to balance public pressures for service improvements with their larger public expenditure goals.[14] Joint planning had been a central theme in the build-up to the 1974 reorganisations of the National Health Service and local government.[15] And as far back as 1962, the Ministry of Health had asked local authorities to submit plans for the development of health and welfare services, which were to be subject to annual reviews.

Ten years later, soon after the creation of the local authorities social services departments under the Seebohm reforms, the DHSS called upon local authorities to respond to planning guidelines and gave directions on the provision levels to be aimed for. The reorganisation of the NHS was intended to introduce better management and promote better co-ordination between health authorities and local government services.[16] The two authorities were required to set up Joint Consultative Committees and Joint Planning Teams to promote joint initiatives in planning and to facilitate the collaborative development of services. The introduction of joint finance in 1976 was also designed to encourage social services departments to engage in collaborative planning with health authorities. It initially provided earmarked funds to pump-prime service developments which benefited the National Health Service but the scope of the funds was subsequently extended to include developments in housing, education and voluntary agencies.[17] Despite this succession of attempts to achieve the comprehensive planning of social and health care, each had fallen well short of expectations due to a lack of vision, insufficient funding and inadequate monitoring. Local authorities felt unable to fully involve themselves in these initiatives as they had no firm indication of future resource levels.[18] Thus it was that the community care initiative of the late 1980s sought to build upon, and to transcend the limited achievements of these earlier attempts. While Sir Roy Griffiths was able to characterise community care as 'everybody's distant relative but nobody's baby', local authority personal social services planning prior to his inquiry did not even have a distant relative.[19]

Organising for effective planning

The legacy of this long history of attempted planning meant that most social services departments already had some sort of strategic planning mechanism in place, based on a model of services for the main client groups. For example, in Hertfordshire joint planning teams, based on clear lines of accountability, provided a focus for resource planning at strategic and operational levels. Four such teams for mental handicap services were already in operation as early as in 1987. The social services department had the lead responsibility for the provision and management of residential, day and respite care, for adults and children with a mental handicap. Notwithstanding the lead role of the department, the joint planning teams sought to enhance participation by other statutory agencies to include district councils, family practitioner committees (now the Family Health Services Authority), voluntary organisations and housing associations.

Other ways in which existing mechanisms provided the basis for the new approach included a review of the role and membership of the existing joint planning groups. The strategic role of joint planning groups was to define the aims and objectives of care groups; develop policies for such groups; give guidance to local planning and development groups; and to advise district health authorities and the local authority through the joint care planning teams. Essentially their task was to support the strategic role of the local and health authorities rather than concerning themselves with the local operational management of services.

Relating to health authorities

Three purposes for planning were defined for community care: to support local service managers and policy-makers in working up strategies for the development, provision and review of local services; to enable local authorities to communicate their plans clearly to their electorate; and to provide a means by which progress towards the achievement of national objectives could be monitored. The government's white paper had emphasised the need for SSDs, health authorities, family practitioner committees (now FHSAs) and housing authorities to ensure that their community care plans complemented each other and did not conflict.

One of the crucial questions for local authorities was how to develop shared plans with health authorities. For this to be possible it was necessary to collect, share and agree upon basic information such as demography, dependency characteristics, and the scale and scope of need within geographical areas. But it proved difficult for a local authority to agree a set of principles when there was more than one district health authority within its boundaries, each with its own management approach.

The view of some authorities was nevertheless that the production of a single plan would be most appropriate. 'Failure to grasp the nettle of working together' would diminish the possibility of achieving better services for people, said one social services director. Elsewhere, in an attempt to collaborate with its five district health authorities to produce a single joint plan, Birmingham city council put forward two important arguments. A single plan would symbolise the commitment to work together and encourage collaboration between authorities. Secondly, it would give the authorities the responsibility of planning for the most effective use of resources along a continuum of care. It was argued that if approached positively, a single plan would avoid unnecessary duplication of service as well as break down traditional agency boundaries in the provision of services. Generally, there were strong arguments for a single community care plan. Common understandings across different authorities could be more easily developed and sustained. Such a plan was to enable authorities to identify some core values and objectives and deal with some of the boundary issues and problem areas.

Apart from the issue of single or separate plans, difficulties for local authorities also arose from differences in approach and experience. Developing planning agreements was not going to be easy if there were no basic definitions from which to work. A major concern expressed about *Caring for People* was that it had done little to clarify the boundary between health care (by the NHS) and social care (by local authorities), or consider the financial mechanisms required for transferring clients across this boundary. Several authorities at the time of the study were involved in developing appropriate definitions of health and social care. Clarification of such concepts was considered essential to establish responsibility and accountability for the provision of particular services and to indicate budgetary responsibilities.

There were many other issues between health and social care which needed to be clarified in practice. For example, there were long-running uncertainties about budget allocations for nursing home placements. There was also concern about the extent to which hospital consultants and GPs might seek nursing home placements in homes in which they have a financial interest. Of immediate concern, however, was that some health authorities were already looking carefully at cost-benefits of provision they had made for elderly and long-term mentally ill people. A health service decision not to provide would have serious implications for local authorities and for many dependent people, and especially for their carers if state benefits failed to meet the full cost of alternative private care. Social care would become increasingly the responsibility of local authorities who would have to assess the needs of each client, devise a package of care relevant to those needs, and then ensure that the package was put together to meet those needs.

Other difficulties arising from joint planning related to different managerial languages and organisational cultures; from different political decision-making systems; from different planning cycles and different geographical boundaries. Health authorities were already moving rapidly towards the role of purchasing authority with provider units delivering care across different user groups. The political structures supporting the two agencies were also quite different - the district health authorities have appointed members as opposed to the local authorities' elected councillors. Such differences could be a source of conflicts in many authorities.

Although much of the commentary on community care centred upon the relationship between local and health authorities, the need to engage with other statutory and independent players extends beyond these limits. For example, while a wide range of agencies need to work together if community care is to be effective, this is even more crucial when the housing dimension is included as a central component.

Housing associations and community care

The White Paper recognised that good quality housing is a key to independent living. In September 1992, a joint circular on housing and community care from the Departments of the Environment and Health reiterated the importance of housing perspective in community care, called for a 'complete reassessment of the way agencies work together' and argued that 'there must be greater knowledge of each other's roles and objectives'.[20] Housing and social services authorities were required to co-operate fully, bringing in other providers in both the public and voluntary sectors, especially housing associations.

Yet integrating housing into the community care agenda was not one of the key tasks for health and social services in planning community care implementation for 1992/93. Many of the problems of ineffective joint working identified by the Audit Commission in 1986 were still at that time characteristic of community care.[21] There was a widespread concern that housing was still marginalised in the community care agenda. Debates centred upon building a framework for action in housing and community care emphasising the importance of shared vision and common language, collaborative structures, common agendas and key tasks and leadership.[22]

In March 1993 the Community Care Support Force (set up by the Department of Health) in its paper *A Framework for Integrating the Housing Agenda*, proposed a model framework for the housing elements of a community care plan and argued that 'a culture of jointly owned goals and real joint working is essential to the successful delivery of community care'.[23] Likewise, a number of models for assessing housing needs have also been constructed to inform housing strategies and care plans. Some have proposed a 'bottom up' approach in which an overview is built up from data collected on individuals, and based on the user's own assessment of their needs.[24] Others have suggested models which integrate national and local data, such as the 'pathways model' constructed by Watson and Harker, which had already been applied to people with learning difficulties.[25]

Thus, there has been an increasing recognition of the place of housing on the community care agenda. It would be consistent with the philosophy of community care that housing associations, for example, should figure prominently at the forefront of service provision.

Moreover, the housing association movement has long experience of operating in precisely this sort of partnership mode, providing an integrated housing and care service. They might therefore be expected to respond readily to the challenge. How in fact does this work in practice?

To date, little evidence has been available as to the actual involvement of housing associations in community care planning and provision. Initiatives to date have been patchy and more often concerned with involving housing authorities in consultation than actively seeking to involve them in planning and assessments. While this need for joint working between agencies is widely accepted the obstacles have proved to be considerable. Inter-agency collaboration within housing and community care agenda at present faces a number of practical problems. There is still some degree of pre-occupation of separate authorities with different priorities, each tending to pursue its own strategy in isolation. Housing needs are seen differently by the various agencies involved in setting priorities and deciding on the distribution of resources. As one council explicitly stated in its housing strategy, 'Considerable work remains to be done if real progress is to be made on integrating the housing agenda fully into community care planning and implementation.'

Another study, conducted for the Joseph Rowntree Foundation in 1993, pointed to the importance of effective integration, and attempted to examine these links between the various agencies involved.[26] The report argued that decisions often 'failed to tackle care and housing needs as interdependent' and revealed evidence of a 'lack of understanding of what each individual agency could offer'. The study noted a widespread scepticism about the capacity of the joint planning system to address housing issues.

Certainly, there appears to have been a large measure of distrust and confusion in the initial implementation stages. An NFHA report by Blake and Ghosh outlined some of the difficulties faced by housing associations. The authors concluded that 'what community care has done so far is to hurl obstacles into the stream'. They reported that 'organisations frequently felt that their contributions were ignored, often after they had spent considerable amounts of time making detailed proposals'.[27] All of these findings about the role of housing associations in community care appear to be equally true of the voluntary sector at large.

Involving the voluntary and private sectors

Voluntary organisations have long played a complementary role alongside the statutory sector. Prior to the introduction of community care, their services were already widely purchased by local authorities on a contractual customer-client basis. In some authorities, these relationships were particularly close and collaborative, easing the transition to the new service planning regime.

For example, in Hammersmith and Fulham the SSD made extensive use of the voluntary sector in supporting people locally - in providing a package of service for individual clients, and in developing new services. This relationship was being developed further by the voluntary sector producing discussion papers on advocacy, to serve as a model of good practice for the social services department. Joint study days were organised with voluntary groups on methods of assessment, including separate days for those groups working with black and minority ethnic communities. The council was also developing policies on service level agreements with voluntary organisations. A joint working party of the voluntary sector and the social services was defining a framework to examine where service level agreements would be appropriate, and drawing up a code of practice for the council and for the voluntary sector in putting such agreements together.

These relationships were unusually close, although examples of such joint initiatives with voluntary organisations are found in other authorities as well. In some, social services departments have introduced service level agreements (SLAs) with voluntary organisations, often ranging in size from large national agencies to small local agencies, to provide a framework for more clearly defined working relationships with the voluntary sector. Such agreements spell out what services the council can expect an organisation to provide in return for funding. More generally, however, voluntary organisations have not responded to the invitation to become service providers to the degree envisaged in *Caring for People*.

Service level agreements have both advantages and disadvantages. For local authorities the advantages are that they enable stabilisation of costs and provide economies of scale, in addition to strengthening purchasing power and reducing case management workload. For the voluntary sector, such agreements clarify their role and enable a sounder financial basis with a greater degree of certainty and planning in the future. There are, on the other hand, disadvantages in that local authorities could become committed to a particular spending level, and could have limited choice, while there is a possibility of potential monopolies arising where there was an insufficiently wide range of such agreements. Equally, the weak negotiating position of voluntary organisations could lead them to take on work outside their capacity or original terms of reference, simply in order to obtain funding.

Collaboration with the private sector prior to the introduction of care in the community was less common. Where it existed, the main private sector emphasis was on residential care. Many areas of provision - the care of highly dependent people and day care being prime examples - have proved unattractive to the private sector. Private agencies often tend to choose their areas of operation and the people they would serve. This could leave local authorities having to provide services to areas and groups which, for whatever reasons, appeared unattractive to other agencies - another variant of residualisation. They will only enter the market when commercial considerations can be satisfied, which have proved far more elusive in respect of domiciliary and day care than in relatively lucrative residential care.[28] Similarly, they will readily withdraw if they encounter threats to their financial viability. For these reasons, few in local government felt that a wholesale shift towards the private sector would guarantee improvements in quality and choice.

Assessment for services

Section 47 of the NHS and Community Care Act, 1990 placed a duty on local authorities to carry out an assessment of each client before providing services for him or her. The purpose of the assessment was to identify, with the active participation of the client and any carer, the wishes and needs of both parties, taking into account the carer's ability to continue to provide care.

Councils were required to decide when a formal assessment process was necessary. Such an assessment was to cover all those who need social care and support which they cannot arrange for themselves, taking account of their problems, needs and circumstances. The objective was 'to determine the best available way to help the individual', focusing on what the individual can and cannot do, and could be expected to achieve, 'taking account of his or her personal and social relationships'.[29] Decisions on service provision were to take account of what was available and affordable. Every local authority was required to monitor the outcomes of its assessment process and the implications of these outcomes for the future development of services.

The guidance principally dealt with assessment, and emphasised that this was to be integrated into the wider case management procedure which authorities were expected to create. It stated that 'case management should be practised through systems developed over time that incorporate a range of graduated responses according to the level and complexity of need'. Thus, where an individual's needs are complex or where significant levels of resources are involved, SSDs were expected to nominate a 'case manager' to take responsibility for ensuring that individual's needs are regularly reviewed, that resources are managed effectively and that each service user has a single point of contact.

The assessment of need

Local authorities had until April 1992 to submit detailed plans. Yet there were so many unresolved questions about the changes that it was difficult for them to look ahead with any certainty. For example, the demand for assessment and case management was unknowable. Nor was it clear who would make up the manager cadre and whether they would have the necessary skills.

Some SSDs sought to get ahead of the game by making progress in addressing these issues prior to the appointed date for introduction. In Kent county council, care management for elderly people had been introduced on a pilot basis as early as 1987. The scheme was subsequently extended to cover people with mental handicap. The county council also developed their own criteria to determine the eligibility for assessment and the range and level of services to provide. In the late 1980s Kent's social services department already had about 150 care managers dealing with about 5,500 elderly people living in their homes across the county.

Most SSDs favoured giving the case manager responsibility for budgetary management. 'A devolved system makes it easier to cope with resource problems, as one can identify more clearly where money is being spent', said the social services director of a county council. Local control of budgets was vital in order to facilitate a speedy and flexible response, and so provide for effective case management. There were, however, fears that case managers might see devolved budgets as a largely finance-led bureaucratic exercise, especially if they had to work within tight guidelines in respect of what they could spend their budgets on. *Caring for People* had portrayed the devolution of budgets, as near to the user as possible, as a strength and as leading to a more creative use of resources. Devolution was intended to bring greater realism to the assessment process and provide greater choice for user and carers. But it was left to each local authority to determine the pace at which, and the level to which responsibility for the allocation of resources was to be devolved.

Determining eligibility was central to the assessment process, although assessments which were needs-led also depended on the extent, nature and availability of resources requested. Again, some SSDs had anticipated the introduction of community care and already developed systems of assessing eligibility for services. In Surrey the SSD developed a 'care equation' to examine the balance between needs and resources. The model was used to measure need, to consider how to meet those needs and to show the resource implications of meeting them, including the extent to which the department provided care for the carers (for example, relations looking after elderly relatives). The model comprised definitions of different levels of need, assessment of how much support was needed, care packages to meet different levels of need and priorities for service provision.

Despite these developments across the county, the introduction of case management was not however possible in advance of resources being transferred to local authority social services departments from the Department of Social Security in 1993. This was because under case management the assessment of need and the purchase of services have to be integrated, while the services themselves are provided by other branches of the social services department, or by the independent sector.

Multi agency co-operation in assessment

Effective assessment and case management was to depend largely upon the degree to which agreements and procedures developed through inter-agency collaboration. This meant that local authority social services departments were required to relate to the other departments, such as housing and education; to outside agencies, in particular health authorities and FHSAs; and to the independent sector.

Joint assessments became a common feature of inter-agency co-operation. In order to make such assessments effective, health and local authorities developed agreements and mutual understandings of what constituted social and health care. Without this, problems would arise for care managers when putting together care packages for clients at the margins between the two agencies, especially when the service provided by one agency was free at the point of delivery, while another might carry a means-tested charge. It would also create difficulties for allocating finance if the agencies in one collaborating area, for instance, moved at a faster rate than in other areas while transferring people from hospital to social care.

Several other problems with assessment arose in relation to elderly people. The new proposals for assessment and provision of packages of care did not define clearly the responsibilities for financing care between health and local authorities. There appeared fewer incentives for health authorities to offer long-stay care to elderly people, and many elderly people and their carers could find themselves with no statutorily defined eligibility for funds, and with the possibility that local authority budgets would not be adequate to ensure provision of care for all those who need it.

The views of users and carers

One common thread running through the new public management, and frequently invoked by Conservative ministers in the 1990s, was concern for the 'customers'. In the case of community care, it was the government's intention to involve users and carers more fully, placing them at the centre of care plans and establishing a greater sense of partnership with them. This whole new approach to assessment and case management meant a change in attitudes for management and staff in local authorities, who had to recognise the importance of involving users and carers in the process of assessment.

In practice, more involvement is less straightforward than it sounds. It is likely that service providers would assess needs from the point of view of service availability rather than from the point of view of client preferences. Rarely do those involved in assessment for service provision believe that client needs can be met in a less than ideal world. Paradoxically, the proposed benefit of the new assessment system might well be in improving the psychological well being of users who respond to being *cared about*, even if their expectations cannot be met in terms of being *cared for*.[30]

Commenting on the philosophical base from which the new arrangements should operate, the director of the Carers' National Association has argued that:

> The aim of the community care policies should be to enable carers and people who need care to have their separate and combined needs met within a framework of consultation, negotiation and choice. Caring is associated with obligations undertaken as part of a personal relationship and this should always be borne in mind when services are being planned.

Services could be improved through greater responsiveness and sensitivity:

> It is too easy to allow service providers the excuse that 'if only there were more resources they would provide better services, but as there aren't they can't'! Changing attitudes to carers and to those for whom they care can result in a better deal for them. Even in a climate where unlimited resources were available, we would still have to tackle the difficult problems of balancing needs, family and society expectations and unresolved relationships.

Research carried out for the LGMB in 1992 indicated that user groups were not much involved in the preparation of community care plans. And while almost all SSDs claimed to encourage user and carer groups, rather fewer lent them tangible support; a minority also afforded them representation on decision-making bodies. On the other hand, the same survey suggested that very substantial changes in user/carer involvement in the assessment process had been achieved. Table 5.1

summarises some of these changes; it is noticeable that SSDs were proceeding with caution in respect of user self-assessment.

Table 5.1
Assessment practices in social services departments

	adopted %	considering %	neither %
Target times for assessment	58	36	4
Carers' needs separately assessed	74	21	4
User/carer access to records	74	23	1
Assessment appeals procedure	35	42	18
Interpreters used as appropriate	77	13	5
User self-assessment	23	28	45
Joint assessment with health staff	76	18	2

Source: LGMB, unpublished data.

User and carer input was always likely to be constrained by provider judgements about resources. The assessment procedure would do little to enhance choice if the SSD staff had the discretion to decide what is available and affordable, and if they were limited by existing contracts for residential and domiciliary care. Would choice in reality be available only to those who could afford to pay for it? Or would choice be available only to those whose assessed needs accord with their wishes? Much would depend on sufficient funds being available to ensure that the costs of care could be met appropriately. Age Concern warned that

> Shortfalls are concealed by elderly people living in overcrowded and inadequate housing and 'topping up' by relatives and charities of residential and nursing home care. The choice at the moment for people with limited means is often between inadequate support at home or selection from one or more places in residential or nursing home care, an option which is often rendered impossible by lack of finance or by lack of appropriate, local vacancies.[31]

Establishing quality: inspection and complaints

The issue of quality assurance was perhaps the most important element of the community care reforms and the one which underpinned all the changes introduced by the legislation. While inter-agency collaboration, partnership arrangements, effective assessments and the management of needs were taken as key indicators of high quality care planning, monitoring and evaluation by inspection and complaints procedures were crucial to checking and judging outcomes.

Inspection arrangements

The requirement for SSD to establish inspection units was contained within Section 50(7)(a) of the National Health Service and Community Care Act, 1990. Further details were provided in the draft guidance also issued in 1990.[32] In the view of the Department of Health the guidance was rightly to be kept to a bare minimum. It was not for the DoH to tell authorities how to implement policy in detail; that was for them to decide. Advice was however given by the Social Services Inspectorate, whose *Inspecting for Quality* explained the broader remit given to inspection (which had hitherto been confined to dealing with private care homes), and set out a range of considerations covering service aims, reporting arrangements, and procedures for acting on inspection reports.

Of these issues, reporting lines were of particular importance, as a number of radically different models were proposed, from an inspection unit reporting directly to the director of social services, to location outside the authority. Wherever located, inspection units were to be at arm's length from the day-to-day operational management and ultimately accountable to social services directors. While it was possible for inspection units to be located outside the department altogether, the requirement for them to account to the director would make it likely, in the SSI view, that they would in practice form a part of the social services department.

What was required was an independent inspection unit in each SSD to set and evaluate common standards of quality assurance for residential services across all sectors and so secure consistency of approach. They were to respond to the demands and opportunities for quality control of contracted-out services and undertake their duties even-handedly, efficiently and cost-effectively. The guidance pointed out that the tasks of the inspection units included quality control in relation to residential care, but this 'emphasis on quality control' was not to 'deny the importance of management systems rooted in quality assurance'. Additionally, the guidance noted that the Department of Health did not expect authorities' quality control measures to stop at residential care. The role of the national Social Services Inspectorate (SSI) was strengthened; apart from advising social services departments on the setting up and operation of their inspection unit, it was to continue to monitor developments, providing support and advice as dictated by local needs.

The local authorities faced several problems in responding to the inspection requirements. There was a perceived tension in relation to the independence of inspection units; whilst the staff of the inspection unit retained their independence via the management line through to the director of social services, they could have conflicting responsibilities to the local authority as their employers. There was also likely to be conflict over the separate functions of inspection and registration units, alongside the support and development aspect of the role. The question of resourcing was equally crucial: the cost of fulfilling the inspection duties would have to be found from within the system. The development and infrastructure costs would be large, and social services departments would need resources to carry out the changes.

Staffing the inspection function was another serious problem for most authorities. There was diversity not only in the range of tasks (inspection, registration, advisory, quality control) to be undertaken but also in the client groups covered by the procedures (elderly, children, mentally ill, people with learning difficulties) and in the range of service providers (local authority, private and voluntary sector). Although the staffing of the inspection units would draw in people with expertise and experience in the service areas and with the client groups with which the unit was concerned, it was not an easy task for most SSDs to gear up for this task in the absence of a pre-existing skill base.

London and metropolitan social services departments had particular problems finding enough appropriately skilled staff for the inspection units whilst maintaining existing services. A large number of staff were needed to undertake the volume of work required if more than just a minimalist approach was to be adopted. Birmingham city council, for example, had over 300 residential care homes in the public and independent sectors to be inspected twice a year. Furthermore, in an authority as large and diverse as Birmingham - geographically, socially, economically and culturally - the range of options for the structure of inspection units, their place in the organisation and the framework of accountability within which they were placed were numerous and complex. The city council's inspection unit was to be responsible not just for the residential sector but also for the children's rights services and for managing and monitoring complaints procedures as well. Strategies needed to be developed to link the outcomes of the process of independent inspection and quality audit to the day-to-day management and operation of residential units.

Under the circumstances which prevailed in most authorities, a conventional location within the SSD was an obvious arrangement. But as Table 5.2 shows, it was not universal. The authorities visited had all chosen to run their inspection units as an integral part of the social services department. Inspection was widely seen as lying within the wider context of quality management, and as part of the quality strategy within a social services department. For example, the London borough of Hammersmith and Fulham established its inspection unit within the social services department, managed on a day-to-day basis by an assistant director. It was felt that to locate the unit outside the department would encourage a perception that the specific quality control work of the unit, and the more general quality assurance role, were marginal activities not directly applicable to the department's own mainstream service provision.

Table 5.2
Location of the inspection unit

	%
Within the SSD:	
reporting to Director	65
delegated responsibility	24
Elsewhere in authority	5
Voluntary organisation	1
Provided jointly with health authority	1
Some other arrangement	4

Source: LGMB, unpublished data.

Some of the other authorities visited explored a collaborative approach to inspection, based on the creation of a joint inspection unit. It is thought that this would be more cost-effective, would provide a single point of reference on registration for independent sector operators of residential and nursing homes, and would enable a better structure to be created for the unit. In addition, such a unit would meet the various registration requirements of the Children Act, and would also look at issues of quality over the whole operation of special services provision, including those elements of community care where there is no legal duty to inspect. Despite these advantages, Table 5.2 shows such joint inspection arrangements to be rare.

Resource implications

The requirement to establish inspection units had implications for the local authority's role as a provider of residential accommodation. In a large number of authorities, physical standards and staffing levels of residential homes are far below those applied in registering private residential care homes. Local authorities are required to bring their own accommodation up to the standards currently applied to the private sector. The need for capital investment in residential homes was clearly substantial. At the same time there was a great deal of uncertainty about whether there will be sufficient resources available to local authorities to meet the increasing demands. Many authorities considered the option of transferring their residential homes in their entirety therefore to the independent sector, and in some cases, for example Dorset, did so.

Other authorities found other solutions. One created a housing association to take over the responsibility for council residential homes together with day centres where these were integral to the residential building or site. It would also develop other accommodation as required by the council, subject to the financial viability of the association. The new association would also take responsibility for all services associated with residential care: catering, cleaning, provision and maintenance of furnishings, fittings and equipment, laundry and building maintenance. Such a transfer was seen as bringing enormous financial benefits because the association would be able to draw additional grants from the housing corporation, the district health authority and other charitable sources. The council would still maintain direct control over the provision and quality of personal care and through this ensure that it is able to discharge its legal obligations to accommodate the residents who are most frail, disturbed, and difficult to care for.

When local authorities entered into contracts with the independent sector after 1 April 1993, they faced very high unit costs as a result of standards set by their own inspection units. There were also cost implications for the authorities' own services, and the desired outcome - unit costing arrangements which are both fair to the local authority in-house providers and to independent sector providers - was to prove elusive.

Complaints procedures

The National Health Service and Community Care Act, 1990, the Children Act, 1989, and the guidance issued by the Department of Health gave recognition to the growth in recent years of a more consumer-oriented approach among social services departments. The growing belief that users should have a much bigger say in the way that services are provided, has been paralleled by a growing awareness of the need to take specific action to promote the quality of service delivery.

Complaints procedures are at the interface between these two strands of concern. They are, said a Department of Health official interviewed, 'inescapable requirements if we are serious about responding to the individual and about securing and safeguarding the necessary quality of services'.[33] Complaints procedures, which were required to be implemented in the first phase by 1 April 1991, offer a channel not only for correcting mistakes made by a social services department but also for getting feedback from service users about the way services are delivered. They help quality control and give users more say over their own lives. They are not, however, a substitute for other, more extensive ways of involving service users and they form only one part of a quality management strategy.

Some authorities developed comprehensive complaints systems. Durham county council instituted an overall representation procedure designed to be simple and to apply to all types of representations including complaints. Its objectives included the provision of an effective means of allowing service users, carers or their representatives to comment on the services provided to them; satisfying the practical, financial and emotional needs of the person making the representation; providing mechanisms for service users and their carers to appeal against the outcomes of an assessment carried out by the department; and aiming to resolve complaints as quickly as possible and as close to the point of service delivery as appropriate.

To ensure that users and their carers have a proper channel through which to express their needs for, and concerns about, the services, Surrey county council established a 'commissioner for social services users and carers', accountable to a joint advisory committee involving county councillors and members of the Surrey voluntary services council executive committee, together with users and carers. Most authorities adopted a more conventional approach, based on publicity leaflets and posters. They probably rarely went far enough to meet the requirements of complaints procedures, which really required authorities to review fundamentally their department's information service to the public.

Establishing quality: purchasing and contracting

In developing the enabling role and thereby promoting the mixed economy of welfare - the basic aim of *Caring for People* - local authorities are required to act as the facilitators and commissioners of the services, which they agree are needed to meet local priorities, and the provision of which they will set out as objectives in their care plans. The enabling role implies discovering and working with all the resources at the disposal of the local community to make appropriate service arrangements to meet local needs within the set priorities and targets. This, in turn, means a separation of the purchaser function from the provider function, which leads to service arrangements or contracts to secure services for individuals. In line with other forms of guidance issued by the Department of Health on community care plans, assessments and inspection units and in the guidance on purchasing and contracting, the Department set out in a non-prescriptive way what the enabling role comprises, leaving it to local discretion how best to develop this role through different forms of contracts with different kinds of service providers.

The practice of purchasing services and using suppliers outside their own departments was not entirely new to many social services departments. What *was* unfamiliar was the scale and variety of arrangements necessary to implement care in the community. Overall, experience provided an insufficient base for coping with community care, and the House of Commons Health Committee judged their preferences quite harshly in its sixth report, calling for 'further work' and 'better guidance'. The Act assumes that the statutory sector will continue to play an important role in backing up, developing and monitoring private and voluntary care facilities, and in providing services where this remains the best way of meeting care needs. The government decided against extending compulsory competitive tendering to social care, but a clear distinction between the purchasing and providing functions is still required to be made.

The purchaser/provider split

By 1992 more than half of the SSDs in England and Wales had restructured their organisation on the basis of a purchaser/provider split. In the authorities visited there was initially much confusion and uncertainty about how this separation would operate. It was not always clear to SSD managers who would be the purchasers and who constituted the providers. In contrast to health authorities, where existing structures (districts, with their constituent units) facilitated the split into purchasing and providing roles, local authority structures, and the role of elected members in committees, did not readily lend themselves to the distinction. Moreover, the separation raises many questions about areas of activity which are unfamiliar territory to authorities: market-making, market failures, external quality control and other aspects of contract management.

Although the concept of a purchaser and provider split is fundamental to the Thatcher government's strategies for local public services, many social services directors remained unconvinced that it would necessarily improve either the quality of service to clients or value for money. In-house service provision, good management, standard-setting and internal monitoring of performance were generally thought to be as effective in bringing about beneficial changes in services as outside purchasing of particular elements of service for individual clients.

There were also difficulties in separating roles where services were currently integrated. The problems were seen as an over-emphasis on organisational structures; possible communication problems; over-concentrate on contracts rather than service delivery; the possible marginalising of the in-house provider role as purchasing became dominant; and a lack of in-house skills and experience. As was reported in one SSD visited: 'The separation of purchaser and provider roles creates a tension within the organisation which may actually be counter-productive: the separation may leave the consumer as a victim of declining standards, as emphasis is placed on meeting contracted budget costs'.

Those authorities who accepted the logic of an organisation with a clear differentiation of the care planning and provision sides felt that, in the present setting, the discipline imposed by the need to persuade people to buy services, with the possibility of going out of business as a consequence, would make providers more responsive. They expected there to be real competition to keep charges for quality services under reasonable control, especially if the department continued to run some of each type of service in-house to reduce the chances of monopolies developing in the independent sector. The separation would also give the independent sector a fairer chance to compete. The purchaser/provider split seemed to offer a clarification of respective roles and establish clear lines of accountability. It could encourage cost consciousness and value for money and encourage even-handedness in contract decisions and genuine competition between in-house and external service provision. It was claimed to stimulate more innovative service provision which is needs-led rather than matching people to existing services, and to improve quality monitoring of in-house provision. A separation of functions also enabled case management decisions to be made independently.

The purchaser/provider split raises questions about the development and potential failure of 'markets' for care provision. It was not obvious that there would be a large number of providers eager to enter the social care market place at a price that local authorities can afford. Social care service users do not have the same opportunity to 'exit' from the service as do the users of other kinds of goods and services and can hardly be thought of as market planning. Considerable effort was required of the SSDs in market-making activity if the goals of quality and choice were to be achieved.

Developing a contract culture

Some of the issues can be highlighted by looking at one particular example. One of the most significant changes arising from the community care white paper is the development of a 'contract culture' surrounding the provision of services. It covers the full range of agreements that organisations make and involves complex issues such as service specifications, letting of contracts and relationships between care purchasers and in-house providers. It represents one means of safeguarding standards of service and is intended to complement good management practice.

Kent social services department was further advanced than most in making the necessary changes in its ways of working. When the government delayed the implementation of contracting, Kent decided to go ahead with these changes on schedule in the interests of service users and the authority. The county council's approach was one of maximum competition, in which a list of approved suppliers was available for selection by care managers and service users. The county council planned to move towards an inter-dependent contract culture involving more settled relationships with a more limited number of suppliers. One advantage of such an approach was that the authority would be more likely to be able to obtain high quality service as part of a settled relationship, with procedures for early diagnosis and rectification. Supply was also thought less likely to be disrupted by the unexpected withdrawal of suppliers and this would make possible continuity of provision. In addition, it was felt that the closer relationship would allow the authority, and care managers in particular, to provide better information to service users about making choices.

A contracting culture requires the ability to specify the standard of service required as well as the volume and price. Kent completed the specifications for all the major residential care groups, as well as for day care and domiciliary care, at a early date. Methods of identifying which service providers meet Kent's service specifications through the administration of a specific questionnaire were piloted. The county has a large private sector providing residential care for the elderly, much of which has an interest in contracting with the council. Kent established different contracting arrangements with its in-house suppliers of services using service level agreements (SLA) - a form of contract specifying the level, quantity and price of services. SLAs had, in the past, been used with voluntary organisations and proved successful, having the advantage that service providers have to justify their services and costs.

More general issues are raised by this example. The 'contract culture' follows directly from the clear separation of purchaser and provider roles. Under the uncertain conditions of the early stages of community care implementation, the behaviour of purchasers could create anxieties for voluntary associations. What purchasers need are providers who will deliver low-cost but high quality service. Increased competition between voluntary organisations means that their proposed schemes will increasingly have to demonstrate to the funders that they are good value for money. In particular, many small housing associations do not have the infrastructure and planning capacity to tender for contracts in competition with larger and longer established organisations. Not only do they lack financial management and tendering skills but often do not have the necessary information to enter the contracting process.

Many voluntary organisations fear that they will have no financial security beyond payment for contracted services, leaving them with no resources for other service developments, all of which have characterised the sector for many years. The uncertainties for independent providers can be seen in the contract conditions offered by one authority visited which explicitly stated that it would consider terminating the service level agreements in the event of 'changes in the needs of service users resulting in a reduction in demand for this service'. Likewise, in the 'absence of adequate funds to support the services agreed' the council would once again consider termination.

As Sue Goss has shown in relation to housing associations, the dominance within community care planning of a purchaser/provider split does not always make sense. Local authorities have found it hard to find a fit and housing associations have sometimes been told that they are simply providers who have no legitimate role in the care planning process.[34]

This 'provider focus', however, tends to overlook the particular value of a thriving and a diverse voluntary sector. Voluntary organisations of all types have an important potential role to play. As representatives, they are in a position to put forward the views of carers and users within the community care planning process. In order to do so their voice would have to be heard in a process from which they have been largely excluded. In respect of community care planning, voluntary bodies can contribute by providing advice and advocacy in respect of unmet needs. In order to do this they should have sound information on needs. Developing better information for their own planning purposes will also enable them to contribute to the formulation of local strategies. Their role as service providers, then, is just one among many.

Central prescription or local freedom?

The community care reforms differ from those considered elsewhere in this book in being highly technical, professionalised, and progressed at one remove from the political agenda. Yet the community care legislation has substantial implications for social services departments, both in the services they continue to provide themselves and in the move to 'enabling', 'purchasing' and 'facilitating' other service providers. These changes were driven by legislation which was designed to achieve enhanced consumer choice and high quality services. To that extent, the philosophy underlying community care is consistent with that driving change in other areas. It exemplifies the broad approach of the Thatcher and Major governments to the management of public services.

It is, however, a highly complex area. Collaboration between different service agencies and the development of local plans in consultation with the local community was necessary to promote better outcomes for clients. The new arrangements for the assessment and management of care have the effect of giving greater recognition to users and carers as active partners in care management. The introduction of inspection units and complaints procedures are an inescapable corollary of the enabling role which the government sought to promote. Two basic themes underpin that approach to community care: that policies should be directed to meeting individuals' needs rather than supplying in-house services, and that this objective can best be met by replacing local authorities and health authorities' provision with a more balanced and flexible range of alternative services.

The flexibility required by community care, together with the need to provide more diverse services, presented major organisational challenges to social services departments. The principles of the new community care programme were not new, and many social services departments were working towards them long before the white paper was published. Indeed, in the government's own view,

> The plans are not proposing anything entirely novel: all they are seeking is the general adoption of best practice in all aspects of planning and management, but that would be a real achievement and will take time and effort by managers.[35]

There will be major pressures on social services departments to achieve the required aims.

Behind the concern for 'best practice' lay the government's intention that local authorities should minimise their activities as service providers. Instead, they were to 'enable' and 'regulate' the community care provisions, working alongside a host of different bodies from the public, private and voluntary sectors. The evidence suggests that many authorities were apprehensive about divesting themselves completely of their care providing role. They were tempted to seek to continue to run at least some of each type of service even in the long run. Social services directors argued that there was no guarantee that the independent sector would be prepared to provide the full range of services, of acceptable quality at prices competitive with in-house costs. There was also felt to be a danger that where there was no in-house service, the development of the independent sector monopolies would force up the charges for services beyond the rate of increase of in-house service costs. Many SSDs sought to retain a minimum capacity to support direct provision as an insurance against failures in the emerging 'market for care'.

Taking account of diversity

The new mechanisms and organisational arrangements proposed in the new legislation set the ground for healthy pluralism but, the difficulties in arriving at a set of shared values were underestimated. Differences in approaches and philosophies presented problems in joint planning. Cross-sector co-operation was retarded as health managers concentrated their efforts on NHS changes (with their emphasis on acute hospital care and self-governing trusts) while local authorities struggled with uncertainties arising from delays in social security transfers.

Voluntary organisations, for their part, were uncertain about their contractual relationships with local authorities, having been traditionally involved with 'advocacy', for and on behalf of service users. Whilst the new 'contract culture' offered the opportunity for voluntary agencies to become more effective, there is also the danger that their objectives and methods of operation would be displaced.[36] An additional consequence would appear to be that the sector is itself becoming more differentiated, and segmenting into contract-dependent providers and other bodies who choose, or who are forced, to stand outside the community care regime.

It is in the context of these difficulties in conflicting purposes and values, that local authorities have sought to establish and promote effective partnerships with other statutory agencies, and with the voluntary and private sectors. The challenges involved in the role were considerable. Yet the response to them was not merely defensive. Some key social services directors sought to develop the philosophy of enabling in a context of locally rooted welfare concerns. Foremost among them was Herbert Laming, then director of social services for Hertfordshire, and former adviser to Sir Roy Griffiths:

> Enabling is about empowering other people and organisations to play their part in it, which means sharing information; letting others take part in decision making; and encouraging others to play a much wider role. It is not primarily about organisational change but about philosophical change; about the role of the state in meeting the needs of the people. It is about the power of the professional in relation to users of the services and their carers; about striking a better balance and helping the state not to dominate. How services are provided and by whom are important but secondary. More broadly a major philosophical change is necessary in the whole of the public sector in trying to move away from doing things for people to doing things with people; giving them good information; helping them understand the options and their implications.

Tension between central and local government

Despite the apparent convergence around the idea of enabling there was an inherent tension between central prescription and local freedom in the community care legislation. The break with the past lay in the fact that the government's policy guidance aimed to do no more than set the framework of what local authorities should achieve, while avoiding telling them how they should do so. Ostensibly, 'policy guidance is aimed at being the minimum essential to enable authorities to get on with the job locally with the maximum flexibility'. Previously such documents usually contained prescription for policy and practice rather than proposing local planning based on the needs and the priorities of the local community.

This new guidance regime was itself a source of conflict, because while directors did not wish for detailed direction from the centre, they were scarcely able to cope with the general exhortations. The bridge was to be built through the provision of more illustrations of good practice, which subsequently assisted local managers to frame their approach without diminishing the scope for local flexibility in implementation. Some benchmarks were essential, for otherwise the language of community care could too easily become empty rhetoric. Unlike other areas considered in this book, such as national curriculum or HATs, in the field of community care it is paradoxical that complaints were of too little central prescription, not too much.

The intrinsic tensions between central and local government in community care would have been clarified if the government had implemented two of the Griffiths' proposals which it instead ignored. The first was to allocate specific funds to each local authority for community care (not just for mental illness, which it has agreed to do). Sir Roy Griffiths proposed ring-fencing because he was anxious to ensure a close link between resource allocation and planning. The second important recommendation in the Griffiths review was to appoint a minister for community care. Undoubtedly, a separate appointment would have raised the profile of community care and improved interdepartmental co-ordination. Instead, the failure of the government to act on these two recommendations by Sir Roy Griffiths resulted in 'altogether a weaker structure which both reduces the capacity of central government to steer local developments, while also distancing its direct responsibilities for such action'.[37]

Tensions these may have been, but they were far from the struggle between irresistible (central) force and immovable (local) object that characterised other areas of the new public management. In community care, the Thatcher government almost fell victim to its own rhetoric of enabling, in which central government set out a guiding regulatory framework, specifying standards and ensuring resources for adequate services, which local authorities would apply in the light of their own local circumstances.

Problems of joint planning

Community care was based on the premise that all the key local players could and should work together within a common planning framework.[38] Experience has shown this to be more complex than supposed, and when assessed in the light of local evidence, the government's assumptions do indeed seem 'breezily optimistic'.[39] In particular, the problems of clarifying the responsibilities of health and local authorities with regard to health and social care issues appear to have been insurmountable in the face of competing pressures. Conflict between the respective professions, their differential status, the tendency to cost-shunting to protect budgets, all served to impede effective collaboration. Although the DoH stated that the ability of health and local authorities to work together would be a key feature of the changes, the authorities remain separately accountable for their performance. DHAs and FHSAs, for example, are accountable to the Secretary of State through their regional health authorities, while local authorities are conscious of their immediate local accountabilities. Recent changes in the NHS have probably exacerbated the pre-existing problems of organisational collaboration. As the House of Commons Select Committee on Health noted:

> The increasing number of NHS trusts and GP fundholders are also shifting the parameters of organisational collaboration and adding to the agenda for both health and local authorities.[40]

These problems - different boundaries, different accountabilities - appear to have affected the success of joint working. The 1992 LGMB survey of social services directors found that only a third of directors in areas where boundaries with the health authority were not co-terminous thought the lack of a common area to be a problem. Yet, as Table 5.3 shows, the responses of directors in such areas to the proposition that the different basis of accountability impedes joint working between social services departments and health authorities were more negative than those in co-terminous areas.

Even the Audit Commission recognised that the system lacked incentives for collaboration. The organisational and financial fragmentation between agencies and confusion over the boundaries between social and health care tend to promote divergence. Nothing less than a 'cultural revolution' would be required.[41] The magnitude of the change required

was also well demonstrated in evidence to the House of Commons Select
Committee on Health, when the Institute of Health Service Managers
pointed to the 'different perspectives', language barriers and different
understandings of continuing care and the purchaser/provider split.

Table 5.3
The effects of different accountabilities

*The different basis of
accountability impedes joint
working between SSD and HA(s)'*

	co-terminous boundaries %	non co-terminous boundaries %
strongly agree	7	8
agree	33	53
neither agree nor disagree	30	15
disagree	21	25
strongly disagree	5	-

Source: LGMB, unpublished data.

Over and above the more obvious difficulties of joint planning, there
are problems arising from a fundamental flaw in the idea of a single
strategy document meeting all purposes, including accessibility to users,
carers and the general public. So the limits to the joint planning process lie
deeper than the construction of a common text. Community care plans in
their nature have been provider documents with varying degrees of service
user comment incorporated. But what is needed is something more akin to
a *purchasing intention* document if community care planning is to achieve
its goal of managing the market so as to draw upon the capabilities of the
full range of providers.[42]

In the light of these difficulties, it is notable that the majority of
directors of social services surveyed in 1992 were able to cite progress in
all the relevant areas of joint working. Notwithstanding the reported
problems which the lack of common boundaries caused for working
relationships, Table 5.4 reveals both just how widespread was actual joint
working even at that time, and how relatively minor an impediment in
practice was the lack of co-terminosity.

Table 5.4
Progress on joint working,
by co-terminosity with health authority

SSD and HA(s) are making progress on:

	Joint assessment %	Joint purchasing %	Joint provision %
Boundaries are co-terminous	97	68	62
Boundaries are not coterminous	97	68	53

Source: LGMB, unpublished data.

Resources

The most fundamental barrier to a co-ordinated strategy for community care in recent years has been the incompatibility of policies on services and on resources. Controls on local government expenditure have been incompatible with the extension of local authority responsibilities in community care.[43] The availability of financial resources was to be a major influence on the implementation of community care proposals. The processes involved in drawing up plans, care specifications, training initiatives and partnership agreements were complex and costly. Few local authorities believed they would have sufficient resources to implement community care adequately. 'We are committed to the white paper but we do feel that the level of resourcing must reflect the level of need', was the comment of one director.

There was a deep contradiction between the government's commitment to extend the community-based services and the limits it placed on resources for community care. As Tessa Jowell put it:

There is a deep seated tension in the legislation - between objectives of self determination and independence and the need to ration services; maximising choice for individuals and their carers, while at the same time targeting services to those in greatest need.[44]

Needs-led planning requires buoyant resources, but these were unlikely to be forthcoming.[45] This tension between needs and resources arises in all aspects of implementation of community care - for example, maintaining high standards in residential homes while having limited resources for investment in them, and the general requirement to provide high quality services while keeping within limited budgets.

During the implementation period social services departments struggled with multiple reorganisations; all were required to come to terms with the changes in the National Health Service and the Children Act, as well as implement purchaser/provider splits in their own organisations. With the transfer of social security funds delayed until 1993 local authorities were faced with a period of uncertainty about the level and method of researching. Even now, it is apparent that SSDs have responded in a variety of ways to the transfer of DSS funding. Some will have sought to guarantee the same price as the 1992/93 DSS period. Others will seek to control prices through tendering, while yet others will not even seek to regulate placement costs. Each will be responding to its own local conditions, including the extent to which it has created semi-independent trusts.

At the end of the day, the test of community care would be its impact upon consumers through the resources available, and the extent to which the changes in training, information, provision to the public and responsiveness to consumers' concerns are managed at the local level. The government's guidance on community care implementation provided 'little more than re-statements of sentiments for good practice in service provision'. More was needed to form the framework within which users and providers could develop new systems of working, and through which users and providers can judge whether what is provided is what they might be entitled to expect. Age Concern England, spokesperson for the most numerous of all the vulnerable groups affected, called on the government to prescribe the processes which local authorities should follow for continuing consultation with users, carers and voluntary organisations, both about their existing needs and about how they will participate in providing for those needs.

There was from the initial stages concern about the difficulties of older people seeking services, when the various authorities responsible for such services were responding to different pressures and requirements from central government.[46] Of immediate concern was whether the funds available would be sufficient to buy a service relevant to the person's needs, or whether care in the community would be used as an instrument of economy by pushing the care of dependent people back onto informal carers.

Crucially, the uncertainty for consumers arises from the fact that all welfare resources are scarce, and have to be rationed. This can be done according to any one of the three distinct routes to care: the Health Service route - service universally available and free, but rationed by waiting lists and medical decisions; the residential home route - service available to anyone, but they may have to pay the excess so there is some rationing, and the state contribution is not cash-limited, so the system can grow to meet demand; the bureaucratic planning route - service package to be decided by a benevolent authority, but that authority will be cash-limited.

Community care is not a new concept. Both political parties have been committed to promoting it for more than a decade. But its particular expression in the Griffiths' report, in *Caring for People* and in the subsequent legislation marked a real break with the past. Not least, this full-scale launch of community care coincided with the promulgation of the philosophy of the enabling authority. Devoid of overt ideological content, community care nevertheless proved to be the most significant opportunity to root the new approaches to public management in fertile soil. As such it provides the clearest example of an emerging professional and political consensus. Significantly, that consensus places the local authority in the centre of the field. Anathema as it was to Mrs Thatcher, the lead role of the local authority made community care the best exemplar of how the new welfare pluralism would emerge.

In its application at the ground level, the critical issue continues to be the extent to which local authorities succeed in introducing the policy changes in a way that benefits those needing, or receiving, community care. Social service departments deal with powerless and vulnerable people who are often not able to exercise significant choice, and those services must now operate within a more complex and diverse framework. Successful management of the financial resources available to social services departments, in this pluralistic setting will involve recognising complexity and responding to the viewpoints of other agencies and groups. This - like the many other challenges facing social services departments - will not be easily resolved. The House of Commons Select Committee on Health foresaw a major stalemate of inadequate providers of residential care, forcing the reputable authorities to 'manage down' the market in ways that minimise the impact on those receiving care.

A substantial degree of inter-dependence will continue to exist between central and local government, and the implementation of community care will depend upon recognising and responding appropriately to that reality. In the course of time, the absence of an ideological impulse in the promotion of community care may well provide it with greater staying power than the Conservatives' other initiatives in the fields of housing, education and competition.

Notes

1. Griffiths, Sir Roy, *Community Care: Agenda for Action, A Report to the Secretary of State for Social Services by Sir Roy Griffiths*, London, HMSO, 1988, para 1.3.4.

2. Department of Health and Department of Social Security, *Caring for People: Community Care in the Next Decade and Beyond*, Cm 849, London, HMSO, 1989, para 3.4.6.

3. G. Wistow, M. Knapp, B. Hardy and C. Allen, 'From Providing to Enabling: Local Authorities and the Mixed Economy of Social Care', *Public Administration*, Vol. 70, Spring, 1992, pp. 25-45.

4. D.J. Hunter and G. Wistow, *Community Care in Britain: Variations on a Theme*, London, King's Fund, 1987, p. 61.

5. Department of Health and Social Security (also Scottish Office, Welsh Office and Northern Ireland Office), *Growing Older*, Cmnd 8173, London, HMSO, 1980.

6. National Audit Office, *Community Care Developments, Report by the Comptroller and Auditor-General*, London, HMSO, 1987; House of Commons Social Services Committee, *Community Care*, Vol. 1, Report HC 13-1, London, HMSO, 1985; Audit Commission, *Making a Reality of Community Care*, London, HMSO, 1986.

7. *Community Care: Agenda for Action.*

8. Department of Health and Department of Social Security, *Caring for People: Community Care in the Next Decade and Beyond*, Cm 849, London, HMSO, 1989.

9. *Hansard*, Cols. 999-1014, 18 July 1990.

10. *Insight*, 18 July 1990.

11. 'Delays in Care Reforms Criticised', *The Times*, 11 July 1990.

12. M. Henwood, T. Jowell and G. Wistow, *All Things Come (to those who wait?): Causes and Consequences of the Community Care Delays*, Briefing Paper 12, London, King's Fund Institute, 1991.

13. P. John, *Recent Trends in Central-Local Government Relations*, London, Policy Studies Institute for Joseph Rowntree Foundation, 1990, pp. 53-56.

14. B. Hudson, 'Community Care Planning: Incrementalism to Rationalism', *Social Policy and Administration*, 26(3), September 1992, pp.185-200.

15. G. Wistow, 'Collaboration Between Health and Local Authorities: Why is it Necessary?', *Social Policy and Administration*, 16(1), 1982, pp. 44-62.

16. Although the main aim of the reorganisation was to unify health services, responsibility for services delivered in the community was now

divided between the health and local authorities, arguably creating further boundary problems for the management of community care.

17. G. Wistow, 'Joint Finance and Community Care: Have the Incentives Worked?', *Public Money*, 3(2), 1983, pp. 33-37.
18. Hudson, 'Community Care Planning: Incrementalism to Rationalism'.
19. ibid., p. 188.
20. Departments of the Environment and Health, *Joint Circular - Housing and Community Care*, Circular 10/92, DOH LAC(92)12, London, HMSO, 24 September 1992.
21. Audit Commission, *Making a Reality of Community Care*, London, HMSO, 1986.
22. P. Fletcher, 'Housing and Community Care: From Rhetoric to Reality', Community Care Planning and Management, 1(5), December, 1993.
23. Housing and Community Care Officer Group, *Implementing Community Care: A Framework for Integrating the Housing Agenda*, Leeds, Department of Health Community Care Support Force, March 1993.
24. P. Arnold, H. Bochel, S. Brodhurst and D. Page, 'Accommodation Addressed', *Community Care*, No. 978, 5 August 1993.
25. L. Watson and M. Harker, *Community Care Planning: A Model for Housing Need Assessment with Reference to People with Learning Disabilities*, London, NFHA, 1993.
26. P. Arnold, H. Bochel, S. Brodhurst and D. Page, *Community Care: The Housing Dimension*, York, Joseph Rowntree Foundation, 1993.
27. J. Blake and S. Ghosh, *Housing and Community Care: The Loose Connection?*, London, NFHA, October 1993.
28. D. Townsend, 'Managing the Local Market: A View from Social Services', in I. Allen and D. Leat (editors) *The Future of Social Services: Accountability, Planning and the Market*, London, Policy Studies Institute, 1994, pp. 10-16.
29. Department of Health, *Caring for People: Implementation Documents, Draft Guidance: Assessment and Case Management*, CCI 8, Department of Health, 1990.
30. G. Wilson, 'Users and Providers: Different Perspectives on Community Care Services', *Journal of Social Policy*, 22(4), 1993, pp. 507-526.
31. Age Concern England, *Community Care: Memorandum to the Social Services Committee,* December 1989.
32. Department of Health, *Caring for People: Implementation Documents, Draft Guidance: Inspection Units*, CCI 9, Department of Health, 1990.
33. S. Hiller, 'Inspection Units and Complaints Procedures: An Introduction by the Department of Health', in I. Allen (editor) *Inspection Units and Complaints Procedures*, papers from a series of seminars organised by the Policy Studies Institute for the Department of Health and

the Association of Directors of Social Services on Policy Guidance and Implementation, Volume Four, London, Policy Studies Institute, 1990, p. 9.

34. S. Goss, 'Become Part of the Community', *Inside Housing,* 15 October, 1993.

35. Department of Health and Department of Social Security, *Caring for People.*

36. C. Heginbotham, *Return to Community: the Voluntary Ethic and Community Care,* London, Bedford Square Press, 1990, p. 58.

37. Henwood, Jowell and Wistow, *All Things Come.*

38. 'The planning framework must start with a fundamental re-assessment of *needs.* Authorities must review needs together and develop objectives and priorities for meeting these needs, setting out their intentions in plans. They must also manage policies into practice, setting in place service commissioners and assessment procedures, aligning arrangements for *co-ordinating care* between authorities'. Audit Commission, *Community Care: Managing the Cascade of Change,* London, HMSO, 1992.

39. Hudson, 'Community Care Planning: Incrementalism to Rationalism', p. 193.

40. House of Commons Select Committee on Health, *Community Care: The Way Forward,* Sixth Report, Vol. 1, London, HMSO, 1992/93, para 119.

41. Audit Commission, *The Community Revolution: Personal Social Services and Community Care,* London, HMSO, 1992.

42. For a discussion of this point see Townsend, 'Managing the Local Market', p. 14.

43. Hunter and Wistow, *Community Care in Britain: Variations on a Theme.*

44. T. Jowell, *Challenges and opportunities,* paper to five ministerial conferences to launch the community care policy guidance, January 1991.

45. D. Leat, 'Community care planning and mental illness specific grant: A report of the discussion at the two seminars', in I. Allen (editor), *Community Care Planning and Mental Illness Specific Grant,* papers from a series of seminars organised by the Policy Studies Institute for the Department of Health and the Association of Directors of Social Services on Policy Guidance and Implementation, London, Policy Studies Institute, 1990.

46. Age Concern England's Comments on the *Draft Implementation Guidance,* Ref. ACECCI 1, (not dated).

6   An Overall Assessment

The distinctive policy agenda of the third Thatcher administration was to radically restructure and redevelop Britain's post-war welfare state. Chapters two to five have shown how, through privatisation, market deregulation and consumer empowerment, the aim of establishing a strong free-market framework within which public sector could operate more efficiently and effectively was pursued. Legitimation was given to these policy shifts by the concept of the 'enterprise culture', characterised by the virtues of individualism, independence and self-help and, above all, by an attack on the collectivism and corporatism that was seen as a major cause of Britain's decline. In these ways, Thatcherism posed a new moral order. The new public management, with its enabling authorities - not fostering dependence but valuing the consumers and responsive to their desires - was thought to be the mode of governance appropriate to securing it.

How effectively did the reforms of the late 1980s transform the classic welfare state, which had remained so remarkably resilient until 1987? To what extent did Mrs Thatcher's policies realise their ideological aspirations? If Thatcherism was committed to encouraging private and individual enterprise and promoting 'vigorous virtues', how far did it succeed? The purpose of this chapter is to assess, in the light of these questions, the extent of policy change which occurred during the third Thatcher and Major administrations, and to examine the successes and failures of the policy areas in broad terms.

A turning point

With so grandiose a programme of governmental reform, it is perhaps surprising that so little was seen of its effects during Mrs Thatcher's first decade in power. Indeed, despite strenuous efforts,

> the basic structure of the welfare state in 1987 was much the same as in 1979. The vast majority of the population was still served by state-funded and state-provided systems of education, health care, social services and social security. Even the proportion of national resources going into public welfare did not change significantly; in 1987/88 it was exactly the same proportion of the Gross Domestic Product (23 per cent) as it had been in 1978/79.[1]

Overall, with the notable exception of housing and some aspects of social security, the measures of inputs, outputs and outcomes right across the territory of the welfare state remained surprisingly resilient through Mrs Thatcher's first two administrations.[2]

True, it was scarcely possible to abolish the State overnight. The programme was rather to reform and tame it. The problem lay in the realm of means, rather than ends. Until the late 1980s, there was no clear and coherent view of how the apparently relentless onward march of welfare could be halted. Public expenditure seemed to have an inertia that could survive even the most savage 'cuts'. But from 1988 a distinctive approach began to gain ground - and here Nicholas Ridley might be considered as much the architect of late Thatcherism as Sir Keith Joseph was of the earlier period. The key to the new approach was later dubbed 'quasi-markets': forcing public sector officials to emulate private sector decision-makers by exposing them to something of the disciplines of the market.

Quasi-markets differ from both traditional forms of government and from true free markets. They differ from the first in being decisively different in their operation from that of the monopolistic decision-maker in a public bureaucracy (who differs in turn from the private monopolist in his possession of legal authority). They replace that monopoly power with a competitive pluralism. They differ from true markets in three ways. First, the competing providers may well be public sector agencies or 'third sector' not-for-profit bodies. Secondly, consumer purchasing power is expressed less in cash terms than in terms of some surrogate measure, which is later translated into a transfer payment within the public sector ('cash following the patient/pupil/student'). Thirdly, the desires of the consumer are often not directly expressed, but are spoken for by proxies, such as general practitioners, or care managers.

The introduction of quasi-markets after 1987 - rightly seen as a turning point in the history of public management in Britain - was characterised by fundamental changes in the rules of the game of service provision. These rule changes produced entirely different dynamics within agencies, who were exposed to pressures and disciplines hitherto unknown to them. A corollary of this process was the imposition on the public sector of styles of management and operation which reflect an idealised notion of private sector management techniques. Managerialism - as it is now commonly known - is more than the traditional concern to promote efficiency in public sector practices. In the words of one of Mr Major's own ministers, it

> aims to transform the way public services are run, moving away from the old command structures to more open, responsive management by clear and published contracts, which empower managers with the authority to run their organisation in the way that best suits the needs of those who actually use the service.[3]

This new ethos of public sector management is itself clearly influenced by Osborne and Gaebler's fashionable *Reinventing Government*.[4] It reflects a wider, international move towards an enabling role for government, which the Thatcher and Major administrations followed and to some extent, shared.[5] The impact has been profound: the new rules and the new style of managerialism produced an upheaval in the everyday lives of what used to be called public servants.

The strategies for welfare pluralism

To what, then, did the Thatcher government turn after 1987? In this book, the concept of *welfare pluralism* is used to bring together and give focus to what might otherwise seem simply a range of apparently unrelated initiatives, pursued since 1987 by Mrs Thatcher and her successor, John Major. How might this concept help us to discern a theme in those programmes?

Welfare pluralism at its most basic derives from the thinking of the IEA and of Friedrich von Hayek, whose intellectual stamp was so clearly apparent upon Margaret Thatcher and her mentor, Sir Keith Joseph. It sees markets and bureaucracies as in fundamental opposition. Markets only operate with a plurality of players, a free market being characterised by a multitude of individual decisions taking place within an atomistic social order. A good society, then, can only be defined in terms of a state of affairs in which people decide for themselves how best to provide for themselves and their families. Socialism, as Mrs Thatcher understood it, was the polar opposite: a *disabling* state in which decisions were taken by the few, on behalf of the many. For her, politics was nothing less than a crusade to 'remoralise' Britain.

The problem for Thatcherism was to move decisively away from bureaucratic decision making and allocation towards a freer market. This inescapably involved a shift of power, and it is in this sense that Mrs Thatcher saw her problem in the third term as essentially a problem of government. The nature of this shift involved the introduction of pluralism, achieved by two means. The first involved an *outward* or lateral shift, bringing in competition to challenge the hitherto monopolistic position of public agencies. This was exemplified by the introduction and progressive extension of CCT which, as we have seen, brought about a thorough-going transformation of the ways in which local authorities operated. It is also seen in the moves towards a pluralisation of landlords through voluntary transfers, in the requirement to bring the independent sector more centrally into the provision of care in the community, and in the provision for opting out of the locally maintained schools sector. Tenants' choice was intended to permit council tenants to opt out of local authority control and manage their estates themselves.

The second strategy was to shift power *vertically downward* to enfranchise or empower the consumer of public services, thus tempering the continuing monopolistic position of the local authorities. In education it was seen in the way that the principles of funding following the pupil and school-based decision-making enabled parental choice to drive the system on the basis of consumer sovereignty. In housing, the modified HATs proposals gave dissatisfied tenants the right ultimately to choose a different landlord. At an individual level, tenants could become true consumers by exercising their right to buy their homes. The requirement to involve user and carer representatives in community care, and to bring the individual user into the assessment process and decisions on care provision, reflected this theme of consumer empowerment.

In any of the packages of reforms introduced during Mrs Thatcher's third term and developed thereafter, these elements of decentralisation through diversification of providers and devolution to consumers are inter-twined. It is apparently paradoxical that these shifts of power outward and downward should have required such strong central intervention to achieve them. Many interpret the Thatcher years as an era of unmitigated centralisation, and see her rhetoric of decentralisation as inauthentic. This is to misunderstand the nature of the project. Mrs Thatcher never appeared uncomfortable with her centralising measures, and her memoirs make frequent allusion to the need for central intervention to liberate people from their local authorities. But was the project successful under Mrs

Thatcher? And how far, and in what ways, has it been pursued since her departure?

In housing, despite voting arrangements which are heavily weighted in favour of a change of status, tenants showed remarkably little interest in a transfer away from local authority control or in favour of HATs. Tenants' Choice had become an embarrassing failure, to be abandoned in 1996.[6] All six of the local authority housing estates initially earmarked by the DOE for HAT status failed to get off the ground in the face of tenant opposition. Although two HATs were subsequently negotiated, they were a significant departure from the original model, and involved compromise between central government and local authorities.

The government also hoped to see an expansion of homes in the housing association sector, but it is still unclear whether housing associations will be able to meet the requirements for social housing that the government has in mind. In mid-1995, the Major government announced in the white paper *Our Future Homes* its intention to bring forward measures to encourage new forms of landlordism. More choice is to be provided through the encouragement of new types of landlord. It will be possible to form local housing companies to take on the transfers of housing from local authorities, and themselves to provide new cheap rented housing. As well as transferring existing publicly owned housing to a wider range of landlords, the government also proposes to involve them in building new homes for renting, which it intends to achieve through an extension of subsidy. Legislation is expected to allow profit-making companies and other bodies to compete alongside housing associations for funds to provide social housing:

> The social rented sector will diversify. New types of landlord will provide and run social housing alongside traditionally-structured housing associations: local housing companies and commercial developers and landlords.[7]

Determined to 'sustain the revival of the private rented sector that deregulation has achieved', *Our Future Homes* also promises legislation to introduce housing investment trusts to encourage the financial institutions to invest in housing for rent. Further deregulation of the private rented sector is promised to make it easier to let property on assured shorthold tenancies and to speed up the time in which a landlord may recover possession.

In respect of one of the principal aspirations of the Thatcher governments, to expand owner-occupation, considerable progress was indeed made. Reflecting closely the Conservative themes of self-reliance and independence from the state in the welfare area, owner occupation rose very substantially. Accounting for 55.3 per cent of households in 1979, home ownership has shown a remarkable increase to 68 per cent in 1994. The right to buy undoubtedly played a major part in this achievement; in *Our Future Homes*, the right to buy is extended to housing association tenants. A target has been set of bringing a further 1.5 million new buyers into the system over the next decade.

A similar broad pattern of mixed success is discernible in education policy. If the object was to free schools from LEA control and enable them to achieve grant maintained (or self-governing) status, the Conservative government fell a long way short. The few studies of the working of opted out schools appeared to confirm their success. Yet with around a thousand schools having voted to opt out by the end of 1994, interest appeared to be falling off rather than increasing.[8] Under John Major the commitment remains. The opting-out process has been further streamlined and the LEA role reduced further. The Education (Schools) Act, 1992, contained provisions to make it easier for schools to opt out, and created two new Funding Agencies for Schools - one for England and one for Wales - through which grant maintained schools will in future receive their funding. With regard to LMS, after a halting start in some areas, the transition to local self-management has been made, and the revised, decentralised, system of local education appears to be firmly established. Proposals for the identification and treatment of failing schools have been put in place. Poorly performing schools may be taken over by education 'hit squads' who will attempt to identify and remedy problems and thus raise standards. The first use of this new power was announced in July 1995 when a five-person team was appointed to take charge of Hackney Downs School in North London.

Overall, do these moves towards diversity and decentralisation, towards competition and consumerism, amount to the replacement of bureaucratic decision-making by market processes? Taking the reforms as a whole, the result is a patchy one. In competition it has proved possible to make markets, and steadily increase the prospects for commercial competition. Although the CCT arena actually constitutes a wide range of distinct markets in any one locality, there is both scope for, and evidence of, true market development. Housing management may be an exception. Although full implementation is still some way off, it is evident that potential returns are limited, risks high, and the capacity to provide scarcely developed.

In relation to internal markets, success has proved far more elusive. Purchaser/provider splits can be required by statute, and implemented with varying degrees of compliance; it is less certain that they will in themselves generate the patterns of behaviour which are appropriate to a quasi-market situation. One of the defining characteristics of markets is uncertainty; and it is precisely that uncertainty, unfamiliar as it is to many public service providers, which inhibits the rate of development of a market approach. To take an obvious example, the take-up of right to buy is crucially dependent upon judgements as to future changes in house prices and interest rates. Similarly, potential tenderers for CCT contracts may hold back, judging the behaviour of the local authorities to be too unpredictable to justify their bidding. In social care, the under-development of the independent sector disposes SSDs to strive to maintain pre-existing purchasing relationships and contracts.

A new consensus?

Mrs Thatcher's aim to change the way in which Britain was governed was ambitious. Certainly a turning point was reached, even if, as we have seen, the record of achievement was mixed. It was left to John Major to consolidate these reforms with his Citizen's Charter initiative, launched in July 1991.[9] With its emphasis on the principles of 'choice, ownership and responsibility', the Charter initiative sought to improve the quality of responsiveness in public sector provision by improving the provision of information and enhancing rights to redress and recompense. Its aim was to create 'greater transparency in the aims, performance and delivery of government services'.[10] Its impact on local government was to be strongly felt. As the Audit Commission explained:

> The Citizen's Charter presents local authorities with a challenge they should not ignore. It offers them an opportunity to use the publicity generated to develop an informed dialogue with their residents about the services they offer and the policies they adopt. This is the start of a process which could help to strengthen local democracy by empowering people with information and increasing their interest in local affairs.[11]

The spirit of the Charter initiative is one which unites, rather than divides, the major political parties. Indeed, Labour claims to have pioneered the charter principles locally, in such local authorities as York. There are, then, two independent streams of political initiative leading to much the same result. This is just one of several key issues on which Labour and the Conservatives have converged. In respect of the issues covered in this book alone, there are signs of an emerging consensus around the new public management.

The election of Tony Blair as leader of the ('new') Labour party has propelled his followers into concurrence with a number of the Thatcher third-term reforms. Opted-out schools have been largely accepted, and during 1995 the teacher unions struggled to come to terms with their apparent popularity. Blair's espousal of attainment targets similarly reflects an acceptance of the Conservative reforms. It seems unlikely that the benefits of competitive tendering, now appreciated by the Labour leadership, will be lightly forsaken. The principle of a division of roles between 'purchasers' and 'providers' has evident attractions, even if its particular application in the NHS and in community care may not survive a change of government.

Mrs Thatcher's larger agenda had been to transform party politics in Britain. She sought to change the dynamics of British government and of the British political system. When she came to power, the Labour party was closely associated with the defence of the public services. She saw it as 'producer capture' writ large. Under Tony Blair, the vulnerability has been lost, as Labour jettisoned one after another of the old shibboleths and accepted the terms of the new debate. That such a convergence should have come about speaks eloquently of the extent to which Mrs Thatcher's third administration transformed the landscape of political debate in Britain.

Notes

1. J. Le Grand and W. Bartlett (editors), *Quasi-Markets and Social Policy*, Basingstoke, Macmillan, 1993, p. 2.
2. ibid., p. 3.
3. *Hansard*, 25 November, 1992, Col. 870.
4 D. Osborne and T. Gaebler, *Reinventing Government*, Harmondsworth, Penguin, 1992.
5. A recent study of health care reforms in seven European countries showed signs of convergence to the contract model and a reliance upon markets. See J. Hurst, 'Reforming Health Care in Seven European Nations', *Health Affairs*, 10, 1991, pp. 7-21. See also C. Propper, 'Quasi-markets, Contracts and Quality in Health and Social Care: the US Experience', in Le Grand and Bartlett, *Quasi-Markets and Social Policy*, pp. 35-67.
6. In eight years, only 981 council tenants out of a possible six million had opted to transfer control of their estates from their local authorities, and in only two cases - Westminster and South Buckinghamshire - did these moves involve estates of more than ten homes. Faced with so stark a disparity between the results of the scheme and its high administrative costs, the repeal of Tenants' Choice was provided for in the 1996 Housing Bill.

7. Department of the Environment and Welsh Office, *Our Future Homes*, London, HMSO, 1995, p. 30.

8. In the six months to the end of May 1993, 385 schools held ballots on GMS, with parents voting in favour of opting out at 302 of them. The corresponding figures for 1994 were 176 and 104. *House of Commons Debates, 1993/94*, Vol. 244, Col. 506.

9. For an assessment of John Major's impact on local government, see K. Young 'Local Government', in D Kavanagh and A Seldon, *The Major Effect*, London, Macmillan, 1994, pp. 83-98.

10. White paper on *Open Government*, Cmnd. 2290, 1993, p.1.

11. Audit Commission, *Citizen's Charter Indicators: Charting a Course*, London, HMSO, 1992.

Bibliography

Adam Smith Institute, *The Omega File on Education*, London, 1984.

Age Concern England, Comments on the *Draft Implementation Guidance*, Ref. ACECCI 1, not dated.

Age Concern England, *Community Care: Memorandum to the Social Services Committee*, December 1989.

Annan N., *Our Age: Portrait of a Generation*, London, Weidenfeld and Nicolson, 1990.

Arnold P., H. Bochel, S. Brodhurst and D. Page, *Community Care: The Housing Dimension*, York, Joseph Rowntree Foundation, 1993.

Ascher K., *The Politics of Privatisation: Contracting out Public Services*, Basingstoke, Macmillan, 1987.

Audit Commission, *Adding the Sums 2: Comparative Information for Schools*, London, HMSO, 1993.

Audit Commission, *Community Care: Managing the Cascade of Change*, London, HMSO, 1992.

Audit Commission, *Losing an Empire, Finding a Role: The LEA of the Future*, Occasional Paper, No. 10, December 1989.

Audit Commission, *Making a Reality of Community Care*, London, HMSO, 1986.

Audit Commission, *Managing the Crisis in Council Housing*, London, HMSO, 1986.

Audit Commission, *Realising the Benefits of Competition*, London, HMSO, 1993.

Audit Commission, *Securing Further Improvements in Refuse Collection: A Review by the Audit Commission,* London, HMSO, 1984.

Audit Commission, *The Community Revolution: Personal Social Services and Community Care,* London, HMSO, 1992.

Audit Commission, *The Local Management of Schools,* London, HMSO, 1988.

Audit Commission, *Citizen's Charter Indicators: Charting a Course,* London, HMSO, 1992.

Baker K., *The Turbulent Years: My Life in Politics,* London, Faber, 1993.

Barnett C., *The Audit of War,* London, Macmillan, 1986.

Bash L. and D. Coulby, *The Education Reform Act: Competition and Control,* London, Cassell, 1989.

Blake J., and S. Ghosh, *Housing and Community Care: The Loose Connection?,* London, NFHA, October 1993.

BMRB Ltd, *CCT: the Private Sector View,* London, Department of the Environment, 1995.

Bogdanor V., 'Power and Participation', *Oxford Review of Education,* 5(2), 1979.

Brindley T., and G. Stoker, 'Housing Renewal Policy in the 1980s: the Scope and Limitations of Privatisation', *Local Government Studies,* 8(3), 1988.

Brown S., and L. Baker, *About Change: Schools' and LEAs' Perspectives on LEA Reorganisation,* Slough, NFER, 1991.

Bullock A., H. Thomas and M. Arnott, 'The Impact of Local Management of Schools: a View from Headteachers', *Local Government Policy Making,* 19(5), May 1993, pp. 57-61.

Bush T., M. Coleman and D. Glover, 'Managing Grant Maintained Primary Schools', *Educational Management and Administration,* 21(2), April 1993, pp. 69-78.

Bush T., M. Coleman and D. Glover, *Managing Autonomous Schools: the Grant-Maintained Experience,* London, Paul Chapman, 1993.

Bush T., M. Kogan and T. Lenney, *Directors of Education: Facing Reform,* London, Jessica Kingsley Publishers, 1989.

Central Office of Information, *Britain 1989: An Official Handbook,* London, HMSO, 1989.

Cheng Y.C., 'The Theory and Characteristics of School-based Management', *International Journal of Educational Management,* 7(6), 1993, pp. 6-17.

Cline P.C. and P.T. Graham, 'School-based Management: an Emerging Approach to the Administration of America's Schools', *Local Government Studies,* 17(4) July-August 1991, pp. 43-50.

Coopers and Lybrand, *Local Management of Schools: Report to the Department of Education and Science,* London, 1988.

Davies B., and L. Ellison, 'Delegated School Finance in the English Education System: an Era of Radical Change', *Journal of Educational Administration,* 30(1), 1992, pp. 70-80.

Department for Education, *Local Management of Schools,* Circular 2/94.

Department of Education and Science, *Better Schools,* London, HMSO, 1985.

Department of Education and Science, *Parental Influence at Schools,* London, 1984.

Department of Education and Science, *Teaching Quality,* London, HMSO, 1983.

Department of Education and Science, *The Taylor Report,* London, HMSO, 1978.

Department of Health and Department of Social Security, *Caring for People: Community Care in the Next Decade and Beyond,* Cm 849, London, HMSO, 1989.

Department of Health and Social Security (also Scottish Office, Welsh Office and Northern Ireland Office), *Growing Older,* Cmnd 8173, London, HMSO, 1980.

Department of Health and Social Security, *NHS Management Inquiry,* London, HMSO, 1983.

Department of Health, *Caring for People: Implementation Documents, Draft Guidance: Assessment and Case Management,* CCI 8, Department of Health, 1990.

Department of Health, Caring for People: *Implementation Documents, Draft Guidance: Inspection Units,* CCI 9, Department of Health, 1990.

Department of the Environment, *Competitive Tendering for Local Government Services: Initial Experiences,* HMSO, 1991.

Department of the Environment, *Local Authority Housing in England: Voluntary Transfers Consultation Paper,* November 1992.

Department of the Environment and Welsh Office, *A New Financial Regime For Local Authority Housing in England and Wales: A Consultation Paper,* Welsh Office, 27 July 1988.

Departments of the Environment and Health, *Housing and Community Care,* Circular 10/92, DOH LAC(92)12, London, HMSO, 24 September 1992.

Dixon R., 'Local Management of Schools', *Public Money and Management,* 11(3), Autumn 1991, pp. 47-52.

Dixon R., 'Repercussions of LMS', *Educational Management and Administration,* 19(1), January 1991, pp. 52-61.

Doling J., 'British Housing Policy: 1984-1993', *Regional Studies,* 27(6), 1993, pp. 583-586.

Domberger S., S. Meadowcroft, and D. Thompson, 'Competitive Tendering and Efficiency: The Case of Refuse Collection', *Fiscal Studies,* Vol. 7(4), 1986, pp. 69-87.

Ernst and Young, *Analysis of Local Authority CCT Markets,* London, Department of the Environment, 1995.

Fletcher P., 'Housing and Community Care: From Rhetoric to Reality', *Community Care Planning and Management,* 1(5), December, 1993.

Flynn N., 'Direct Labour Organisations', in S. Ranson, G. Jones and K. Walsh (editors), *Between Centre and Locality: The Politics of Public Policy,* London, Allen and Unwin, 1985, pp. 119-134.

Golby M., and R. Appleby (editors), *In Good Faith: School Governors Today,* Tiverton, Fair Way Publications, 1991.

Goss S., 'Become Part of the Community', *Inside Housing,* 15 October, 1993.

Griffith J.A.G., *Central Departments and Local Authorities,* London, George Allen and Unwin, 1966.

Griffiths, Sir R, *Community Care: Agenda for Action, A Report to the Secretary of State for Social Services by Sir Roy Griffiths,* London, HMSO, 1988.

H.M. Inspectorate of Schools, *Good Teachers - Education Observed,* London, Department of Education and Science, 1985.

H.M. Inspectorate of Schools, *The Implementation of Local Management of Schools,* HMSO, 1992.

H.M. Inspectorate of Schools, *The Implementation of the National Curriculum in Primary Schools: a Survey of 100 Schools,* Department of Education and Science, 1990.

H.M. Inspectorate of Schools, *The Quality of Training and Support for Governors in Schools and Colleges: September 1990 - April 1991,* London, DES, 1991.

Halpin D., J. Fitz and S. Power, 'Local Education Authorities and the Grant-Maintained Schools Policy', *Educational Management and Administration,* 19(4), October 1991, pp. 233-242.

Halpin D., J. Fitz and S. Power, *The Early Impact and Long-term Implications of the Grant-Maintained School Policy,* University of Warwick, Department of Education, March 1992.

Halpin D., S. Power and J. Fitz, 'Opting into State Control? Headteachers and the Paradoxes of Grant-Maintained Status', *International Studies in the Sociology of Education,* 3(1), 1993, pp. 3-23.

Halsey J., 'The Impact of Local Management on School Management Style', *Local Government Policy Making,* 19(5), May 1993, pp. 49-56.

Ham C., and P. Spurgeon, 'The Development of the Purchasing Function', in P. Spurgeon (editor) *The New Face of the NHS,* Harlow, Longman, 1993, pp. 1-22.

Hartley K., and M. Huby, 'Contracting Out Policy: Theory and Evidence' in J. Kay, C. Mayer and D. Thompson (editors), *Contracting Out Policy: Theory and Evidence in Privatisation and Regulation - The UK Experience,* Oxford University Press, 1986.

Hegarty S., 'Taking Steps Towards LMS', *Public Finance and Accounting,* 10 June 1988, pp. 23-29.

Heginbotham C., *Return to Community: the Voluntary Ethic and Community Care,* London, Bedford Square Press, 1990.

Henwood M., T. Jowell and G. Wistow, *All Things Come (To Those Who Wait?): Causes and Consequences of the Community Care Delays,* Briefing Paper 12, London, King's Fund Institute, 1991.

Hiller S., 'Inspection Units and Complaints Procedures: an Introduction by the Department of Health', in I. Allen (editor) *Inspection Units and Complaints Procedures,* papers from a series of seminars organised by the Policy Studies Institute for the Department of Health and the Association of Directors of Social Services on Policy Guidance and Implementation, Volume Four, London, Policy Studies Institute, 1990.

Hillgate Group, *Whose Schools?: A Radical Manifesto,* London, Hillgate Group, 1986.

House of Commons Select Committee on Health, *Community Care: The Way Forward,* Sixth Report, Vol. 1, London, HMSO, 1993.

House of Commons Social Services Committee, *Community Care,* Vol. 1, Report HC 13-1, London, HMSO, 1985.

Housing and Community Care Officer Group, *Implementing Community Care: A Framework for Integrating the Housing Agenda,* Leeds, Department of Health Community Care Support Force, March 1993.

Hudson B., 'Community Care Planning: Incrementalism to Rationalism', *Social Policy and Administration,* 26(3), September 1992, pp. 185-200.

Hunter D., and G. Wistow, *Community Care in Britain: Variations on a Theme,* London, King's Fund, 1987.

Hurst, J. 'Reforming Health Care in Seven European Nations', *Health Affairs,* 10, 1991, pp. 7-21.

Institute of Public Finance, *Competitive Tendering and Efficiency: The Case of Refuse Collection,* IPF, 1986.

John P., *Recent Trends in Central-Local Government,* London, PSI for the Joseph Rowntree Foundation, 1990.

Karn V., 'Remodelling a HAT', in P. Malpass and R. Means (editors) *Implementing Housing Policy,* Buckingham, Open University Press, 1993, pp. 74-90.

Knight C., *The Making of Tory Education Policy in Britain, 1950-86,* Lewes, Falmer Press, 1990.

Kogan M., D. Johnson, T. Packwood, and T. Whitaker, *School Governing Bodies,* London, Heinemann, 1984.

Lawlor S., *Away with LEAs: ILEA Abolition as a Pilot,* London, Centre for Policy Studies, 1988.

Lawton D., *The Tory Mind on Education, 1979-94*, Lewes, Falmer Press, 1994.

Le Grand J., and W. Bartlett, *Quasi-markets and Social Policy,* Basingstoke, Macmillan, 1993.

Leat D., 'Community Care Planning and Mental Illness Specific Grant: A Report of the Discussion at the two Seminars', in I. Allen (editor), *Community Care Planning and Mental Illness Specific Grant,* papers from a series of seminars organised by the Policy Studies Institute for the Department of Health and the Association of Directors of Social Services on Policy Guidance and Implementation, London, Policy Studies Institute, 1990.

Lee T., 'Where is LMS Taking Us?', *ACE Bulletin,* 39, January/February 1991, pp. 7-9.

Lee T., *Carving Out the Cash For Schools: LMS and the New Era of Education,* University of Bath, Centre for the Analysis of Social Policy, Social Policy Paper, No. 17, November 1990.

Letwin S.R., *The Anatomy of Thatcherism,* London, HarperCollins, 1992.

Levacic R., 'Local Management of Schools: Aims, Scope and Impact', *Educational Management and Administration,* 20(1), January 1992, pp. 16-29.

Local Government Information Unit, *CCT on the Record: A Review of the Experiences of CCT Under the Local Government Act, 1988,* London, LGIU, 1994.

Local Government Management Board, *A Survey of Internal Organisation Change, 1992: Report of the Corporate Survey,* unpublished, 1993.

Local Government Management Board, *CCT Information Service Survey Report No 6,* 1992.

Local Government Management Board, *CCT Information Service Survey Report No 8,* 1993.

London Research Centre, *Housing in Kensington and Chelsea: Living in the Royal Borough,* London, LRC, 1988.

London Research Centre, *London Housing Survey 1986-87: Full Report of Results,* London, LRC, 1989.

Lowe R., *The Welfare State in Britain Since 1945*, Basingstoke, Macmillan, 1993.

Maclure S., 'Forty Years On', *British Journal of Education Studies,* 33(2), June 1985.

Maclure S., 'The Endless Agenda: Matters Arising', *Oxford Review of Education,* 5(2), 1979.

Maclure S., *Education Re-formed: A Guide to the Education Reform Act 1988*, London, Hodder and Stoughton, 1988.

Malpass P., *Reshaping Housing Policy*, London, Routledge and Kegan Paul, 1989.

Marren E., and R. Levacic, 'Senior Management, Classroom Teacher and Governor Responses to Local Management of Schools', *Educational Management and Administration*, 22(1), January 1994, pp. 39-53.

Maychell K., *Counting the Cost: The Impact of LMS on Schools' Patterns of Spending*, Slough, National Foundation for Educational Research, 1994.

Meredith P., 'The Education Act, 1993: Further Development of the Grant Maintained Schools System', *Education and the Law*, 6(3), 1994, pp. 125-131.

Morris R., '1944 to 1988', in *Central and Local Control of Education After the Education Reform Act, 1988*, (editor R. Morris), Harlow, Longman, 1990, pp. 5-20.

Morris R., *Choice of School: A Survey, 1992-93*, London, Association of Metropolitan Authorities, 1993.

Morris R., E. Reid and J. Fowler, *The Education Act, 1993, A Critical Guide*, London, Association of Metropolitan Authorities, 1993.

Morris R., *School Choice in England and Wales: An Exploration of the Legal and Administrative Background*, Slough, National Foundation for Educational Research, 1995.

Mullen P., 'Planning and internal markets', in P. Spurgeon (editor), *The New Face of the NHS*, Harlow, Longman, 1993, pp. 23-45.

Mullins D., P. Niner and M. Riseborough, 'Large-scale Voluntary Transfers', in P. Malpass and R. Means (editors) *Implementing Housing Policy*, Buckingham, Open University Press, 1993.

Mullins D., P. Niner and M. Riseborough, *Evaluating Large Scale Voluntary Transfers of Local Authority Housing: An Interim Report*, London, HMSO, 1992.

Municipal Journal, *Compulsory Competitive Tendering in '93*, London, 1994.

Murie A., and P. Malpass, *Housing Policy: Theory and Practice*, London, Macmillan, 1987.

Murie A., and R. Forrest, *An Unreasonable Act?*, University of Bristol School for Advanced Urban Studies, 1985.

National Audit Office, *Community Care Developments, Report by the Comptroller and Auditor-General*, London, HMSO, 1987.

National Audit Office, *Value for Money at Grant-Maintained Schools: A Review of Performance*, London, HMSO, 1994.

Office for Standards in Education, *Grant Maintained Schools, 1989-92*, London, HMSO, 1993.

Osborne D., and T. Gaebler, *Reinventing Government*, Harmondsworth, Penguin, 1992.

Paddon M., 'Management Buy-outs and Compulsory Competition in Local Government', *Local Government Studies,* 17(3), May/June 1991, pp. 27-52.

Price Waterhouse, *Management and Employee Buy-outs in Local Government: a Brief Introduction,* not dated.

Propper C., 'Quasi-markets, Contracts and Quality in Health and Social Care: the US Experience', in Le Grand and Bartlett, *Quasi-Markets and Social Policy*, pp. 35-67.

Randall S., F. Birch and R. Pugh, *Large Scale Voluntary Transfer of Housing: Key Legal and Practical Issues,* London, Lawrence Graham, 1992.

Ranson S., 'Education', in N. Deakin and A. Wright (editors), *Consuming Public Services,* London, Routledge, 1990.

Ranson S., and H. Thomas, 'Education Reform: Consumer Democracy or Social Democracy?' in J. Stewart and G. Stoker (editors), *The Future of Local Government,* London, Macmillan, 1989, pp. 55-77.

Rao N., *Managing Change: Councillors and the New Local Government,* York, Joseph Rowntree Foundation, 1993.

Rauta I., and A. Pickering, *Private Renting in England 1990,* London, HMSO, 1992.

Ridley N., *The Local Right: Enabling Not Providing,* London, Centre for Policy Studies, 1988.

Robinson J., 'Reforming the Reforms', *New Law Journal,* 142(6552), 15 May 1992, pp. 685-686.

Rogers M., 'Opting Out: A Flagship on the Rocks?', *Local Government Policy Making,* 19(5), May 1993, pp. 35-39.

Sackney, L.E., and D.J. Dibski, 'School-based Management: a Critical Perspective', *Educational Management and Administration,* 22(2), April 1994, pp. 104-112.

Secretaries of State for the Environment and Wales, *Housing: the Government's Proposals,* Cm 214, London, HMSO, 1987.

Sexton S., *Our Schools - A Radical Policy,* Institute of Economic Affairs Education Unit, 1987.

Shaw K., J. Fenwick and A. Foreman, 'Client and Contractor Roles in Local Government: Some Observations on Managing the Split', *Local Government Policy Making,* 20 (2), October 1993, pp. 22-27.

Sked A., and C. Cook, *Post-War Britain: A Political History,* fourth edition, Harmondsworth, Penguin, 1993.

Sleegers P., and A. Wesselingh, 'Decentralisation in Education: a Dutch Study', *International Studies in the Sociology of Education,* 3(1), 1993, pp. 49-67.

Szymanski S., and T. Jones, *The Cost Savings from CCT of Refuse Collection Services,* London Business School, 1993.

Thatcher M., *The Downing Street Years,* London, HarperCollins, 1993.

Thomas G., 'Setting Up LMS', *Educational Management and Administration,* 19(2), April 1991, pp. 84-88.

Thomas H., and A. Bullock, 'School Size and Local Management Funding Formulae', *Educational Management and Administration,* 20(1), January 1992, pp. 30-38.

Townsend D., 'Managing the Local Market: A View from Social Services', in I. Allen and D. Leat (editors), *The Future of Social Services: Accountability, Planning and the Market,* London, Policy Studies Institute, 1994, pp. 10-16.

Walsh K., and H. Davies, *Competition and Service: the Impact of the Local Government Act, 1988,* London, HMSO, 1993.

Walsh K., *Competitive Tendering for Local Authority Services: Initial Experiences,* London, HMSO, 1991.

Watson L., and M. Harker, *Community Care Planning: A Model for Housing Need Assessment with Reference to People with Learning Disabilities,* London, NFHA, 1993.

Whitehead C.M.E., and M.P. Kleinman, *Private Rented Housing in the 1980s and 1990s,* Cambridge, Granta Editions for the University of Cambridge, Department of Land Economy,1986.

Whitty G., and I. Menter, 'Lessons of Thatcherism: Education Policy in England and Wales 1979-88', *Journal of Law and Society,* 16(1), 1989.

Williams N.J., and F.E. Twine, 'Increasing Access or Widening Choice: the Role of Re-sold Public Sector Dwellings in the Housing Market', *Environment and Planning A,* 24(11), November 1992, pp. 1585-98.

Willmott P., and A. Murie, *Polarisation and Social Housing,* London, Policy Studies Institute, 1988.

Wilson G., 'Users and Providers: Different Perspectives on Community Care Services', *Journal of Social Policy,* 22(4), 1993, pp. 507-526.

Winkley D., 'The LEA and the Primary School: Changing Relationships', *Local Government Policy Making,* 18(1), July 1991, pp. 14-19.

Wistow G., 'Collaboration between Health and Local Authorities: Why is it Necessary?', *Social Policy and Administration,* 16(1), 1982, p. 44-62.

Wistow G., 'Joint Finance and Community Care: Have the Incentives Worked?', *Public Money,* 3(2), 1983, pp. 33-37.

Wistow G., M. Knapp, B. Hardy and C. Allen, 'From Providing to Enabling: Local Authorities and the Mixed Economy of Social Care', *Public Administration,* Vol. 70, Spring, 1992, pp. 25-45.

Wood B., 'Privatisation: Local Government and the Health Service', in C. Graham and T. Prosser (editors), *Waiving the Rules: The Constitution under Thatcherism*, Oxford University Press, 1988.

Young. K., 'Local Government', in D. Kavanagh and A. Seldon, *The Major Effect*, London, Macmillan, 1994, pp. 83-98.

Index

This index covers the introduction as well as the main text, but not the bibliography. References to tables are indicated by italics.